HEADS IN BEDS

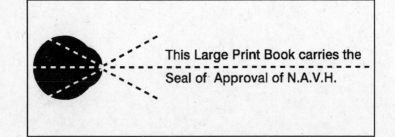

HEADS IN BEDS

A RECKLESS MEMOIR OF HOTELS, HUSTLES, AND SO-CALLED HOSPITALITY

JACOB TOMSKY

THORNDIKE PRESS

A part of Gale, Cengage Learning

Farmington Hills, Mich • San Francisco • New York • Waterville, Maine
Meriden, Conn • Mason, Ohio • Chicago

GALE
CENGAGE Learning®

LIBRARY OF CONGRESS CATALOGING-IN-PUBLICATION DATA

Tomsky, Jacob, author.
   Heads in beds : a reckless memoir of hotels, hustles, and so-called
hospitality / by Jacob Tomsky. — Large print edition.
      pages cm. — (Thorndike Press large print peer picks)
   Reprint of: New York : Doubleday, [2012].
   ISBN 978-1-4104-7397-4 (hardcover) — ISBN 1-4104-7397-X (hardcover)
   1. Tomsky, Jacob—Anecdotes. 2. Hotel clerks—United States—Biography.
3. Hotels—Employees—Biography. 4. Hotels—United States—Humor.
5. Large type books. I. Title.
TX911.3.F75T66 2014
647.940922aB—dc23   2014029535

Published in 2014 by arrangement with Doubleday, an imprint of
Doubleday Knopf Publishing Group, a division of Random House, LLC, a
Penguin Random House Company

Printed in the United States of America
1 2 3 4 5 6 7 18 17 16 15 14

AUTHOR'S NOTE

To protect the guilty and the innocent alike, I have deconstructed all hotels and rebuilt them into personal properties, changed all names, and shredded all personalities and reattached them to shreds from other personalities, creating a book of amalgams that, working together, establish, essentially, a world of truth. I mean, *damn,* I even change my own name.

INTRODUCTION: "WELCOME TO THE FRONT DESK: CHECKING IN?"

I've worked in hotels for more than a decade. I've checked you in, checked you out, oriented you to the property, served you a beverage, separated your white panties from the white bedsheets, parked your car, tasted your room service (before and, sadly, after), cleaned your toilet, denied you a late checkout, given you a wake-up call, eaten M&M's out of your minibar, laughed at your jokes, and taken your money. I have been on the front lines, and by that I mean the front desk, of upscale hotels for years, and I've seen it all firsthand.

How does one fall into the pit of hospitality? How is it that nearly every dollar I've ever earned came from a paycheck with a name of a hotel written on it somewhere (or of course in the form of cash from the hand of a generous hotel guest)? Call it an accident, like catching a train with the plan to go across town, but as the platforms smear by one after the other, you come to realize you've broken city limits, the train is not stopping, and you're just going to have to ride this life until the doors open. Or until the conductor stops the train and throws you out on your ass.

After a certain amount of years in the hotel business (and I'll go ahead and mention this up front), you're just too useless and used up to do anything else.

I grew up military: navy mother, marine father. When I was a child, it was two years maximum in any given city, and then we'd be on the move again, changing schools, checking into a hotel in L.A., a hotel in Jacksonville, a hotel in Asheville, a hotel in San Pedro, looking for a new "permanent" residence. I grew up like a spun top, and, released into adulthood, I continued spinning, moving, relocating.

Those two-year episodes of my childhood left me feeling rootless, lost in the world; perhaps that's why I stubbornly pursued a degree in philosophy. I cannot explain the idiocy behind my choice of major. Shit, if I had chosen business, I might be in business right now. Perhaps you'd think one main goal within the philosophy degree itself would be the ability to argue unequivocally why a philosophy degree is not a complete waste of time. I never learned that argument. Garbage. My degree was garbage stuffed inside a trash can of student loans.

So someone, some asshole, suggested I earn some money in hospitality. Hotels were willing to ignore my dubious degree and offer great starting pay, and I will say this: it's an ideal career for the traveler. I love travel in every way: new people, new sounds, new environments, the ability to pick up and disappear. (My top is, even now, spinning, and though it's digging a nice divot into Brooklyn, the balance is beginning to lean, and once that tip finds traction, it's going to rocket me off the continent.) Plus, hotels are everywhere: kidnap me, duct tape my face, drop me out of a plane, and I promise you I will land in a parking lot adjacent to a hotel and in less than a day I'll be wearing a suit, assisting guests, earning a nice check, and making friends at the local bar.

Hotels are methadone clinics for the travel addicted. Maybe the only way I can even *keep* a home is to hold down a job surrounded by constant change. If I'm addicted to relocating, then how about I rest a minute, in a lobby echoing with eternal hellos and good-byes, and let the world move around *me*?

And that is exactly what I did. From New

Orleans to New York, I played by hotel rules and, in the process, learned every aspect of the industry. Due to the fact I just don't care anymore, here is one of my objectives: I will offer easy and, up till now, never publicized tips and tricks. Want a late checkout? Want an upgrade? Guess what! There are simple ways (and *most* of them are legal ways!) to get what you need from a hotel without any hassle whatsoever. It's all in the details — in what you need done, whom you ask to do it, how you ask them, and how much you should tip them for doing it. Need to cancel the day of arrival with no penalty? No problem. Maybe you just want to be treated with care and respect? I understand, dear guest. Come on, now, calm down, you fragile thing . . . take my hand . . . good . . . okay, now put some money in it . . . *very* good . . . thank you. Now, that's a proper hospitality business transaction.

And when all is said and done, you will understand the hotel life, what we do, and how we do it. Though why we *continue to do it* may be harder to grasp. All of this will be beneficial to you because the next time you check in with me (and believe me, I get around; I've probably checked you in a couple of times already), the next time we meet, a comforting, bright light of total understanding will be shining in your eyes, and I will help you and you will help me, and reading this book will give you the knowledge you need to get the very best service from any hotel or property, from any business that makes its money from putting "heads in beds." Or, *at the very least,* it will keep me from taking your luggage into the camera-free back office and stomping the shit out of it.

As a hotelier, I am everywhere. I am nowhere. I am nameless . . . except for the goddamn name tag.

But first, let's talk about names. Let's talk about changing the names to protect the innocent. Let's talk about how innocent *I* am and how much *I* need protecting.

My name is Jacob Tomsky. But in the hotel world we are all registered with our last name first. Jacob Tomsky becomes Tomsky, Jacob. So, in the spirit of self-preservation, Tomsky, Jacob — for the purposes of this book — becomes Thomas Jacobs.

Good luck, little Tommy Jacobs.

CHAPTER ONE

I am standing on St. Charles Avenue, uptown New Orleans, a few months out of college and a few weeks into summer. It's already extremely hot in the full sun. Which is where I have to stand: in the sun. Next to the valet box. All day.

I took a valet-parking job at Copeland's restaurant to shake off my college-loan laziness, to climb out of the educational womb and stand on my own two feet as a money-making, career-pursuing adult. Educated in the useless and inapplicable field of philosophy, I quickly deduced that my degree looked slightly comical on my already light-on-the-work-experience résumé. Perhaps it was even *off-putting.* To a certain eye, hell, it probably made me look like a prick. But I had to start somewhere. So I started at the bottom.

This job is not good enough. Why not? First of all, I'm parking cars. Second, we have to turn in all our tips. I imagined I'd get off the first night with a pocketful of ones to take to the French Quarter, not that you need much money in New Orleans. As it turned out, however, attached to the valet box that houses the car keys, like a wooden tumor, is a separate slot for us to jimmy in our folded tips. All of them. Attached to *that* box, like a human tumor, is the shift boss, back in the shade at a vacant umbrella table, sipping a noontime drink that most definitely contains alcohol. It also has chipped ice and is sweating in his hand, sweating in a much different way than I am sweating.

A lunch customer hands me his ticket. I find his keys easily in the box and take off at an impressive run. His car is not easy to find: the valet company has not rented a nearby lot to service the restaurant, and so we, certainly unbeknownst to the clients, just drive around the area and try to parallel park the vehicles as close to Copeland's as possible. Once the vehicle has been parked, it's up to the valet to draw a silly treasure map on the back of the ticket so another valet can locate it. My co-worker Chip draws every treasure map like this: #*. Every single one. And finding the car is never easy. But I bring it back and slide up

14

to the curb, holding the door open, the car's AC pouring like ice water on my feet, and receive a neatly folded bill from the customer.

"It's damn hot out here, son. This is for you running like that."

It's a twenty-dollar bill. Chip, now back and posted by the valet box, holds a salute against his brow, trying like hell to make out the bill. I walk up to the tip tumor and start to wiggle it in when Chip says, "No. *No!* What are you doing, Tommy? Don't you keep a dollar handy to swap it out with? Please don't put that twenty in there. Please. It's for you. That dude *told* you it was for you."

"Actually, it's for Copeland's Valet Parking Corporation," the human tumor says, setting his drink down wet on the valet box.

"Are you seriously drinking a mudslide?" Chip asks.

I use a car key from the box to vanish the bill completely and post up next to Chip. Back in the sun. The shift boss sinks back into the shade.

"I am *way* too old for this. Sharing tips? Forty percent to management leaves 60 percent of the tips to us, divided over twenty runners, on a check, with taxes taken out, and guess who's running the math, guess who's counting up the tips? A grown man drinking a goddamn mudslide." He must have been talking to himself previously because now Chip turned to me: "You think he's gonna turn in that twenty? Or just keep it for himself? We *never* get good tips out here. You know what I heard? There's a new hotel opening up downtown. You heard that? It's supposed to be *luxury*." He said the word as if it were mystical and perhaps too good for his own tongue: *"luxury."* "And they're looking for parkers. Copeland's customers don't tip for shit."

Chip, with a wide smile, accepts a claim check from an emerging lunch customer and locates the keys in the box. "It's a fucking Mazda, dude," he says quietly to me. And then to the customer: "You won't be long in this heat, sir! I will run for your vehicle!" Then he takes off sprinting: it's almost vaudevillian how he tears ass around the corner, his body at full tilt.

Chip cruises the Mazda back in record time, gliding up to the curb. "AC running and classic rock on low for you, sir."

The customer drops something into his cupped palm. Something that makes Chip's face contort.

Chip stands upright, essentially blocking the customer from entering his own vehicle,

16

and spreads open his palm to let the two-quarter tip flash in the sun.

With a voice strained and tight, as if he were suffering intense physical pain, he says, "Why, thank you so very much, sir."

Then he pivots slightly and extends his hand, palm flat, quarters in the sun again.

Then he drop-kicks both coins. Kicks the shit out of them into the street.

They arc over the road and land on the rough grass of the neutral ground, settling in before a streetcar rocks by.

I can see the shock on the customer's face — the confusion, the horror. Chip just walks off with determination, crossing St. Charles and onto the neutral ground. After picking the quarters out of the grass, he crosses the tracks to the far side of the street and starts bearing down Napoleon Avenue, toward Mid-City: the job, the restaurant, the shift boss, me, all of us in his rearview mirror.

I finished my shift. Then I took his advice about the hotel job.

Whether I knew it yet or not, it was one hell of an important moment for me, watching Chip snap at what seemed like such a minor affront, seeing that much emotion applied to a single low-quality tip. And then watching him bend down, fish the quarters out of the dirt, and take them with him. I didn't understand any of it. Not yet.

Here we go.

Hotel orientation. Human resources pretty much hired everyone. Everyone who passed the drug test.

I passed, thank you.

Chip did not.

The River Hotel, connected to a brand known for luxury, known for being out of almost everyone's price range, was being built right there on Chartres Street, in downtown New Orleans. It was three weeks from opening and still under construction. Yet they hired us all, tailored our uniforms, and started paying us. A week ago I was *earning* money and *giving* it to an idiot who pounds mudslides. Now I wasn't even working, but I was collecting a check. A good check. And no one had even said the word "valet" yet.

Not that our new managers weren't saying any words. Honestly, they couldn't *stop* saying some words: "Service." "Luxury." "Honesty." "Loyalty." "Opulence." And mid-length phrases such as "Customer Feedback" and "Anticipating Needs." And then longer, million-dollar phrases like *"Fifteen-Hundred-Thread-Count Egyptian Linen Duvet Covers."*

Management ran classes every day on service, administered in the completed conference rooms, the tables draped with what we assumed to be Egyptian fabric and adorned with iced carafes of water, which we poured into crystal goblets to wash down the huge piles of pastries they fed us. They were hell-bent on teaching us how to identify something called "a guest's unmentioned needs."

"A man needs his car, he don't need to speak a word. Get that claim check out. Get that dollar out, feel me?"

That came from the back of class. I turned my head to get a look at who I assumed were to be my co-workers: three black guys not really adhering to the "business casual" mandate for these orientation classes.

"Tommy, can you give me an example of a guest's unmentioned need?"

I wasn't even wearing a name badge: these hospitality maniacs had actually learned everyone's name.

"Well, ma'am —"

"You can call me Trish. I'm the front office manager."

"Well, ah, *Trish* . . ." That got a low laugh from the back of class. "Maybe they pull in a car, it's dirty from the drive, and we could get it washed?"

"Perfect example."

"Wait up. You want I should drive the car back to my driveway in the Ninth Ward to wash it? Or bring in quarters from home?"

"Perry; correct?"

"Yeah, Perry."

"Perry. You come to me anytime, and I'll give you hotel money to wash a car, change a tire, or buy them a CD you know they'd like for the drive home. Anything you think of, you can come to me."

"Well, goddamn."

The day before the grand opening the hotel closed off a block of Chartres Street (pronounced "*Chart*-ers," by the way, completely disregarding the obvious Frenchness of the word; we also pronounce the street Calliope like "Cal-e-ope"; Burgundy comes out not like the color but "Ber-GUN-dy," and just try to stutter out Tchoupitoulas Street or Natchitoches even close to correctly). We were collected into parade groups, our new managers holding up large, well-made signs indicating our departments. Front desk. Valet. Laundry. Sales and marketing. Bellmen. Doormen. Food and beverage. And housekeeping of course, by far the largest group, about 150 black ladies dressed as if they were going to a club. The valets hung

20

together in a small clot, not saying much to each other, looking up at the finished, renovated hotel.

The vibe was celebratory and overwhelmingly positive. We were let in, one department after the other, and we hustled up a stairwell lined with managers clapping and cheering as if we were the goddamn New Orleans Saints. They threw confetti, smacked us on the back, and screamed in an orgy of goodwill and excitement. By the time we crested the third floor and poured into the grand banquet hall, every single one of us had huge, marvelously sincere smiles stuck hard on our faces. And we held those smiles as we took turns shaking the general manager's hand, who, no shit, wore a crown of laurel leaves. As a joke, I suppose.

"I'm Charles Daniels. Please, call me Chuck."

"All right, then, Chuck," Perry said in front of me and waited while Mr. Daniels located the gold-plated name tag that read "Perry" from the banquet table beside him.

Mr. Daniels didn't go so far as to *pin on* the name tag, *anoint us,* as it were. But we were in such a rapturous state during the event I believe we would have readily kneeled before him and let him pin it to our naked flesh.

And then there was an *open bar.* Not sure where they shipped in this opening team from; they certainly weren't locals. Neither was I, but I'd spent my young life traveling, moving so often I'd learned the skill (and believe me it is an incredibly useful skill) of assimilating into any new culture, whatever that culture may be. I am a shape-shifter in that way. And as I approached my four-year anniversary in Louisiana, just about my longest stretch anywhere, New Orleans had already become the closest thing to a home I'd ever had. And the open bar was a nod to this town, a town that runs on alcohol, and much appreciated. This is a city where you can find drink specials on Christmas morning. Not that you could find me on Bourbon Street Christmas morning; I didn't drink at the time. I stayed sober all through college while pursuing my degree and hadn't had a drop since I was fifteen and used to take shots of Jack Daniel's in my basement during school lunch. But an open bar in New Orleans? People got *tore up.* Housekeeping got *tore up.*

Now that it was revealed which department we fell into, we tended to group up for the party, getting to know each other.

"Dig this general manager. He look like a

slave owner with that headpiece," Walter said.

"Nah," Perry said. "Chuck a cool mother-fucker. You just enjoy that free drink you got," and then he took a long finishing pull from his own bottle of Heineken.

Everyone was smiling. Everyone was friendly. Everyone had a name tag on. It was like a big crazy family, and we opened tomorrow. We were all in this together, and everyone in that banquet hall, after two weeks of service training, two full paychecks for *nothing,* couldn't wait to unleash their skills on a real guest. The managers had whipped us into such a frenzy that if any actual guests had wandered into that party, we would have serviced them to death, mauled them, like ravenous service jackals.

Already the hotel had created the possibility of a home for me, a future. It seemed so glamorous, all the linens and chandeliers and sticky pastries. The hotel was beautiful, and I was honored to be a member of the opening team. It was at this very point I realized my life of constant relocation had led me to this nexus of relocation, this palace of the temporal where I could now stand still, the world moving around me, and, conversely, feel grounded. I studied Mr. Daniels as he circulated the party, all conversation politely cutting off when he unobtrusively joined a group. That was the position I wanted. That was a life I could *own.* And I distinctly felt, because this is exactly what they told us during orientation, that if I performed with dedication and dignity, took the tenets of luxury service to heart, hospitality would open herself up to me and I could find my life within the industry. I wanted to be king. It was *possible* to be king. I swore that day I'd be the general manager of my very own property.

This excitement carried over and crashed like a wave on the following day, the day the hotel opened. But before we were able to molest our first guest, we had to sit through the opening ceremony.

One thing about hotels: once they open, they never close.

I don't mean they never go out of business; certainly they do. But the fact that a hotel could fail to be profitable astounds me. Why? The average cost to turn over a room, keep it operational per day, is between thirty and forty dollars. If you're paying less than thirty dollars a night at a hotel/motel, I'd wager the cost to flip *that* room runs close to five dollars. Which makes me want to take a shower. At home. That forty-dollar turnover cost includes cleaning supplies,

electricity, and hourly wage for housekeepers, minibar attendants, front desk agents
(and all other employees needed to operate
a room), as well as the cost of laundering
the sheets. Everything. Compare that with
an average room rate, and you can see why
it's a profitable business, one with a long
history, going back to Mary and Joseph running up against a sold-out situation at the
inn, forcing him to bed his pregnant wife in
a dirty-ass manger.

The word "hotel" itself was appropriated
from the French around 1765. Across the
ocean, a hotel, or *hôtel,* referred not to
public lodging but instead to a large govern-
ment building, the house of a nobleman, or
any such place where people gathered but
no nightly accommodation was offered.
America, at the time, was filled with grimy
little inns and taverns, which provided beds
for travelers and also functioned as a town's
shitty dive bar. Having a monopoly on the
alcohol game was a boon, one given to
tavern keepers in gratitude for putting up
travelers, something no one wanted any part
of. It wasn't until George Washington
decided to embark on the first presidential
tour of his new kingdom that spotlights
began to shine on these public houses of
grossness. In order to present himself as a

25

man of the people, he turned down offers to stay with associates and wealthy friends, instead lodging himself in tavern after tavern, sniffing at room after room, frowning at bed after bed. For the first time in American history, townships were *ashamed* of their manner of accommodating travelers. The country was unified and expanding. Something had to be done about our system of lodging.

So, in 1794, someone, some asshole, built the very first "hotel" in New York City: a 137-room job on Broadway, right there in lower Manhattan. It was the first structure built with the intention of being a "hotel," a word that was quickly replacing the terms "inn" and "tavern," even if it only meant that swarthy innkeepers were painting the word "Hotel" onto their crappy signs but still sloshing out the booze and making travelers sleep right next to each other in bug-ridden squalor. The first big hotels failed monetarily or burned to the ground or both. It wasn't until railroad lines were getting stitched across America's expanding fabric that hotels, big and small, began to prosper and offer people like me jobs.

So, profitability aside, what I am referring to here is not the fact that once a hotel opens it will never close (or be burned to the ground!) but that once we cut the ribbon on the hotel, once we opened the lobby doors, they never closed again. In fact, they unchained them because they were built without locks, as almost all hotel lobby doors are. Three o'clock in the morning — open. Christmas Eve, 3:00 a.m. — open. Blackout — open. World War Whatever — open (with a price hike).

The mayor was kind enough to attend the opening ceremony, going down the line of sharp-dressed employees and shaking hands (or giving elaborate daps, depending on ethnicity). And then in came the public, and there we stood, smiling, proud, ready. The locals poured into the Bistro Lounge, strolled through the lobby as if it were a museum of classical art, put handprints on fresh glass doors, and began to scuff, mark, and mar the pristine landscape, putting their asses in chairs, creasing and bending the leather, scraping and marking the cutlery as they bit down hard on steak-tipped forks.

For a long while at the valet stand, well, we didn't have shit to do. We stood those first few hours, feet spread and planted at shoulder width, arms behind our backs with our hands clasped, as we were taught to stand. Then we began to shift on our feet. Then we began to talk quietly out of the sides of our mouths. Then to turn our heads and talk openly at a normal volume. Then to go to the back office to check our cell phones. Not Perry, though: he remained at his post, and the most he did was shake his head when everyone started to get restless.

"We ain't making no damn money," Keith said, swinging his fists at his sides, directing the comment at Perry, who had somehow become the de facto leader: not simply because Perry was older, though he had a good five years over everyone else on the line, but because of something in his calmness, the way he held his lean body still, the way his eyes were so white and his face so black and all of him so goddamn calm and cool.

"This *day-one* shit, Keith. Relax yourself."

"Shit, I needs money. We got that full wage last two weeks, but now we on that hourly wage adjusted for tips, ya heard me? I mean, we ain't even seen a car and —"

"Y'all tighten up. Chuck coming through."

And we did. But not just for Perry. Mr. Daniels had an absolutely presidential charisma. I *wanted* to work for him. We all did. He came out through the lobby doors into the porte cochere ("fancy word for covered driveway, shit") and walked down the line, rattling off each of our names like

28

an old friend. But then he stopped, as if he'd forgotten something, and walked back to stand before us on the tiled driveway, the soft rush of the marble water fountain pulsing behind him in the cavern of the porte cochere.

"A bit overstaffed, it seems? Gentlemen, I hate to say it, but when a property opens, especially one as illustrious as ours, known for service, well, we have to overstaff for the first few weeks. You see, people come here, and they want to *see* the service. They actually want to *see* a bunch of employees standing around doing nothing. It's sad but true, believe me. And that's all well and good for the front desk, collecting a full wage regardless, but much harder on people who depend on proper staffing and tips, such as yourselves. Men, I'll be honest. It's going to take some time for our occupancy to build. However, we already have some meetings and parties booked, transient business, some that'll bring 150 cars in and out on the same night. So we can look forward to those. In the meantime, I'll have accounting up your wages to non-tipped status until business starts booming. Which it will, believe me. How's that sound? Also, we will be selecting a valet captain at the end of the month for those who are interested and worthy. Perks include an hourly wage bump and the best shifts. Hang in there, gentlemen. Coincidentally, you look fantastic." He slapped Keith on the arm and walked off into the garage.

"That's my *boy* right there," Perry said, relocking his hands behind his back and smiling at the fountain across the driveway.

Perry was elected valet captain, zero resistance.

After a month, all of Mr. Daniels's predictions played out: occupancy picked up, filling the garage with luxury vehicles and our pockets with ones. The elite New Orleans social scene also played a role, holding banquets, balls, and charity affairs in our meeting spaces, causing tremendous, short-spurt traffic influxes, then again a flurry of tickets coming out at the party's end. When it came to the social scene, a man we named the General quickly became our favorite guest. His chauffeur would pull him up in a canary-yellow Bentley, impossible to miss. Whichever valet was at the head of the line would stand off to the side of the Bentley as the doorman opened the door. The General, poor of hearing, poor of sight, his seersucker suit riddled and blotched with military medals (hence the name), would tilt up his chin and peer through his cataracts, looking for anyone willing to assist him with anything. His liver-spotted hand always held a stack of fresh, sticky two-dollar bills. The valet would post up beside his vehicle, as if intending to park it (even though the chauffeur would rather let us piss on his shoes than let us touch the interior of the Bentley), and the General would peer hard at the parker, mumble something militaristic, and rip off a two-dollar bill for him. All we had to do was *insinuate* we were helping, and we'd get tipped. Press an elevator button, hold a door. Shit, perform a sweeping hand motion as if to usher him along the way, and there was a two-dollar bill coming. Not to mention his vision was so bad you could follow him, executing multiple amped-up, essentially useless functions, and come back to the valet line with ten or more fresh, sticky bills.

Not that we needed bigger pockets to fit all the money. I learned something indisputable about any valet-parking position: the job kind of blows.

Imagine a dark, stuffy, sweltering ten-floor parking garage with no elevator, New Orleans summer heat licking at your neck with a fat wet tongue as you run up ten flights, walk along Level 10 holding the keys up above your head, sweat dripping down your arm, mashing the lock button so the car yelps, helping you locate it. Slip in wet, learn the vehicle, lights on, AC on, throw it in reverse, flop that wet arm over the leather passenger side headrest, and back up, AC only blowing heat on your sweating face, reversing quickly before — SHIT, BRAKE — Keith tears by in a Porsche going god-damn ninety, the tires screaming, hip-hop from a local station shaking the whole garage level. Now you're sweating even more from *fear,* from almost smashing together two seventy-five-thousand-dollar vehicles, but the AC is beginning to work, and, who knows, this is a Mercedes-Benz S500, get it down safe, and all this sweat and fear might be worth it. Now *my* tires are screaming because I'm taking the turns like a maniac, flying down the level ramps so fast my stomach drops (and so does the front end, right into the concrete, but who cares — that's internal and nonvisual dam-age), gunning it on the straightaways, turn-ing up the Vivaldi loud because it makes my reckless driving seem beautiful, and scrap-ing the front end again coming down a ramp (Level 7, something about Level 7, the shit always bottoms out), but I don't hear the scrape, just feel it, because Vival-di's *Four Seasons* is *blasting,* and then —

FUCK, BRAKE — there I am bumper to bumper, my Benzo just about underneath a mammoth black Escalade, its headlights burning my eyes like the end of a white tunnel I almost died inside, Perry perched in the driver's seat, laughing, pointing his long finger at me, so I reverse hard, bringing the back end of the Benzo right up against the wall, maybe some contact there, but nothing that'll be discovered before leaving the hotel. Perry pulls up alongside and lowers the automatic window. "Used to have me one of these big bastards. Back when I moved bricks. Get on down there, Tommy, the Zulu Krewe is wrapping up their ball, and Keith and Walter are stealing all the tickets. That shithead Walter be pulling three tickets at a time. He playing with the wrong motherfucker." And then I pull forward, our two vehicles an inch apart, his side mirror going right over the top of my Benz, and then I gas the fuck out of it, tires screaming, taking it down the last ramp going thirty and then braking it down to five, rolling out of the dark garage ever so slowly, with such care and attention that I have time to make eye contact with my customer, his face crunched with concern for his vehicle.

"Here you are, sir. Enjoy your evening."

"Hm," he says and pushes past me, no intention of tipping, but I smile and close the door softly for him, my eyes already on the valet counter for my next ticket. There it is: another goddamn tenth-floor ticket. Not only is Walter tripling up on tickets; he's handpicking them by floor to minimize running. Another Mercedes-Benz S500. Time to run.

"Okay, listen up. We are getting complaints, gentlemen. No more tire squealing. I understand y'all are trying to do your job quickly, but that garage is like an amplifier, and if you burn tire on 10, we hear it down here. How do you think that makes our guests feel, listening to crazy peel outs while waiting for their cars to come down? No more burns. Take it slow. Number two: do not change the radio station. We're getting complaints that when guests leave and turn on the radio, it's blasting Hot 93. These guests have no interest in listening to Cash Money Millionaires." We all took a second to laugh there. "*Do not touch the radio. Do not change the seat alignment.* Easy, right? Big night tonight, mayor's having another charity dinner, two hundred in and out by 10:00 p.m. ALSO, if you get a hotel overnight valet ticket coming in, park it on 10,

DON'T BE LAZY AND PARK IT ON 2. All that means is you'll be running up to 10 all night for these transient party guests. You see an overnight ticket, park it all the way up. Because it ain't coming back down tonight. Keith, you hear me? Don't think I don't know what's going on down here, you guys."

That was John, the assistant front office manager. Bellmen, doormen, front desk, and valet parking all fall under the front office. John had recently been assigned to us to crack down on all the bullshit. Without a doubt, bullshit was getting ubiquitous down here.

In our back office, where we kept the car keys filed by number in fat yellow packets, we also had a small CD player to motivate ourselves. Our CD collection kept growing and growing. Down comes a Lexus, the guest slips a folded dollar to Walter, and he struts into the back office, pulling a jewel case from his underwear.

"Check this shit out, brah. Now we got some Beethoven up in this bitch. Classical, ya dig? Crackers make mad money listening to shit like this."

And we all knew Keith was stealing pocket money from the vehicles. We'd see him counting up big piles of change in the back office during his shift. Also, he made too much noise when he ran.

Unfortunately, once your vehicle rounds that corner into the cavern of the garage or takes a right at the light, any manner of terrible things may happen at the hand of a valet parker. What's the best way to ensure your vehicle isn't taken advantage of? Well, sorry, not much can be done. When your daughter goes on *this* date, you just have to pray she comes home before midnight and unmolested. However, performing a walk around before your car goes speeding off never hurts. On the valet ticket is a sketch of a vehicle that the parker or doorman uses to mark any already present scars. That way, later, should a guest assume he or she has discovered a new scratch, the valet can quickly prove the scratch was preexisting and already marked on the initial ticket before the vehicle was ever moved (even though the valet might have clipped a pole while parking it later and, you know, marked it then). So performing your own walk around and familiarizing yourself with any present flaws might pay off later. Should something happen, this little bit of surety will come in handy, and if the valet happens to watch you checking your vehicle, he might be more careful not to add anything fresh. If you do see the actual valet getting into your vehicle, it wouldn't hurt to drop a few dollars at the outset, so you are on his mind as he pulls it off. Then again, even if you manage to establish initial contact with the parking valet, the valet who retrieves it later will have no connection to you and all the alone time he needs with your car. If you cannot stand *anyone* having private time with your baby, then you can always leave it in direct charge of the doorman. The driveway is the doorman's domain, and he can, and will, allow certain vehicles to remain parked for hours in his direct line of sight and conveniently ready for departure. How can you secure a coveted spot right out front? Give him a nice crisp twenty-dollar bill. He'll be more than happy to help. Doormen love twenties. They love it even more if your car is luxury and makes their driveway look expensive. If you have a busted-looking Chevy, you might as well give it to Keith and let him steal all your change.

"Dude taking nickels and pennies. That's some low-down poor shit," Perry said. "Listen, Tommy, you know you my boy. Come up in my office to talk some business."

His office was the house car, a black

BMW 7 Series, owned by the hotel to facilitate short trips for VIPs around the city and the occasional airport pickup or drop-off, which Perry was throwing me a lot of recently and I appreciated. Airport trips got you off the line for about an hour, the hotel paid you twenty in cash for the time, and the guests would often tip twenty on top of that. Plus, either there or back you're alone and get to recline the seat, slide open the sunroof, and listen to whatever you want as you pimp through New Orleans in a black BMW 7 Series. The hotel gave one airport gig to Walter, *one;* a drop-off, and he came back five hours later. Said he washed the car. But it was clearly still dirty.

Perry put the key in the ignition of the BMW so we could put the radio on low and recline the seats.

"Tommy, you know Trish, right?"

"Front office manager?"

"Right, the FOM. She's looking for someone to bring up there and was asking me about everyone. I told her you're good with the guests. That's why I been putting you on those airport gigs heavy, because you good with the guests. I've told everyone about the position, but she might have her eye on you. Play cool for a time down here. A few more weeks and maybe Trish will bring you upstairs. Inside the hotel proper. What you think?"

"What do I know about front desk? But I guess I want to advance." A sparkling vision of being a GM flashed quick in my mind. Just a few months on the line had already laid dust on my dream. I'd begun to see the hotel for what it really was and gotten an idea of just how many rungs were on the ladder. "And I like it down here, working with you. Why should I leave?"

"Money. Career. It's the right thing to do. Listen, I'd do anything for my baby girls, and that's why I nailed down this captain gig. I know you ain't got no family, but do it for you. And do it now. A man should always want the best for himself. It's goddamn hot out here. Get up inside that air-conditioning, ya heard?"

"I'll think about it."

"See that you do. Now get out. Imma get our baby here detailed from my boy uptown."

Definitive fact concerning cutthroats in any tipping business: nothing makes turn-jumping, gig-stealing, tip-snatching hustlers angrier than having it done unto them.

I don't know who was up for the ticket, Walter or Keith. I was last in line and had just received a generous ten-dollar tip from (if you can believe it) a Honda enthusiast. Walter grabbed a set of keys from the ticket pouch and walked off calmly toward the garage. Keith said, "HEY," nice and loud so that it reverberated through the porte cochere, drawing the attention of Sanford the doorman and Perry, as well as the group of five or so guests sitting on the marble benches, waiting for their vehicles. "*I'M* UP, MOTHERFUCKER," Keith ripped out, now taking off in stiff-legged strides toward Walter, who was still strolling calmly, just as before.

I think Perry knew what was about to happen. I believe he deliberately *let* it happen.

About a foot behind Walter, who had not turned his head an inch, Keith raised his arms and wrapped his hands around Walter's throat from behind. He was, in full view of everyone, choking him from behind. Walter twisted under his grip, spinning quickly, and planted his own thumbs on Keith's throat. Perry started to say, "Whoa, whoa," but still had not moved from behind the key dispatch counter. They brought each other to the ground, hands crushing each other's windpipes, rolling around on the tile floor, squeezing, cursing, the guests standing now, mouths gaped in pure shock.

New Orleans Times-Picayune want ad: Two Valet Positions Available at New Luxury Hotel Downtown. Drug-Free Workplace. Competitive Hourly Wage + Tips. Please Fax Résumé. Psychopaths Tolerated. Up to a Point.

Two new valets started the following week. One looked like Eddie Munster and couldn't drive a stick shift. Pretty damn crucial. He would run all the way up the stairs and then walk all the way back down, keys hanging sadly from his hand, shaking his head. "I couldn't get it to move, you guys."

"Damn, Perry. He's jamming everything up."

"At least he ain't *choking out co-workers,* ya heard me? But, yeah. Listen, keep an eye out for a stick-shift overnight ticket. Something grimy, not too nice. Take him up to the top stretch, and learn him on it, dig?"

And that's what I did. We burned the life out of a guest's clutch teaching Eddie to drive. It smelled like a metal-and-oil barbecue up there.

Turns out that was just the beginning of Eddie's problems. Now that he could *drive* everything, he could efficiently *wreck* everything. He scraped five front bumpers taking the tight turns in the garage. He put a scratch down the side of our house car, nice and long. I saw the stress in Perry's face when his BMW was damaged. It was all he could do to avoid reverting to his old ways and pistol-whipping Eddie into a coma. Perry was doing a seven-year bid in Orleans Parish Prison while I was attending seventh-grade social studies.

"This dude is a moron. My man, I almost miss Walter and Keith. Least they was men. Look at this head-hanging, little-boy shit-head."

Then Eddie managed to do it right. He set a record, I would wager, still unmatched in that garage. While trying to pull it out of a tight spot, he artfully embedded a Porsche's front end *deep* into a deluxe van's automatic side doors. The vehicles had more than ten thousand dollars in damage. Each. ("Oh, shit, Lord Jesus Christ.")

But even that wasn't the end for him. It was a busy Friday afternoon, plenty of guests arriving for the weekend, pulling in to the driveway to unload luggage and drop off their vehicles. The situation called for a little extra hustle. So Eddie jumped into the driver's seat of a car and threw it in reverse, hoping to slip it out of the line and get it up into the garage. But he failed to check the rearview mirror. Had he thrown it a glance,

42

he might have seen the rear window obstructed by the trunk, which was still popped. He might have then intuited that someone might be digging around inside that trunk for the last of his or her luggage. But Eddie failed to look and jammed his tiny foot down hard on the gas, backed up the vehicle, and, to the shock and terror of every single human being in the porte cochere, scooped up the guest who was, in fact, removing the last of his luggage from the trunk. The guest screamed as the back bumper lifted him off the ground by his knees, and that scream became muffled once the guest, still at the mercy of Eddie's backward momentum, was face-planted into his own trunk, into his own goddamn luggage.

It wasn't until *that* scene Eddie left his valet position.

Management promoted him.

They had to take that boy's tiny foot off the pedal. So they put a phone receiver in his baby hand, taking valet dispatch calls and lining up the tickets for us to bring down.

They took my foot off the pedal, too. My dedication, positive attitude, and lack of thievery, violence, and drugs had made a favorable impression on the executive committee. Trish came down one pleasant autumn afternoon, into the coolness of the porte cochere, and asked me if I might be interested in a front desk position.

I said yes.

A promotion to be proud of. Tennis shoes to dress shoes. "From ashy to classy," Perry said to me my last night on the line. He put his hand around my arm, smiling so proudly, as if I were his son. Then he let his hand fall back to his side, took a hard look at me, his eyes focused, and said, "Don't forget where you came from, Tommy."

I never have. Valet 4 Life, motherfuckers.

CHAPTER TWO

I attended the Monday morning 7:00 a.m. meeting, held in the offices behind the front desk. I stood in a circle with my new co-workers, looking like an idiot in my valet uniform and dusty black tennis shoes. Everyone seemed to be looking down at my sneakers. Less than a week ago I'd been running for a ticket and kicked what I thought was a shoe in the middle of the Level 8 straightaway. But when I followed the projectile, brown and certainly *shoe-like,* it rolled over heavily a few times and then righted itself, assuming its natural *rat-like* posture, and waddled off, wounded, to the far corner of the garage. I looked down at my shoes, shivering again at the meaty memory of that rodent slammed against my black K-Swiss.

"I would like to introduce you to Tommy," Trish said. "His uniform suit is being tailored, so today he will stay back here, in the heart of the house, and train on the system. Please assist him with any questions he may have." That was the first time I heard the term "heart of the house," which refers to the back offices and hallways, the storage closets and freight elevators, the white-painted rooms filled with dirty off-white sheets to be cleaned, as opposed to "the front of the house," meaning the polished marble foyers, vacuumed Oriental rugs, gold-plated railings shined to perfection, and the lobby's center table sagging with fresh-cut flowers that cost the hotel thousands of dollars a week. Trish then continued the meeting, reading off the meeting sheet, something I would grow very familiar with, containing all events for the day, hotel occupancy broken down by check-in/check-out, as well as a healthy dose of company service training, very similar to the two weeks of classes we'd received prior to opening. That whole "party line" fell apart in the garage, but up here they were still pounding the Kool-Aid. And I was taking my first sip.

One member of the staff had just finished reading a service story off the meeting sheet from a sister property in Florida: something about an employee buying a chew toy for a guest's puppy and the guest cried from joy or whatever. "Ladies and gentlemen, have a wonderful day. Start the show," Trish said, and with that the crew dispersed, some pushing through the door to the front desk and lobby to relieve the solitary overnight agent, others down the hallway to man PBX, or the operator stations. Trish told me to head to the general manager's office for a brief meeting with Mr. Daniels.

"Take a seat," he said to me and indicated a plush coffee-colored leather chair in front of his desk, the same type that populated the Wine Bar in the lobby. "Welcome to the hotel proper, my boy. You handled yourself wonderfully down there in the garage. I heard you witnessed 'the choking.' Things can get pretty fucked down there, right?"

"Yes, sir." I appreciated the profanity, the deformalization of the situation. This man knew exactly what he was doing.

"Now you are truly in the hotel business. Front desk. The brain center of the hotel. You'll learn how a hotel operates, son, from check-in to checkout: billing, room features, upgrades, taxes, cash handling, amenities, VIPs. Lots to learn. You excited?"

"Absolutely."

"Good. I started at front desk myself. Should an employee have his heart set on my position right here, GM, and believe me, this gig is fantastic, front desk is half the battle. The other half is housekeeping. If you know how to get a guest into the right room and know everything about what it takes to make sure that room is spotlessly cleaned, then you can run a hotel, end of story. But you can't run a luxury hotel. Luxury is more than chandeliers and horrible oil paintings of horses. Obviously, it's about service. And that is what I want you to learn, Tommy. Take care of our guests. They will love you for it. I will love you for it. I know you heard that lie we told you that every employee, every day, has a large available budget to service our guests in creative ways? It's actually true. Use it. We will support you in your decisions. Now get your ass out of that leather chair and embrace our property management system. Learn the system so you can rule the world. Go get 'em. I'm very proud of you."

Chuck a cool motherfucker.

I walked back down through the lobby and pushed open the door to the heart of the house, determined to prove myself, ready to execute my vision.

"I hope your brain isn't as dusty as your shoes, homey."

And with that, Andy, who was waiting for me in the back office, began training me on the property management system (or, uh, PMS for short). A strange thing to see a hotel translated into a program, every room and floor represented, every guest assigned a profile, rate, and requests. A portion of the work involved learning the room codes: NT = No Tub. NC = No Closet. SB = Small Bathroom. And here is a great one: NE = Near Elevator. Or another guest favorite: NV = No View.

Andy set me up on the test system, the exact program (different color screen!) running for some reason on an arbitrary date in 1983, and there I could create reservations, assign rooms, check guests into one room and then move them to another, check them out, post and remove charges, and generally screw things up nice for all the fake 1980s guests.

"Okay, okay," Andy said, "you've got this." I think he was disappointed. Maybe he had planned to close the door to Trish's office, assume a relaxed seated position that indicated they were close, friendly, almost equals, and say, "Listen, this new kid, the valet? Ain't got the brain for it, Trish," and then brush some dirt off his crossed knee, a disappointed frown on his face. It never turned out that way for him.

So Andy led me down the hall to PBX, or

the operator department, explaining this portion of our job on the way. "So, at most hotels, the front desk agents are just agents, and the phone operators are just operators. But here, they are smarter about it. FDAs operate the phone system. Now, why do you think that's a smart move?"

"Well, I suppose if the guest dials zero and needs something from the front desk, the operator doesn't have to transfer the call? They can take care of everything from the first point of contact?"

"Where did you learn that term, 'point of contact'?"

"That's not really a hotel term, is it? And I learned it in college."

"Oh, college. You went to college," he said and nodded at me, actually frustrated.

Andy, apparently, was an elitist prick. Which is exactly why he was picked as front desk trainer, because it takes a superior prick like that to really *get off* on telling you everything you need to know. It's sad, but he got his rocks off knowing more than a new hire, who knows nothing. Which actually makes him an effective choice: I was getting thoroughly trained.

"And make sure that red light is on before you talk some shit because otherwise the guest can hear you, and you don't want that, so keep an eye on the red mute light here in PBX, and also no one knows why it's even called PBX, but some people say it's phone booth exchange because —"

"Actually," Trish said from the doorway, looking pretty, leaning casually, "it stands for private branch exchange, going back to when the systems were operated by hand. Not that I was around back then, of course."

"Of course not, Trish. You weren't at all," Andy stuttered out.

"Anyone know what's wrong with this moron?" I asked rhetorically, but, you know, internally, making sure my red light was on and all that.

"Suit's ready, Tommy. Let's wipe the valet off you."

As soon as they had a suit on me, they escorted me out to the desk and stood me in front of my very first front desk terminal.

Oh, Mr. Anderson. The very first guest I ever checked in. I remember you.

That's a lie. I don't. It was a blur, a simple check-in that bled into the five million other check-ins I would come to perform in my life.

I was nervous, though; *that* I remember. Andy posted up behind me while I prepared myself, staring down at the system, room codes and F-key shortcuts racing through my head, my check-in verbiage piled up in a heap that I hoped to extract and hand over phrase by phrase in the appropriate order, all while smiling and not sweating.

Sanford the doorman came around the corner, pulling a gold bell cart behind him stacked with luggage. He was my favorite doorman. As big as a bear, when he grabbed your hand in greeting and pulled you to his chest for the half hug, he'd rip you forward, and you'd bounce off him. Apparently, he spent almost all of his tip money at Foot Locker. "Tommy, I got over five hundred pairs of tennies. My son, he got about fifty pairs. I got a shoe problem, me."

Now he caught sight of me posted up behind the front desk. "Look *here*. All in a tie and shit! Tommy! You look sharp, son."

"Thanks, Sanford," I said, and we shook hands over the desk. "Waiting on my first check-in."

"I got your boy right *chere*," he said, looking down at a luggage tag. Andy flinched behind me, hearing garage language used in his lobby. "Anderson. Man, I gots to tell Perry. Have him come up here and scope you out. We all proud of you. Believe that. Here come this dude now."

Sanford began superfluously adjusting luggage on the cart until the guest approached the desk. "Mr. Anderson, this is Tommy for your check-in. I'm going back downstairs, sir."

"Fine. I'm checking in. Anderson."

I didn't even see Sanford slip off without a tip. I was busy pulling up the reservation, swiping the credit card, and issuing phrases one after the other, voice a bit shaky, fingertips a bit wet, but functional nonetheless.

Done. He walked off ahead of his luggage, a bellman falling in behind. Just like that. Done. Baby's first check-in. That one was for Chuck Daniels.

The next check-in I dedicated to me. The one after that for Perry. The one after that for Trish. After that for Chip and all those who never made it. After that for the human tumor, fuck it. After that for me again. After that for Louis Armstrong, why not? After that for Andy, I guess. After that for posterity.

And every check-in after that?

For the paycheck, son.

I'm getting ahead of myself with that last line. Never for one minute in New Orleans did I work for my paycheck. I worked for my company, my GM. And I had a tremendous talent for it.

The front desk really *is* the brain center

of the hotel. After a few months I saw the hotel itself as a puzzle: king-bed pieces, bathtub pieces, views-of-the-Mississippi-River pieces. And then there's the predatory, demanding horde of 350 checking-in guests who all want king beds with bathtubs overlooking the Mississippi River. I wanted to make them all happy, but in the puzzle of a hotel not everyone can be an edge piece, not everyone gets a corner suite.

Service is not about being up-front and honest. Service is about minimizing negatives and creating the illusion of perfection. Here's how it's done: Lie. Smile. Finesse. Barter. Convince. Lie again. Smile again.

I learned mind control, how to persuade guests they want something other than what they booked. You demand a king bed? But are you sure you don't want double beds (BARTER)? I only offer because double-bed rooms are larger, more square footage (LIE), and you can use the second bed to spread out your clothes (FINESSE) or use it to relax on and still have a fresh bed to crawl into (CONVINCE). I'm glad I have a double-bed room for you too, sir (SMILE). It was absolutely my pleasure (LIE AGAIN). Enjoy your stay (SMILE AGAIN). The guest leaves happy, and that makes *me* happy.

I came to learn the system by heart, how to utilize every single feature. Within a PMS, perhaps the trickiest yet most helpful representation of the hotel is the matrix or tape chart. Basically, every room is listed vertically on the left with a horizontal row extended out representing that room on future dates. A currently checked-in reservation for a specific room is usually represented as a long red bar, which, let's say, takes up three nights, then after that a hole for two nights, and then an upcoming res pre-blocked in that same room, usually represented as a green bar: and that lets me see the hotel as a whole, allowing me to drag reservations from this room to that, filling in holes so as not to leave one-night vacancies I cannot fill unless I have a one-night guest. In those first months I was actually naive enough to ask guests if they would like to stay in one room for tonight and move to another tomorrow for the rest of their stay. They sure as hell would not.

I also learned how to fully operate the phone system, which was simple. Days assigned to the PBX station were days of spinning around in the chairs, wearing a headset, talking idly to co-workers, balling up printer paper and throwing it at the mailbox slots, throwing it at each other. The calls come down the line in order, one agent after the next, so, should there be four agents working, after you take your call — which could be as simple as "What time is check-out?" — the next three calls were up to your colleagues, and it might not come back to you for a good ten minutes, depending on the time of day and occupancy. I once used a stopwatch to time my workload, starting the counter when I picked up a call and stopping it the moment I disconnected. Then I would go back to throwing paper and spinning around in the chair. After timing the entire day, I calculated my hourly wage based on actual time worked, and it came to over $200 an hour, which, taking the math further, would have given me over $400,000 a year.

Interestingly, though, operators were also in charge of the in-room movie systems, which were separate back then, so removing charges and canceling orders had to be done at a separate console.

"Good afternoon, thank you for calling the front office. This is Tommy, how may I assist you?" How many times has that phrase chunk come out of my mouth? If you wedged open my skull and pressed the point of a souvenir hotel pen into the right spot in my brain, I guarantee that phone greeting will spurt out of my mouth on auto-repeat.

"Yeah, I'm in room 1205. I accidentally ordered a movie. Can you take it off the bill?"

"Certainly, sir."

Over to the movie console to cancel *Asian Secretaries Rike It Rough,* two minutes and seven seconds into playback. I guess the opening credits were sufficient.

Worry not. The systems have changed, and we can no longer see the movie titles. I mean, we know the new releases cost $12.95 and the sexual releases cost $14.95. We just no longer have access to your specific fetishes. Not that we judge you (LIE).

These were my first glimpses into the lives of strangers, something I was coming to realize was a side effect of this business (or perk, depending on the predominance of your voyeuristic tendencies). Want to know what people are really like? What their strange habits are? How they treat people when no one they deem important is watching? Ask their desk agent. Basically, ask their servants: because that is what we are, an army of servants, included with the price of the room.

I was having a lovely time, though, learning to navigate life through the eyes of someone who serves but is unseen. César Ritz, the "king of hoteliers and hotelier to kings" and founder of what would become the Ritz-Carlton empire, is quoted as saying, "People like to be served, but invisibly." If a guest wanted to be gruff and shout out orders, I was accommodating, all stiff movements and sharp, quick head nods, handling his business efficiently. If a guest wanted to assume we were friends, call me by my first name, and tell me about a street performer he saw last night on Bourbon Street, I would lean on the desk, chin in hand, and listen, laughing at the same exact description I heard yesterday from another guest, about the same exact street performer.

I was infinite. All things to all people. Uniform impeccable. Providing exceptional service. Working overtime.

I learned how to defuse anger.

I learned how to take all the blame and smile.

We worked hard through the mild New Orleans winter, through the seasonal drop in occupancy, which allowed me to focus on each guest interaction and master the system. As spring took hold, the heady fragrance of flowers *almost* overcoming the debaucherous odor of the Quarter, we steadied ourselves for our first run through

New Orleans's premier tourist event: Mardi Gras.

Nothing is more universally misunderstood than Mardi Gras. The image associated with the event usually boils down to . . . well, tits. Tits and beads. But that's like saying the island of Manhattan boils down to popped-collar trust-fund date rapists, just because you've only been to the Upper East Side. Or the whole city is Chinese, just because you got off at the Canal Street N train stop. Breasts, without a doubt, are available for viewing, but only in a very small strip of the French Quarter, on a single street. The rest of the city couldn't be more lovely this time of year. It's a time for families (and everyone is family), parades, and getting together as a city to celebrate life and, most important, *take time off work.* And, yeah, also, *drink.*

"Care to join us for a libation, Tommy?" This polite request came from Gordon the bellman, a true southern gentleman, over six feet tall, gaunt, flamboyantly gay, and exceedingly kindhearted.

"I don't drink."

"I need *me* a drink. I can't stand this job." That admission came from Mark, another bellman: black, very young, and constantly unhappy with his position. The money wasn't enough for him: dragging people's bags around made him feel subordinate, I suppose. Most people would put up with a lot more for the kind of cash a bellman can earn, but Mark was openly humiliated by his duties. ("What a gorgeous job for a guy . . . Carrying people's suitcases and waiting around for a tip." — Holden Caulfield.)

We snapped off our name tags, changed out of our uniforms, and exited through the employee entrance, right into the French Quarter. Since Mardi Gras weekend was approaching, everyone's neck was roped with beads, from the McDonald's fry cooks to the janitors to the homeless. Another rarely mentioned effect of the beads: they brought us all together. We drained the seriousness out of our individuality by wearing cheap, gaudy plastic beads.

Five bellmen, Sanford the doorman, and three other FDAs rolled into the Alibi bar, a service industry spot on the west edge of the Quarter.

Drinks: dirt cheap.

Clientele: often wearing name tags and/or aprons (waiters on break from fine dining restaurants in the area rolled in to shove dollars into the video poker, smoke cigarettes, take tequila shots, and generally make the most of their fifteen-minute breaks).

"What you drankin', Tommy?" Sanford asked.

"Just a soda or something. I don't drink."

"You never drank? Ever?"

"I feel sorry for people who don't drink," Gordon drawled out. "When they get up in the morning, that's the best they will feel all day. Frank Sinatra."

"I did when I was younger. In high school."

"Word? What'd you drink then?"

"Whiskey."

"Jack?"

"Jack."

"There it is. Lisa, angel, four Heinekens, five Abita Ambers, and a shot of Jack for my boy here. This dude is on the up-and-up."

There it was before me. I had only one option. A lifting of the glasses and then down it went, hot and nice.

"Nah, nah. I know I didn't just see *that* shit. Tommy, you had you a shot right there? That was Dr Pepper?" Perry asked, striding in from the street, sitting down on a stool next to me. He didn't even have to look at the bartender: she opened two Heinekens and put them both before him immediately.

"Whoa." My breath was still choked with burn. "Yep."

"Yeah, then you drinking one with me too." And with that another was served up, and I took that one down out of respect for Perry.

It was almost Mardi Gras, fuck it.

Later, I sat down drunk on the corner of Carondelet and Canal Streets, listening for the rumble of the streetcar that would take me back uptown to my apartment, watching the evening sun bleed from the streets, the city shifting into night, when it truly became New Orleans: the music, the constant festival, the smell of late evening dinners pouring out, layering the beer-soaked streets, prostitutes, clubs with DJs, rowdy gay bars, dirty strip clubs, the insane out for a walk, college students vomiting in trash cans, daiquiri bars lit up like supermarkets, washing-machine–sized mixers built into the wall spinning every color of daiquiri, lone trumpet players, grown women crying, clawing at men in suits, portrait painters, spangers (spare change beggars), gutter punks with dogs, kids tap-dancing with spinning bike wheels on their heads, the golden cowboy frozen on a milk crate, his golden gun pointed at a child in the crowd, fortune-tellers, psycho preachers, mum-

blers, fighters, rock-faced college boys out
for a date rape, club chicks wearing silver
miniskirts, horse-drawn carriages, plastic
cups piling against the high curbs of Bourbon Street, jazz music pressing up against
rock-and-roll cover bands, murderers, scam
artists, hippies selling anything, magic
shows and people on unicycles, flying cock-
roaches the size of pocket rockets, rats
without fear, men in drag, business execs
wandering drunk in packs, deciding not to
tell their wives, sluts sucking dick on open
balconies, cops on horseback looking down
blouses, cars wading across the river of
drunks on Bourbon Street, the people
screaming at them, pouring drinks on the
hood, putting their asses to the window,
whole bars of people laughing, shot girls
with test tubes of neon-colored booze,
bouncers dragging skinny white boys out by
their necks, college girls rubbing each
other's backs after vomiting tequila, T-shirts,
drinks sold in a green two-foot tube with a
small souvenir grenade in the bottom,
people stumbling, tripping, falling, laughing
on the sidewalk in the filth, laughing too
hard to stand back up, thin rivers of piss
leaking out from corners, brides with dirty
dresses, men in G-strings, mangy dogs, balloon animals, camcorders, twenty-four-hour

3-4-1, free admission, amateur night, black-eyed strippers, drunk bicyclers, clouds of termites like brown mist surrounding street-lamps, ventriloquists, bikers, people sitting on mailboxes, coffee with chicory, soul singers, the shoeless, the drunks, the blissful, the ignorant, the beaten, the assholes, the cheaters, the douche bags, the comedians, the holy, the broken, the affluent, the beggars, the forgotten, and the soft spring air pregnant with every scent created by such a town.

The next morning, after my immaculate liver processed the whiskey like water, I awoke refreshed and ready to work through Mardi Gras at the hotel. There were plenty of call-outs, plenty of extra shifts available; front desk agents with less pristine livers were left bedridden, or they deliberately called in sick to catch their favorite parades. Or ride in them — even *Perry* called out to hold his position in the Zulu Parade, promising to hand me down a coveted painted coconut if I could find him on the float, which I failed to do, since I was working doubles to make sure our desk was adequately staffed.

I worked on and on at that front desk. I turned down tips to prove my level of commitment. Turned down tips? I know, a minute ago I was bitching about the wooden tumor. Now, if I escorted a guest to the elevators, taking the time to personally walk him or her across the lobby, and was presented with a five-dollar bill for my service, I would bow and say, "Please. It's my pleasure," and walk off, leaving the guest with tip in hand and mouth hanging open. That guest will be a loyal customer for life. How does that help me? Well . . . it doesn't. However, I was simply and happily following the company mandate, which demands that I escort. The policy at my hotel was that employees should never point or give directions; they should walk guests to their destination. Hotels are not the only business that secretly implement this policy. Ask any salesperson in Nordstrom where the ladies' shoe department is. You will take him or her, like a dog, on a walk.

But it wasn't all great shifts and great service. It's a hotel, after all: I was learning quickly that shit goes horribly wrong.

I certainly recall the first guest I ever walked. The term "walking a guest" sends shivers down any GM's spine, and multiple front desk agent spines as well. Often (okay, *always*) hotels will overbook whenever possible. The average no-show rate (guests who cancel last minute or simply fail to arrive) is 10 percent, daily. Accordingly, the sales department and reservations are encouraged to book the property to 110 percent capacity, in the hopes that with cancellations and no-shows they will fill every room in the hotel. Putting a head in every bed is called a "perfect sell," and it's not easy to accomplish. After clocking out at 11:00 p.m. and leaving the hotel with only five rooms vacant but ten remaining arrivals, you come in the next morning and ask, "What happened?"

"Perfect sell."

"No shit!?"

But what happens when the numbers game doesn't play in the hotel's favor? Someone gets walked.

Now, a man in my current financial position, a man clocking in and out for a living, would consider getting walked to be a wonderful surprise. Sure, I planned to stay at Hotel A, but Hotel A blew it and overbooked. Management saw the ship sinking around 5:00 p.m. and started calling other comparable hotels in the area, securing rooms under the name Hotel A TBD. So, yeah, Hotel A made a mess, but they will *pay for my entire night's room and tax* (plus one phone call — how cute is that?) and certainly arrange or pay for transportation, even if it's just down the block.

I was once in Boston, during marathon weekend, and when I arrived at my hotel and announced my name at the desk, the agent froze, terrified. She stammered, "Oh, Mr. Jacobs. Oh. Please. Please, just wait here a moment." A manager (easy to spot; different suit, different tie, surname on the name tag) came out from the back office sporting one hell of a frown, holding a folded piece of paper in his hands as if it were my grandmother's death certificate. I knew what it was: the letter I was going to hand to the front desk. The front desk of Hotel B, where I was headed.

"Are you guys walking me?" I asked enthusiastically. That reaction *really* threw them. They must have thought I was psychotic.

"Oh, well . . . yes."

"Relax. I work the front desk. It's all good." Their faces instantly drained of all that fear and trepidation. Plus they gave me twenty for cab fare. And I walked. I saved $350 on the room rate, and that twenty bought drinks in the lobby bar of Hotel B. Well, it bought *a* drink in Hotel B; the cocktail prices were absurd. Hotel B is ridiculously overpriced.

However, that is a man in my financial situation. Why was all that fear and trepidation in their Bostonian front desk eyes?

Because *motherfuckers go ape shit when you walk them.* They are *incredulous.* They *cry.* Honestly, never in their lives has anything like this ever happened to them, ever. Meanwhile, they are one of ten walks for me tonight, and tomorrow is looking like another night "front row at the shit show."

"I will never stay here again, ever."

These people just saved five hundred dollars, and they are *irate.*

(That word was invented for the hospitality business: "irate.")

It was a Japanese couple who broke my walk cherry. And there wasn't much foreplay or romance.

"Mr. Umagawa, I am terribly sorry about putting you in this position. But we have secured alternate lodging for you at the Ritz-Carlton. It is four blocks away, and we will be taking care of the full cost of your room."

"No. *No.* NO. We have contract. You must *honor contract.*"

At this point his wife started yelling at me, loudly. Andy was working the desk beside me, watching it all go down. Soon after, this incident became a famous anecdote, one

68

he'd be asked to re-create in the employee cafeteria.

"So she starts screaming, right? Half Japanese, half English until she boils it down to the phrase 'We sleep on floor! We SLEEP RIGHT HERE ON FLOOR. WE SLEEP ON FLOOR.' At which point the husband, who is doing deep-breathing exercises, draws his hand slowly in front of his wife, silencing her immediately with this tiny little gesture. He started to talk about the con track again, you know, honoring the con track. Your boy Tommy here just kept his head swiveling from one to the other, 'CONTRACK.' 'WE SWEEP RYE HEE ON FROOR.' 'YOU HONOR CONTRACK!' 'WE SWEEP ON FROOR!' "

When Trish finally came out and saw the miserable scene in the lobby, she quieted them down and gave them a room. At Hotel A, our hotel.

Yep. You might have used this argument yourself, because I've heard it an infinite number of times: "Come on, you're telling me there isn't one single empty room in this hotel? It's not even 5:00 p.m., and you are seriously telling me there is not one single goddamn room in this goddamn hotel? Do not bullshit me . . . Tommy."

Notice the use of the name there at the end, the way he paused and fished it off my name tag? A real jerk move. As I said, we get to see how people treat their servants, and it's rarely attractive. But he is right. I have twenty-five vacant rooms at my disposal. Why is Asshole A getting walked to Hotel B? Many reasons:

1. He booked Expedia, hence he has a deeply discounted rate, hence he is less important.
2. We checked: he never stayed here before and might never visit the city again, even without this earth-shattering catastrophic event he is experiencing.
3. He's a one-nighter. You walk a two-nighter, then you have to bring him back the next day, and there is nothing easy or pleasant about that for anyone. He will walk around like a martyr, like Jesus let off the cross.
4. And this one is so much more important than all the others: he is acting like a dick about it. I can break; I can make the call and say, "Sir, I understand, perhaps I could put you in a twin-bed room tonight; would that be okay?" But I'm not going to. He is spitting all over my desk. He's using profanity.

"I will never fucking stay here again, do you know that?"

"Sir, blow me. Please, fuck yourself hard, and never come back," I said, with my red light on of course. And then out loud I said, "I am incredibly sorry, sir. I want to personally apologize, and if you do return, I promise we will take extra-special care of your reservation and ensure you are upgraded." (We say we will do this, but we won't. We will forget. But we will certainly be reminded of our past transgression. A Jesus let off the cross loves to constantly bring up "the cross.")

Each walk was a little nightmare for me. I mean, I was turning down tips. I wanted to do nothing but please these guests. And here they were screaming in my face. It was terrible.

Little did I know, a few years later, in another city, I would walk fifteen people at one time. And I would start it off like this: "OKAY. PEOPLE. EVERYONE QUIET *DOWN* AND *LISTEN UP.*"

But at this hotel, though I had no comparison at the time, things were relatively calm. We didn't often overbook, and perhaps the southern location had a calming effect on most of our guests.

Our southern location also drew a few

71

celebrities, providing me with my first celebrity encounters, if you can call them encounters.

"Paul McCartney is onstage with Clarence. He's doing Beatles songs for heaven's sake!" Gordon the bellman said, eyes wide.

"Cover me," I said and walked around the desk, crossing the lobby to the Bistro Lounge. We'd all seen Paul McCartney come through the lobby (like a canary-yellow Bentley — impossible to miss), and we knew he'd probably get a drink in the Bistro and check out our horn player Clarence, a local musician from the Ninth Ward, backed up by a simple jazz band. Clarence had been garnering recognition and getting good press in the *Times-Picayune.* So, *sure,* Paul gravitates to the music, and, *fine,* he grabs a table to take in some of the set. But now he's onstage performing Beatles classics with Clarence and the band? I could hear his unmistakable voice clearly as I approached. The entrance was already jammed up, and right in front of the crowd was the assistant front office manager, John, saying to every employee who approached: "Next employee who pushes their way into the Bistro is fired. Tommy, I will fire you on the spot. Get back to the desk, *now.*" I did. We all tried to be quiet and hear the performance from across the lobby.

John was very upset at me in particular for attempting to join the crowd. He said that I, above all, should understand that our celebrity visitors might be mobbed by locals but NOT by hotel staff. He was right, but I mean, when something as rare as . . . Okay, he was right.

For the next two weeks John was disappointed in me. But our relationship only lasted another two weeks. Turns out hotels are like the army. They shipped him out to take over the front desk of a hotel in Cleveland (damn). Then they sent my girl Trish to open a new property in Egypt (*damn!*). Now that the hotel was up and running properly, they were shipping out the opening team. We had a new FOM named Chris Bourne, far older than Trish and half the brain. Andy was particularly devastated by this loss.

For his part, Andy turned out to be a decent enough guy. Well, his idiosyncrasies were apparent, unavoidable, and not necessarily *endearing,* but you know the old saying, at least he wasn't choking co-workers to death. And he did have a decent sense of humor.

After a year we started to loosen up at the desk. It was a Tuesday, just past noon, the fire alarm system running a test, the emergency lights in the lobby flashing, sirens yelping out staccato blasts, when this old man walked up to the desk, concerned, dizzied by the loud sirens, his eyes wide in the flashing lights.

"What's going on? Is there a fire?"

"A fire? No, sir," Andy responded.

"Well, what's all this commotion?"

"Well . . . Sir . . . YOU ARE OUR ONE MILLIONTH CUSTOMER!! CONGRATULATIONS! YOUR STAY WILL BE FREE!!!"

Andy also developed a new technique to defuse guests' anger. Dealing with guests' tempers is a big portion of the work at the desk. You can try meekness, but it might fuel their ferocity. You can try pulling back your shoulders with confidence and assuring them you will take care of it ASAP, but that can come off unsympathetic. So Andy developed an experimental method wherein, should a guest approach with a red face, ready to spit with anger all over the desk, well, then, you simply one-up him on the anger.

"I just came back from lunch, and my room has not been *cleaned yet*. Anyone *planning* on cleaning it!? Is anyone actually *working* here!?"

"WHAT?!" Andy hissed. "I cannot BE-LIEVE they FAILED TO SERVICE YOUR ROOM, SIR. Jesus F. . . . NO, no. NO, sir. Trust me, it is NOT OKAY AT ALL. SOMEONE IS GOING TO LOSE THEIR JOB FOR THIS," Andy yelled, jamming his finger down hard on the front desk and rip-ping the phone receiver from the cradle to dial housekeeping.

He broke the guest like a pony. The guest waved his hands before the desk and said, "It's not really that bad. Can't we just get it cleaned now? That would be fine."

There are a thousand ways to complain, a thousand ways to have your problems in-stantly solved. As far as the most effective tactic, would I suggest screaming at an em-ployee? Obviously, I would not.

Here is what I *would* suggest: Before ap-proaching any employee, try to pinpoint exactly what the problem is (You were promised one rate and charged another / A bellman was rude to your wife / Someone must've thought you were finished with the pizza box you left on the floor of the bath-room and threw away the last cold slice), and then, if possible, what solution would make you feel satisfied (Having the rate adjusted to reflect the original booking / Be-ing assured that the issue will be investigated and the bellman will be spoken to / A pizza slice on the floor? It's gone. Let it GO). Though most complaints *should* be delivered to the front desk directly, in person or on the phone, keep in mind that most issues you present will not have been caused by the front desk at all. So briefly outline your problem, offer a solution if you have one, and then ask whom you should speak with to have the problem solved. "Should I speak to a manager about this?" "Should I speak to housekeeping about this?" Those are wonderful and beautiful questions to ask. Most of the time the front desk will be able to solve the problem immediately or at least act as proxy and communicate your unrest to the appropriate department or manager. Want to make sure that the agent doesn't nod, say "certainly," and not do a damn thing? Get his or her name. Nothing tightens up an employee's throat like being directly identified. You don't have to threaten him or her either, just a nice, casual "Thanks for your help. I'll stop by later to make sure everything has been taken care of. Tommy, right?" Whatever you asked me to do I am DOING it.

Lastly, let's try to keep fiery anger out of the lobby. Almost 100 percent of the time the person you are punching on had nothing whatsoever to do with your situation. It's a hotel; nothing's personal. Here is a nice rule of thumb we can all try to remember: a person of culture should make every effort to hide his frustration from those who've had nothing to do with its origin. Boom.

But will screaming get you what you want? Well, probably. Even if Andy hadn't broken the guest by one-upping him on intensity, he was still definitely in the process of calling housekeeping to get the room cleaned, obviously calm now that the guest had wandered off. That's when Mark, the youngest bellman, came from the elevators and stood still in the middle of the lobby, looking down at his feet. I'd just given him a checkout, an upper-level luxury suite, and he'd taken a cart, but now here he was, cartless, breathing hard and looking at the marble lobby floor.

"Mark, what happened? You okay?"

"I can't do this. Anymore. I went to the room you gave me and knocked. This little white girl comes to answer the door, maybe ten years old, wearing a fancy little dress. And so I say, 'Are you ready to check out?' and this tiny girl turns around and says, 'Mommy, Mommy, the servant's here!' "

"Then what?" Gordon asked.

"Then I walked off. I ain't no servant. I'm gonna quit, Gordon. Tommy, I'm quitting." He unpinned his name tag, slid it off his uniform, refastened the pin, and set it on the bell stand. "I'm sorry. Good-bye, you guys. Tell Chuck I'm sorry."

Less than an hour later Chuck wanted to see me. I sat myself down in that same leather chair.

"Tommy, Tommy, Tommy."

"Chuck, Chuck, Chuck."

"Funny. So. What do you think?"

"About what, sir?"

"Your progress."

"I feel I've done well at the desk. I've tried very hard."

"And this business, the hotel business, is it for you? A career man?" He seemed distracted. He was playing with a hotel pen, dismantling it.

"Yes, sir."

"I trust you, Tommy. I'm going to offer you a choice. You're done with the front desk. I heard you've started to loosen up down there, started in with the jokes."

"Oh, well, I hope I haven't —"

"Not to worry. It's natural. You've outgrown the position. So I'd like to offer you two opportunities. Whichever one you want is yours. As you are aware, there is a bellman position recently available. Extremely recently. It's yours if you want it. You are fantastic with the guests. Or."

"Or?"

"Housekeeping manager. Management, Tommy. Take over the evening position down there. You'd be in charge of turndown, scheduling, purchasing, and a thousand other things. A staff of 150."

". . ."

That's all I could say: ". . ."

It was happening: he wanted me to be a manager. I thought back to the party they threw us before the hotel opened. I'd come so far. I didn't have to stop. Now the rungs didn't seem so endless. After housekeeping, perhaps a move to a smaller property to manage the front office, which I already felt would be kind of easy. Then to a larger property to manage the entire housekeeping department. Then I could be a rooms executive, essentially the GM's vice president, overseeing "Rooms Division," which included all of the departments necessary to run a hotel, as opposed to food and beverage, which only dabbled in hotel life when it came to room service. Five to ten years and I could be a GM in any city I chose.

"Let's talk money. Housekeeping means

ten-hour shifts or more, on salary. When you break it down hourly, you will make less than you are making now. You'll have to purchase your own suits. The work is physically demanding, the staff is large and can be difficult. It's a very challenging position. Bellman? You'll double your money immediately and keep the eight-hour shifts. Zero responsibility."

"You think I should take the bellman position?"

"Do that, and you'll never be anything else in your life. Hate to say it, but it's true. I've seen it my whole career: Show me a twenty-year-old kid getting his first job as a bellman, and I'll show you a seventy-year-old bellman who started fifty years ago. You grow accustomed to that pay grade, and taking a step forward will always mean cutting your money in half. No one takes that step."

"Housekeeping," I said.

"Housekeeping?"

"I can do it. I want to do it."

"That's my boy." He slapped his hand down on the desk. "You're a manager now. All kinds of things are going to change. The way your friends treat you will change. The way I treat you will change. This is going to be the worst part of your journey by far. Monday morning, nine o'clock managers'

80

meeting in the River View conference room. Show up in a suit and be ready. Let's get it on."

CHAPTER THREE

"Listen to me, goddamn it," Chuck hissed at everyone in the conference room. "Our occupancy is dropping, and we are *dying* here. Why? Anyone know why? *Because,* in this city, the only bed with a higher rate per night is New Orleans Charity Hospital. Sales department: We need to drop these rates. We need to GET SOME GODDAMN HEADS IN THESE BEDS. DO ALL OF YOU WANT TO END UP IN GODFOR-SAKEN CLEVELAND WITH JOHN? Is any of this clear?"

Holy shit. Mr. Daniels was going *off.* And no one seemed surprised. He stopped speaking and turned his head to the windows. The conference room was on the fifteenth floor, high enough to crest the squat architecture of the French Quarter and offer a view of the Mississippi in the distance, like a fat brown ribbon.

"On a final note," Chuck continued,

quieter now, eyes still focused on the Quarter below, "this is Tommy Jacobs, our new p.m. housekeeping manager. Tommy, this is Terrance, the director of housekeeping. He's a sharp kid, Terrance. Watch he doesn't take your job." He leveled his gaze back to the conference table, surrounded by managers from every department in the hotel. These morning meetings, or staff meetings, are designed to get everyone — Christ, I hate myself for even writing this — "on the same page." Here is the opportunity for front office to mention to housekeeping that all the double-bed rooms are booked for the night, hence the ladies need to clean them, or "flip" them, as early as possible. It's also an opportunity for people in the sales department to pretend they know something about the hospitality business, even though they don't. Accounting might take this opportunity to be complainy and say things like, "Um, as we said before, can you guys, uh, maybe complete the voiding process yourselves instead of just moving it to the accounts-refund folio because that kind of makes a mess for us, okay? We said that last week, but it's definitely still happening."

"All right, let's get to it," Chuck said, wrapping up with a deep breath. "Remember: heads in beds. The only thing that matters in this business. Heads in beds."

And with that we stood. After suggesting Terrance tour me around once the housekeepers were settled, Mr. Daniels motioned for me to remain seated. Everyone poured out of the conference room, leaving just the two of us.

"How'd I do?"

"Pretty intimidating, Mr. Daniels."

"GMs have two personas. Much in the way a president has two personas. He must be loved by the people, the voters, in this case the staff. But he must be feared by management, his cabinet. It's about kissing babies in public and cracking heads in private. So there it is. Terrance is waiting for you on 25. Go."

I'd never even seen the twenty-fifth floor. That was on club level, which began on 20 and continued to the top floor, each level requiring key access. In fact, since the levels were locked, I had to get out on 19 and walk the rest of the way up the stairs. I could have used the employee service elevators, but at that time I was some front-of-the-house "peacock" strutting only through guest areas. Desk agents live in the front of the house. I was about to go deep into the heart.

Not every luxury hotel has a club level,

but should you find yourself with the option and the money, the increase in rate can pay for itself. It's like flying first class. Done properly, club level starts with the doorman. Upon identifying your last name, hopefully cleverly picking it off a luggage tag or, ideally, recognizing you from your last stay, he runs it against the club-level arrivals, a list he receives every morning, often kept taped inside his silly-ass top hat. The doorman then discreetly alerts the valet dispatch, who calls the club level so they can prep. Often, when booking a club res, reservations will inquire about your favorite cocktail, and when, upon your arrival, club receives the advance call from valet, they prepare your fancy drink and place it on a tray next to a hot *oshibori* towel. The doorman, bypassing that pedestrian and disgustingly open-to-the-public front desk, then passes off the guests directly to the bellman, who whooshes them right up to the twentieth floor, where they are greeted at the opening of the elevator doors with the cocktail and hot towel, then seated and checked in by a private concierge.

On average, a club lounge has five food presentations a day, from a simple but filling breakfast to hors d'oeuvres and appetizers throughout the day and ending with the evening dessert. And let's not forget the opulent crystal decanters filled with high-quality alcohol left out day and night, next to mixers on ice. First class: you might have three hours to drink and eat back the extra money you spent. Club level: you can swallow your money back with three vodka tonics and one food presentation, then, over your next night stay, really begin to get value. Which is also why the best possible upgrade isn't always a suite or a view. It's as simple as getting your key juiced, sliding it in, and activating the club level. How do you light that light? How do you get that kind of upgrade? Well, dear guests, you'll have to wait for that one.

Terrance was on 25 berating a housekeeper about the cleanliness of her cart. As I approached, his eyes flicked over, he saw me but proceeded to act as if he had not and continued blowing hard about not storing trash bags on the top level of the cart and making sure the amenities were packed tight enough so they weren't rolling around in a big mess. Just glancing quickly at that cart gave me a glimpse into my new world, which, apparently, was now full of . . . amenities.

The amenities! Ah! From shower caps to shoehorns. All tightly packaged and incredibly stealable. Consider the unmanned housekeeping cart a smash-and-grab situation. Pack your bags full of almond butter hand cream and guava face soap with espresso chips! Take three of everything, and get the hell out of the hallway. Even if you do get caught, just say you were out of shampoo or, even better, out of *toilet paper* and thought you'd save the hotel the trouble by grabbing it for yourself. Think of it this way: these amenities are here for *you;* they are *yours.* We are in no position to dispute the claim that when *you* wash *your* hair, you prefer to dump fifteen bottles of lavender and poppy seed shampoo all over your scalp like some gooey shower freak.

Eventually, Terrance stopped scolding the housekeeper and introduced me. "Nancy, this is the new turndown manager, Tommy. You will show him respect at all times. Clean up this damn cart."

Nancy was the cutest little old lady: black, even darker than Terrance, and super-squat with puffy gray hair and a sweet smile. Despite Terrance's tirade, she smiled and squeezed my hand before starting to right all the overturned shampoo bottles.

One minute into my training and I already disliked my boss. I wasn't sure what kind of manager I was going to be, but I knew what kind of manager I was *not* going to be.

Terrance walked me along the hallways, checking his clipboard for vacant suites. Despite the sheet confirming the room was vacant, he still knocked before slipping in his yellow master key and touring me through the unoccupied rooms.

"This job is very easy," he said, pounding the clipboard against his closed fist to accentuate "very" and "easy." "It's about attention to detail. You see this one hotel room? A hundred and fifty-five different quality points, check points, that make it a clean room. Baseboards, no dust. Hospital-cornered sheets, pulled tight as possible. Vacuumed, stain-free carpet. Streak-free mirrors and glasses. Tipped toilet paper. Here."

He handed me a standard checklist, and it went on and on and on with minute points in a small font, filling both sides of the paper.

"Nancy is one of the best. That's why she has these two top floors on club level. I give her a hard time because I give everyone a hard time. I'm going to give *you* a hard time."

"Great."

"You don't believe me?"

"I certainly do."

Pushing through an unmarked white door to the supply closet, he stopped and turned to face me. This was a man who hits the gym, grunts and screams as he benches 350, and then leaves more angry than he went in. He had one fat vein surging out of his white starched collar, and it ripped up his throat and pulsed in a rage, as if it were filled with hot sauce and pumped that burn right into his brain.

Coincidentally (if you can manage to assimilate this info as well), he was a man who also got pedicures. Three times a week.

"We gonna have a problem?"

"No, sir."

"Heard you started down there in valet parking. I checked up on you. And the boys liked you. But don't think you get a pass with me just because some valet parkers think you're cool for a white boy. Don't test me. And don't let this suit fool you. Now, if you work hard and pay attention to detail, we ain't gonna have problems."

We were going to have problems.

As we toured the hotel from top to bottom, club level to first floor, entering dirty room after dirty room, I saw empty shopping bags, cold curly fries soaked in ketchup on the floor by the bed, a used condom that didn't quite make it and hung sagging from the lip of the trash can, nasty dirty sheets, spilled bottles of beer leaking over the top of a minibar, a pile of bloody towels tucked shamefully behind a bathroom door, and all manner of garbage left by our upscale guests. As we passed cart after cart, we saw housekeeper after housekeeper kneeling in the far corner of the bathroom, scrubbing *behind* the toilet, gathering cold food and garbage, polishing mirrors, rewrapping hair dryer cords, vacuuming, and performing every single action that falls under the word "cleaning."

I was soon to witness unique methods employed by these housekeepers. To put on a pillowcase, they would throw a solid karate chop right down the middle of the pillow and then shove it in, folded like a bun. This method was preferred to the civilian method of tucking it under your chin and pulling up the pillowcase like a pair of pants because these ladies had no interest in letting fifty pillows a day come into direct contact with their faces. In addition, you know what cleans the hell out of a mirror, and I'm talking *no streaks*? Windex? No. Furniture polish. Spray on a thick white base, rub it in, and you'll be face-to-face with a spotless mirror, streak-free. However, I am not recommending you take this tip and apply it in your own home. Though using furniture polish is quick and effective, over time it causes a waxy buildup that requires a deep scrub. So, ladies were treating mirrors like furniture all over the building, but certainly not in front of Terrance. Catching a lady with Pledge in the bathroom was a lecture-inducing event. So they kept this move behind closed doors along with another dirty secret I didn't uncover until much later: I walked in on ladies with Pledge in one hand and a minibar glass in the other. Certainly not all, but some of them were using furniture polish on the *drinking glasses.* Keeping those glasses clean "looking" was also part of the job. Do you see any dish soap on a housekeeping cart? Usually hot water and a face towel equals clean. But to be absolutely sure they won't be singled out for spotty glasses, they might spray furniture polish all over them. So the next time you put a little tap water into the minibar glass and wonder to yourself why it has a pleasant lemon aftertaste, that's because you just took a shot of Pledge. Honestly, furniture polish might be *more* sanitary than simple hot water and a wipe down using the (hopefully untouched) hand towel from the previous guest. Either way, sorry about that.

Be it the good, the bad, or the unsanitary, it was a tremendous amount to take in. I felt overwhelmed but proud. It was this swelling pride that kept my smile almost ever present, despite feeling as if I were sinking fast.

The following morning the reality and sheer size of my new department really smacked me on the ass. At 8:30 a.m. the housekeeping office, as large as a conference room, was packed with more than a hundred housekeepers yelling and laughing.

Besides the room attendants there are two other sub-positions within housekeeping. The housemen: Usually one or two per floor whose job includes helping the ladies "strip" the rooms, meaning pull off and drag out the dirty sheets. They keep the hallways clean and vacuumed, restock the supply closets, assist the ladies with whatever they need, such as refilling their cleaning bottles and restocking their carts with amenities, and, finally, handle most of the room deliveries. If you've ever called for an extra pair of slippers or asked to have a rollaway placed in your room, then you've met a houseman. In fact, speaking of slippers, when the houseman delivers them, drop a few dollar bills on him, and go ahead and ask for another five or ten pairs. Witness how quickly they are delivered. Those posh, hotel-logo, plastic-wrapped slippers make great gifts for people you really don't give a shit about! Like your co-workers! Once you've dropped some money on a house-man, anything his department has to offer is yours for the taking. Yours for the packing in the suitcase and using later. Ten bottles of the lotion you love, an extra pillow to jam in your carry-on and use on the plane, Q-tips and cotton balls, travel lint rollers, a year's supply of nail files, and everything else in the housekeeping storage closets. If word gets out that every time a houseman knocks on your door he gets a few dollars, those men will deliver bootleg DVDs if you ask them. And they have them, too.

The final subgroup is the lobby attendants. They are responsible for, obviously, cleaning the lobby but also all public areas not located on a floor with guest rooms, such as the conference rooms and public restrooms. Heart-of-the-house attendants are within that subgroup as well, ensuring that the back offices and hallways, employee bathrooms, and employee cafeteria are kept up to standard.

Heart-of-the-house attendants have the worst job. Guests can be disgusting, but employees are animals. Our bathrooms and locker rooms can look like train station toilets. We had two dedicated heart-of-the-house attendants, and both of them suffered from physical problems. The first was Charlie, surging well over six feet, 220, and built out of iron. He'd been a star quarterback for LSU, on the fast track to run the New Orleans Saints' offense (so I was told discreetly in service elevators) until the night he'd driven his brother home to the Eighth Ward and the car was shot up by an AK-47, killing his brother, who was active in the drug game, and lodging several bullets into Charlie's limbs and one more into his skull, and all that before the car even crashed. He never played again. He had a scar down the right side of his skull as big as his smile, and he had a *big* smile; he was as kindhearted and gentle as you can imagine. Everyone still treated him like a star quarterback, launching rolls of toilet paper back and forth with him in the back hallways when Terrance wasn't there to rip the roll out of midair and start a lecture on the cost of toilet paper and how it rolls off the dispenser funny once the cardboard tube has been compromised.

The second heart-of-the-house attendant was Roy, one of only two white housekeeping employees. He had cerebral palsy, his body asymmetric, movements strained and loping, but he was 100 percent upstairs. Roy was hard to understand, but once you got the hang of his speech, he was sharp and said some funny, funny shit. Terrance could never understand a word.

"How's it going there, Roy?"

"Be going better if I was banging your wife instead of cleaning these toilets."

Imagine that line is wet ink, smear your thumb over the whole of it, and then read it back. Most of us understood every syllable, though, and held our breaths.

"Well." Terrance clenched his neck muscles in frustration. "See you at the Christmas party?"

"You bet. Bring your wife," Roy said.

Roy had a tattoo of a pistol on his back with a bullet exploding out of the barrel.

Along with Roy, for a brief time, we had a second white employee, a housekeeper in fact. A little white wisp of a lady. An alcoholic. Too many bottles of gin from too many minibars from too many rooms on too many days. We sent her to the Employee Assistance Program, and she came back clean. Clean and dead. Her face was like a white paper bag, her eyes dry. She stopped talking to anyone, cleaned rooms slowly and poorly. Then one day she bounced in, her face full and radiant, smiling and ready to work. They let her go that afternoon: she was drunk.

But before I knew anyone, that very first morning, I was horribly overwhelmed. The housekeepers gathered every day at 8:30 a.m. to receive their "boards," meaning their personal lists of rooms to be cleaned for the day. General instructions were given and small attempts to force down the company Kool-Aid, though you couldn't quite get the ladies to care at all about corporate mottoes. Every morning Terrance would jabber on and on about attention to detail while domestically abusing his clipboard, relentlessly informing the staff their jobs were "Very. Easy."

I said hello to Nancy, the little old lady on club level. She put her small hand on mine and told me not to be nervous about meeting all these new people. She said soon enough I'd learn everyone's name.

Soon enough was not soon enough. A staff of 150, all dressed in uniforms, often losing and switching name tags, perhaps deliberately, just to fuck with me.

"Is this room going to be done by three, Donna?"

"Donna? I'm Debra, listen to this new manager —"

"Oh, sorry. You're wearing Donna's name tag?"

"*Rasis.* You *rasis.* You should be *shamed of yourself,* Tommy. Just kidding, baby. And you know what, you can have this room now. I'm finished."

"Great. Thanks, Debra. A few Mardi Gras travel groups are already in the lobby waiting to check in."

Mardi Gras was a different experience inside the rooms. A couple of guests rented the suite with a claw-footed tub, built a fire below it, and tried to turn the porcelain tub into a deep fryer. Most of the tubs were successfully converted into gigantic coolers and filled with beer. Housemen had no problem nipping a bottle or two and pounding them down in the storage closet. They also had no problem getting a beer from the minibar if nothing better was available.

Minibars. Most people are appalled at the prices. But it comes down to this: that is the cost of convenience. You aren't at home, but you can pay handsomely to simulate the feeling. The high cost of convenience is one of hospitality's master hustles. However, you never have to pay for the items in the minibar. I am going to say that again and, to really drive it home, utilize some serious italics: *you never have to pay for a goddamn thing inside that tiny little fridge of joy.* Why not? Minibar charges are, without question, the most disputed charges on any bill. That is because the process for applying those charges is horribly inexact. Why? Because it's done by people. The traditional minibar, before they invented the sensored variety, is checked (maybe) once a day by a slow-moving gentleman or lady pushing a cart full of snacks. Unlike a housekeepers' cart, often available for a smash and grab, you will never see a minibar cart without its attendant. You might never even see a minibar attendant. They are like mole people. They peer into the confusion of bottles and bags, looking for something that needs to be replaced, looking for something that is *no longer there.* They replace it and put a pen mark on their room chart. These marks are then, at some point in the lazy future, delivered to another fallible human who manually inputs them onto a guest account. Can everyone see the margin for error in this process? Because it's HUGE. Maybe the attendant failed to notice the cashews were consumed Monday but catches it on Tuesday, and the charge is applied to *your* bill on Wednesday, even though you just checked in five minutes ago. Keystroke errors, delays in restocking, double stocking, and hundreds of other missteps make mini-bar charges the most voided item. Even before guests can manage to get through half of the "I never had these items" sentence, I have already removed the charges and am now simply waiting for them to wrap up their overly zealous denial so we can both move on with our lives. And this is why, essentially, you are able to eat and drink everything for free.

Give it a go. Pound a whiskey and ginger ale, then shove a Toblerone down your throat. Upon checkout, or if you feel more comfortable avoiding confrontation like most Americans (God bless us for being so timid), you can call down from the room phone to the front desk and explain that you checked your bill on-screen and noticed the charges are incorrect. It's actually that simple. Don't provide a goddamn alibi or offer to produce medical documentation proving your throat swells like a frog if you even touch an almond. Just say you never had it, and we will take it right off.

Never, ever will the hotel accuse you of lying. That is the absolute last stance hotel management wants to take. You think a respectable hotelier wants to go through your garbage looking for spent M&M's wrappers? If a front desk agent does take it upon him- or herself to insinuate you are lying, then you are staying in a bad hotel. Or at least you have come into contact with a bad desk agent who's getting his or her rocks off by treating you like garbage. We are the front desk: the minibar is not our fight. The hotel buys those items in crazy bulk and charges a crazy increase. And people pay it. But you don't have to be one of those people.

You could be one of these people:

Here is the plan. Check in at the desk and make a strong request for a nonsmoking room, possibly mentioning allergies (but don't go overboard and annoy the agent, please). Refuse help from the bellman (that shouldn't be hard for your cheap ass), and go up to your room unaccompanied. Immediately open the minibar and shove every goddamn item into your suitcase. Take it *all*. Then smoke a cigarette on the bed and gaze out the window. Afterward, call down to the desk and complain about the heavy smoke smell in the room. Request to be moved. I mean, it smells like someone *just smoked* in here. The front desk will send a bellman up with your new keys, and — not that he has been informed, nor would he care — should he pop his head in, he too will smell the odor. Go to your new room, close the door, and get fat and salty and drunk on your suitcase of snacks. The hotel will never trace that minibar to you. Moving rooms in the system, when it's done the same day you check in, leaves almost no trace, no overnight confirmation that you actually ever occupied that suite. Certainly nothing that allows the hotel to track down those five minutes when you stole five hundred dollars' worth of individually wrapped snacks. The minibar attendant will check on the bar in your first room maybe today, probably tomorrow, and then just restock it, no questions asked.

Perhaps you think it would be strange for the attendant to find a completely empty bar? No. Certain guests (alcoholics, the parents of kids without in-room chaperones, and tour managers for famous metal bands from the 1980s that no longer have a famous 1980s metal band budget) are always asking to completely empty out the bar. Just get rid of it all. In fact, on a side note, when a huge company books a block of rooms (a business that provides items often found in minibars, such as a soda or beer company), they will sometimes demand that all competitors' brands be removed prior to the group's arrival. Minibar moles *hate this:* having to remove Coca-Cola products from

101

seventy-five rooms just because Pepsi people want to live under the delusion that they run the market.

What about sensored minibars, that brilliant invention designed to eliminate the human factor? Certainly, the great minibar caper described above should not be attempted with a sensored minibar. All of those charges would immediately fly onto your bill and follow your account when you moved rooms. But, speaking as someone who *personally lived* through the transformation from a human system to the world of sensors, I was ready for the "I never even touched the minibar . . ." complaints to dwindle, hopefully, to zero. They did not. I barely noticed a change. Sensors come with their own problems. Random electronic malfunctions are just the beginning. They are weight sensored and on a brief timer; therefore, if you simply take an item out to examine it, you might get charged, unless you replace it within the thirty-second time limit (or Indiana-Jones-it with a "bag of sand"; in this case pour the, I'm just assuming, *booze* into a minibar glass — or right into your mouth! — and then quickly submerge it into an ice bucket that you've prefilled with water — or tea if you're Indiana-Jonesing whiskey — then screw back the cap and replace it with dramatic showmanship, carefully, slowly, with hands shaky and wet, sweat bubbling on your forehead, racing to get it done before the thirty-second time limit triggers). But don't press it down too hard, or it'll trigger. And don't put anything, like a sandwich, on top, or it'll trigger. And don't take the items out to store your own items, or it'll trigger. And don't move any items around, or it'll trigger. It will always fucking trigger, and that is why, should you ever wake up in terror with a mess of tiny empty bottles by the bedside phone, pistachio shells all over the pillow, and your mouth smeared with Hershey's, never fear. Forgive yourself. Just tell the front desk you "never even touched the minibar," and we will whisk away the charges. Or say you stored your own items and it must have charged you. Or say you took a few items out to look at them and it must have charged you. Get it? *Say anything,* anything at all, and we will make it go away.

Need one more reason the charges could be incorrect? As I said before, housemen steal from the minibar. Even minibar attendants might steal from your minibar, for Christ's sake. We aren't going to accuse you of anything, because we all have access to your snacks. We all have master keys. Any room, anywhere, anytime. We let ourselves in when you are gone. We let ourselves in even when you are there. I walked in on guests having sex, guests who must have heard me knock, guests who seemed to climax at my embarrassment. I saw deliberate robe slips from men and women, young and old. I found bondage gear still attached to a towel holder that had been ripped out of the wall, the prisoner escaped, I suppose, wandering the hallways in a ball gag. (Joking about that last part; in fact, I discovered most people with these proclivities were quite adult, almost professional about them, and had no interest in making a large scene or offending anyone.)

Housekeepers deal with the brunt of these sexual harassment situations. The first week a new housekeeping employee will approach a door, give three loud knocks, throw a throaty "housekeeping department," followed by another powerful hammering on the door, before slowly pushing her way in, face and body protectively shielded by the heavy door, until there is no question the room is vacant and she can confidently whisk herself inside. Six months later, after she has performed the same preliminary announcement on over fifty doors a day, it becomes something more like, "House —"

at this point a light knock occurs in conjunction with a less throaty "keeping," the master key is already slipped in the lock, the light clicks green, and BOOM the door is already opening, and the lady is entering back first, pulling her cart through the doorframe.

"OH MY GOD!! CHRIST, DON'T YOU KNOCK?! OH, GOD!"

"Sorry, ma'am. Sorry. I'll come back in an hour."

Is she really that sorry? Probably not. That housekeeper might have twelve more rooms to clean before she can go home to her family. And though, as a hotel guest, she has every right, that woman taking a luxurious bath followed by a twenty-minute session of staring at herself naked in the mirror is directly slowing down the housekeeper's working day. Off the room attendant goes to blast through another door with minimal warning, attempting to get some work done.

The next time, pulling the cart in, she might be confident the room is vacant, due to a lack of screaming. However, spray bottle already in hand, she turns to face an older gentleman who didn't feel the need to either shout out a warning OR secure the robe properly. There are now three entities in the room: the housekeeper, the man, and the man's penis. Two of these entities are rather pleased with the current situation.

Some guests are dying to be walked in on. Some guests are terrified of being walked in on. But every one of these guests, fundamentally different in every way, lurks there, hidden behind a locked door, doing God knows what. And every door a housekeeper unlocks leads her into the world of the unknown.

Any room, anywhere, anytime. In certain ways I learned more about the true nature of hotels while holding the housekeeping manager position than any other. When I had access to these rooms, these short scenes and snapshots into people's lives, I came to see the hotel for all its uses: guests propose, get married, impregnate each other, turn forty, get divorced, snort heroin, murder, and die in hotel rooms (sometimes in that order). They receive news of a loved one's death from a blinking red light. They sign a fax that begins production on a factory in China. They receive a FedEx box containing everything left of their marriage. A man comes from Tulsa to be a full-on cross-dresser for a week in New Orleans so the rest of his life can remain intact at home. A woman leaves her room at the Marriott checked in and empty, paid for by her company as a travel expense, books a room at our hotel to tryst with the man she *should* have married, spending three days in love and ordering room service before paying our bill in cash and returning to the Marriott to check out of her never-used room and fly home to the husband she no longer has sex with (who, while she was out of town, booked a room at the Days Inn by the airport to snort fat rails of coke, order gay porn, and hire male escorts). Aliases and pseudonyms, clandestine visitors, drug addicts on a professional drug binge, writers, runaways, recent divorcées using the room as a central cry hub, alcoholics, gamblers, and whores. And families on vacation! Newlyweds banging the day away! Any given room, behind any given door, someone else's life was on fire. Not the life lived at home, not the cable-and-bed-by-9:00-p.m. life, waiting around to die. The hotel life: boundless, foreign, debaucherous, freshly laundered, exploratory, scantily clad, imaginative, frightening, expensive, and *brand fucking new.* I wandered the hallways every day like a guard keeper in the house of reinvention. Whatever these people were getting into, whatever their lives had become, I made sure that if they vacated the room for an hour's time, they had clean sheets to do it on, new soap to scrub it off with, fresh towels to wipe it down, a clean robe to cover it up, and a fresh pillow to sleep it off on.

Sometimes, when I was wandering the halls, it was too quiet. There is no question my time as housekeeping manager saddled me with one new sexual fetish (at least). I would hear soft moanings, muffled sex sounds seeping through the walls, and then pause, listening intently because, honestly, it turned me on. It had never surfaced before, but apparently I am always game to hear a couple smashing it out on the other side of a door or wall. Sadly, every single time I heard a sigh or moan from a hotel room it was always, *always* just someone listening to the damn television: "Ooooh, oh, oh, ooooooooh." At this point, excited, I'd freeze and focus my attention just in time to hear "And now back to Afghanistan." Other times, if the hallways were like ghost towns, doors wedged open by abandoned carts, not a houseman to be found, chances were the New Orleans Saints were playing. I'd start hitting the larger suites until I found the one room filled with twenty-five employees, some standing on the damn bed, watching the Saints lose. Terrance would

108

have suspended every single one of them. But me? I let the Saints finish the drive (in a punt) and then escorted them all out, making the last three to leave touch up the suite. Maybe it made me a weak manager, but I never felt disciplinary action was the best corrective. Not so long as the rooms were getting cleaned to standard. I walked in on housemen and housekeepers banging each other and would break up fuck scenes like breaking up a fight: "All right, you two, separate. Jesus. Debra, nylons up. Finish this room quickly, please. The VP of Best Buy and her children are waiting in the lobby for it."

Perhaps I should have suspended or fired them, too. However, when I asked for something, a favor, it got handled. Terrance could ask them to bring up a cotton ball after their shift, and they'd refuse. I could ask them to strip the sheets out of thirty more rooms, and they'd do it quickly so we could all go get drinks together after work.

It was like a big-ass family.

I showed up at the morning meetings and, every day, got to say hello to my friends. Most of the time, however, I worked the turndown shift. Turndown, or second service, is important to any true luxury property. That extra visit by the attendant while

guests are out having dinner really under-
lines the luxury experience: they return to
find the lights dimmed, radio on low, bed
refreshed and cracked geometrically, of
course with the goddamn pillow chocolates
in place (in my apartment I kept three
stolen boxes of turndown chocolate for my
own, you know, personal use), and finally,
masterfully, a fresh rose at the foot of the
bed* (*fresh rose only available for VIP
guests). I was responsible for personally
visiting the VIP suites every evening to
ensure second service had been done properly, that all the boxes were checked. Knocking on door after door after door. The first
month I knocked until every single knuckle
on both hands was rose red and sore as hell,
even my poor pinkie knuckles. After a
month I learned to knock with a pen or my
key card.

I also had celebrity interactions that, if
you can believe it, I'd prefer *not* to have
had. Most of which (at least in the pages of
this book) I won't go into (get me drunk =
another story). But I will mention a certain
cinematic director, lodged on the club level
for a few nights, known for his rather dark,
gothic tendencies. His name, though recog-
nizable in context, is still rather common,
so, when reviewing the VIP list, I figured it

might be him but wasn't certain. I couldn't care less either way, but it was my job to knock on his door, hopefully finding the room vacant so I could slip in and check all the boxes on my list, most importantly ensuring the attendant had laid the VIP rose. I knocked, and, as commonly happens, the guest was there, at which point I simply inquired if he'd received turndown and if everything was satisfactory.

Turns out it actually was that director. He stared back at me blankly. Then he put on an arrogant, frankly derogatory smile and said, "Oh. Oh, I see. Yes, *okay*, everything is *fine*," and then closed the door in my face, taking that arrogant smirk along with him. I stood still a moment more, marking the room off my list, confused. What kind of re-action was that? Was that arrogant smirk directed at me? Then I figured it out. He assumed I was a fan, a fan who had devised some excuse to knock on his door just to meet him. I was just doing my *job* (as I had been for the last twelve hours straight, on my feet, my knuckles bruised), and this ar-rogant prick thought meeting him was my dream come true.

He can suck it. His movies are for dysfunc-tional trust-fund babies who turn fifteen and go goth. And now I've never seen another.

He wasn't the last celebrity who got all of his work removed from my Netflix queue. Another actor, famous during my teen years, spent a full month in the penthouse while filming a movie in the New Orleans area. Well, this actor calls up late one evening and asks for five more potpourri bowls. That's fine. The man digs the scent. However, the large silver potpourri bowls in the penthouse, about the size of a wok, are only in the top-floor luxury suites, and we didn't keep spares. So, since he was a VIP in the penthouse, I first removed the two big bowls from the unoccupied luxury suites. Then, in a move I might have seriously regretted, I knocked on the *occupied* suites, far too late in the evening, and, finding the guests out for the night, stole the damn things from the occupied rooms too. In truth, I did it for him. He'd been in some teen movies that meant *a lot* to *a lot* of people, me included. So I did it for him. I showed up with the five bowls, and when he cracked the door to take them inside and I tried to pass over the fresh bags of potpourri, he pushed the bags back at me and said he just wanted the silver bowls. Said he wanted to eat cereal out of them.

Those goddamn bowls will hold a *full box* of cereal. And why'd he need five? What was that about?

I found out the following day: dude had problems. While running through the penthouse, making sure it had been cleaned to standard, I saw *bags* of pills, gallon Ziploc bags marked with every day of the week, enough pills in the Monday bag to actually *fill you up.* The man was traveling with his "nutritionist" and eating bags of pills (on top of full boxes of cereal apparently, or maybe he filled the big bowls with pills, soaked them in soy milk, and, with spoon in hand, went at them like a maniac). This "nutritionist" (clearly I mean those quotes) actually called down to the concierge on his behalf, requesting that an acupuncturist, a voodoo doctor, and a chiropractor all be sent ASAP to the penthouse. Freak show.

But beyond compelling me to steal those bowls from occupied suites, he wasn't bothering anyone. At least not until the movie production extended and we had to inform him that, though he certainly could extend his reservation with us, the penthouse had already been booked for a night in the future and he would have to vacate for that single evening. First he refused. So we made it as clear to him as possible that yes, motherfucker, it was reserved over a year ago and *you* are moving. Finally comprehending that information, he demanded to be moved to a suite with a view of the Mississippi. There was another issue. All those suites were occupied for that night as well. Trying to solve his own problem, he informed us that his "nutritionist" would be moved to a lesser suite and he would occupy her river-view suite for the evening. That made it two rooms that were now moving. Then we realized when he said *he would move,* he meant that *we would move him,* and not simply send up a bellman with a few carts. I had to gather a group of ten housekeepers to roll up there and move all his unpacked luggage. As I walked the crew of housekeepers down the hall, out he came, wearing a black baseball cap pulled over his eyes, basically creeping along the wall, past the army of ladies who were prepared to drag his underwear and oversized pill bags to the adjacent room, and he didn't even make eye contact, didn't even thank anyone, just hugged the wall with the hat over his eyes like a freak, as if we'd bother him for an autograph. Asshole. I'm still mad about it.

And I don't think his movies are funny anymore. Not even the classic teen movies.

Anyway. How about a good celebrity story? I'm already feeling warmer inside. And this man is a star: Mr. H. I would like to start by saying that his first interaction with the staff involved calling down *politely* to the concierge desk with a single request. What did he ask for? An acupuncturist? A voodoo doctor? Big Ziploc bags? No. Scrabble. He wondered if someone could pick up a Scrabble set. And someone did. And he dropped a hundred-dollar bill on the desk in payment. That's already enough to love the man, but there is more.

As is often the case with the hospitality business, the company I was working for was a management company. In fact, that business model stretches all the way back to the origins of hostelries. There were even some innkeepers who paid the building owner a flat yearly fee to run a property, and any profits exceeding the fee and operational overhead went right into the innkeeper's old-school rough-sewn pockets. Sort of like paying rent on a barber chair, then all the tips and cut money goes right to the barber. But if the barber cuts hair like shit and no customers sit down anymore, he still owes the rent. These days, owners, those who own the building itself, will enter into business with a hospitality company that manages the operations. In this specific case, our owner built himself a residential palace on the top floor: personal movie screening room, grand piano, fantastic, opulent. He was prepared for everything but the weather. You can only stay inside your palace for so long before you have to venture out into a sweltering Louisiana August afternoon. And no amount of wealth can keep that New Orleans sweat from pouring down the back of your neck and soaking your expensive clothes. So he threw together a mansion for himself in Boca, moved out, and let the hotel start renting out his residential palace.

That was where Mr. H. was staying. I ran into Nancy, the lady in charge of cleaning all of our luxury club-level suites, and asked her if she'd gotten around to the owner's apartment yet.

"Oh. Well, the man in there so nice, Mr. Tommy. So nice."

"Who? Mr. H.?"

"Whoever. Listen at this. I go in there to get it out the way early, being the biggest suite and everything. I start to cleaning, and this man comes out to say hello. First he offers me some food. I say no, and he asks me how long it usually takes to clean up the place. I told him little over an hour maybe.

Guess what he made me do?"

"Mr. H.?"

"He made me sit right down for an hour. Wouldn't let me clean, just made me put my butt down and *rest*. Gave me all kinds of food, and fruit too, but you know I don't eat no fruit."

"So he wanted you to relax instead of clean? That's fucking amazing!"

"For about a half hour he played on the piano for me, too. That was nice."

"Mr. H. played piano for you?"

"Whoever. He a nice man. Said to go on and skip his room this whole week."

"You've never seen *any* of his movies? Come on, Nancy!! Mr. H. is the shit!! Unbelievable!!"

"You best calm yourself, Mr. Tommy. Getting all worked up. Listen . . . you gonna tell Terrance he refused service for the week? My points won't add up, and you know he'd toss me off my floors to make it up."

"Of course not. If Mr. H. wants you to take it easy, I do too. Don't mention it to anyone else, though, okay?"

"Mr. Tommy, you sweet. Now get on, I got rooms to clean."

I never told Terrance. In the housekeeping department rooms are worth points, and every housekeeper must clean a total num-

117

ber of points to keep the workload fair. Points are raised or lowered based on the size and difficulty of the room. The owner's penthouse was equal to more than half her board, so getting a week pass on that room ensured Nancy a nice, easy time of it.

These women fight hard for their regular set of rooms, which are referred to as "sections." Some of the more time-consuming portions of upkeep, such as dusting the baseboards and polishing the silver, need not be done daily, so keeping a steady section, keeping the same set of rooms, was a major concern. New hires would never get a solid section but rove around and pick up the uncovered rooms from ladies on vacation or ladies who had called in sick that day, bringing on the inevitable complaints that whatever bitch cleaned their section while they were out sick did a shit job.

But doling out boards wasn't the biggest problem. Try doing the schedule for a staff of 150, most of whom have children with appointments, husbands with court dates, and all of whom want every holiday off. On top of that, I was responsible for purchasing: ordering all the supplies necessary to operate a hotel, from souvenir hotel pens to face towels to Kleenex to trash bags to Band-Aids to cleaning supplies to the big pink bags of liquid soap for the lobby bathrooms. All of these items were lined up on an intense ten-page Excel spreadsheet. I would cross-reference current storeroom supply with the speed at which each item was consumed for the month, tempered with the coming month's *predicted* usage derived from the previous year's usage in order to get a perfect ordering schedule, which then must be handwritten on order forms and submitted to accounting. Christ.

Speaking of Christ, the easiest thing to order was the Bibles. Terrance assigned me the task of ordering 250 more Bibles, and all it took was one phone call to the folks at Gideons International. I said we needed 250 more Good Books. They said they'd arrive next week at no cost. Running out of Bibles isn't really a problem, but you don't want to be the one who fails to order enough toilet paper. And all of those tasks must be completed after you have "turned" or "flipped" the hotel (meaning ensured that every room has been cleaned, with the exception of any "dropped" rooms, which are rooms left dirty overnight due to low occupancy coupled with low staffing), as well as executed turndown properly with no mistakes. Not to mention the front desk is constantly moving guests, causing rooms to fall into the "touch up" category, necessitating a visit from a manager or a housekeeper to verify the guests didn't use the toilet or smush out a quickie before they decided that room wasn't good enough for them.

I was ex*hausted.* Working eleven-to-fifteen-hour days. My new suits were thinning on the knees from constantly kneeling on bathroom floors to search for "dark and curlies." I worked through holidays and once worked a full month without a day off. I was never home anymore, to the joy of my roommate. My drinking, which started so casually at front desk, had now become the only stress release I had. After wrapping up a fifteen-hour shift at 11:00 p.m., I didn't have time to watch television; instead, I'd just limp to the bar to get a bunch of whiskey inside me, then go home and get five hours of sleep before running the boards in the morning.

And then, late one evening, while I was interfacing with that infernal purchasing spreadsheet, the phone rang in my office. It was John, my old manager from the front desk.

"John, you calling from Cleveland?"

"Hell no, Tommy. I wasn't even there a month before they offered me another position in D.C., and now I'm in West Virginia.

The company is opening a new property, and you are speaking to the rooms exec. You believe that?"

"I do, actually. Congratulations."

"So why I'm calling . . . I wondered if you wanted to come out here and work with me. Maybe run my front desk?"

"Front office manager?"

"Yep. From valet to FOM, and that's just the beginning. After you get this handled, I have no doubt they'll find a housekeeping department for you to run. What do you think? Wanna open this motherfucker with me?"

"Well," I started, leaning back in my seat, rubbing at my eyes. My feet were swollen in my dress shoes, and in the harsh fluorescent lights my eyes burned from constant exposure to cleaning agents. I was, as they say, shot to shit. "Virginia?"

"West Virginia. Not going to lie, Tommy, we're a skeleton crew. I am already pulling sixteen-hour days to get this show running, and you will too. But the company will pay your moving costs, and I'll show you how to bump the numbers to give yourself a thousand or so in your account even after the move. Everyone does it. It's kind of like an unofficial signing bonus. So, my man, want to run my front desk?"

I thought I was going to be sick. I couldn't understand exactly why at the time, but then, as I held the phone to my head, I thought I was going to vomit all over the keyboard, slip out of the chair, pass out under the desk, and die.

CHAPTER FOUR

I had taken John's call so late and exhausted
it wasn't until halfway through the following day's shift I remembered the job offer.
In the basement laundry dump, while I
pulled sheet after sheet from the laundry
chute, it came upon me like recalling a
dream (or more like recalling the taste of a
meal on your tongue, the one that made you
ill).

I had my jacket off and hung outside the
dump room because this was physical and
disgusting work. Sometime during the mid-
day rush, when housemen run through the
checkouts to strip the sheets and drop them
down the laundry chute, everything had
gotten jammed up. The floor of the dump
room was half a foot thick with dirty bed
linens, robes, and towels, which I scrambled
over to get to the mouth of the chute. The
chute resembled a frozen white waterfall, a
cone of linens rising up to the metal tube.

When I tugged at a robe hanging halfway out, another spray of linens came down to jam the hole and freeze the fall again.

My hands were uncomfortably hot because I was wearing latex gloves. Why gloves? Because this was a never-ending pile of nastiness. The laundry department has a runner responsible for keeping up with this chute and separating the items into large blue bins for washing: one for robes, one for sheets, one for towels, and so on. Apparently, according to the laundry manager, the runner had been fired that morning. The manager had been inspecting the linen closets, trying to get an idea of what linens the day would call for most, when he saw a pair of black Nikes sticking out from the side of a metal shelving unit. A sheet had been draped over the entire front of the unit, and when he detached it, he found his runner asleep on a row of freshly stacked king sheets, even a pillow under his head. The runner awoke to an execution-style firing. A gentle shake of his shoulder and just as he came to, just as his pupils dilated, "You're fired, Jamal. Get out. Now." Two deadly sins of the hotel business: stealing and sleeping on the job. You can't fight those sins. You will be fired.

As exciting as finding that pair of floating

Nikes was to the laundry manager, he failed to communicate to *my* department that *his* department was currently without a runner. How were we finally alerted to this problem? A houseman, stripping rooms on 10, had opened the chute and found it packed and rising up above his tenth-floor drop slot. Ten minutes later the whole beast was jammed up all the way to 15, just packed full of dirty linen. And housemen on 16 and above were still making it rain sheets. So now here I was, at the very bottom of it all, yanking at soiled linen.

I focused on not touching my face, trying not to instinctively wipe the dripping sweat from my forehead. As I grunted and pulled hard at a sheet, the flow opened, and I hopped back to let the mouth expunge another floor or so of linens, backing up to let the pile spread. Taking a moment to rest, I scanned the billowy off-white pile I stood on, now almost two feet thick. In the mix I saw spots of red (blood) and slimy latex condoms hiding among the folds like greasy snakes (yep).

This wasn't the first time I'd found myself in the shit pit. Items lost in the rooms were also under my jurisdiction. A guest's first instinct, since the beginning of hoteldom, all the way back to the nineteenth century, is to immediately assume the housekeeper is a thief. I cannot stand that. These ladies need their jobs, and never once have I witnessed a situation where a housekeeper put her job at stake for one earring. Usually, the guest lost it, or maybe left it buried in the bed linens, and once the sheets got dumped, I would be sent down here to sort through the pile until I found it. Or didn't. Mostly didn't. I wish I could offer advice on locating lost items, but it's a big world, it's a big hotel; earrings are grains of sand, and white pajama pants are water in the ocean. Utilizing the drawers in the room instead of flinging off your clothes like an excited five-year-old might help. Using the in-room safe for sentimental items instead of tossing valuables over your shoulder like lucky grains of salt, also a good idea. *Messiness* looks like *trash* to housekeepers, so keep papers in a folder or tucked in a briefcase. A hotel room seems to feel like home, that's the plan, but you are not at home. You are in flux. You are in a private/public space. Act accordingly and keep organized.

Catching my breath, I leaned against the far wall from the mouth of the chute, trying to balance on the pile, my dress shoes sinking in, and that's when I remembered John's phone call. Again, an unexplainable nausea overtook me. What was this feeling? Why was my stomach churning and my heart shuddering? Was it the disgusting scent of soiled linens? No. I was terrified. Of work. Of more uninterrupted, thankless work. Hour after hour on my feet and talking. Scheduling, purchasing, cleaning, hiring, firing, and constant door knocking ("Good morning, this is housekeeping." "Good morning, this is housekeeping." "Good afternoon, housekeeping." "Good after-noon, housekeeping." "Good evening, housekeeping." "Good evening, housekeep-ing").

Perhaps now is also the best point to men-tion that this business, the one that cur-rently has me standing on a pile of dirty sheets and blood-borne pathogens, does not pay exceedingly well. At the front desk I made a generous hourly wage and found myself with a close-to-normal amount of free time. Sure, I worked Thanksgiving afternoon and Christmas morning, but I had two days off a week and money to blow. It's actually mid-management that doesn't pay. My weekly housekeeping checks only beat my front desk checks by about the cost of a decent dinner* (*wine and tip not in-cluded). However, in management, I hadn't worked less than an eleven-hour shift in three months. Calculated to a rough hourly wage, that put me earning 60 percent less an hour compared to what I made at the desk. That's why "salary positions" are often jokingly referred to as "slavery positions." But being at work all the time had one monetary advantage: my bank account was, in casual terms, dusty. My money sat there collecting dust. I made deposits and no withdrawals. I hadn't bought anything other than well whiskey in months. I ate every meal in the employee cafeteria, which, though disgusting in practice, was cost-effective. I was never home. I was never out. I was simply on my way to or from work. Or sleeping during my day off, unable to rouse myself to do shit. The idea of walking and talking during my day off seemed excessive, and so there it was in my dusty, untouched bank account: thousands and thousands of dollars.

West Virginia.

I gave one more halfhearted tug at a pillowcase and staggered out of the dump room, snapping off the latex gloves and slinging my jacket over my wet back. I found Terrance in the manager's office, eating a greasy double burger.

With a mouth full of wet meat he said,

"This computer is broken. Look here. The arrow on the screen moves backward, and the buttons aren't even clicking," and then he grabbed the mouse and started smashing it. I saw the cord snaking out from beneath his wrist. His hand moved toward the phone, to call the IT department, I assumed.

"Wait, you're just holding it upside down. The cord should come out from the top. That's why it's moving funny and you can't click."

"What? Oh. Shit. You know, maybe you should get a job in IT, Tommy. How about that for an idea?"

"Because I know how to use a mouse?"

"Don't get smart with me. I've seen you. You know computers. And you ain't cut out for this work down here. You don't have it in you."

"Meaning I haven't been doing a good job?"

"The staff likes you, but that's it."

"That's it?"

He took a second to look me right in the eye. "Basically."

At that moment, still mentally avoiding touching my face, I hated the hospitality business. I hated all of it: servicing overprivileged, whiny guests, the short pay for long hours, dealing with this prick who couldn't operate a mouse and constantly insulted my work. And here I was on the cusp of digging myself deeper, moving to a state I had no interest in, so that eventually I could run a hotel in a city I might have no interest in. I wouldn't have time to *take a shit* in West Virginia while opening the property, much less spend the money I was making, money I was currently making for, apparently, no reason. The business had even eliminated my desire to spend any of it. I saw what the other managers bought with their money: mostly finding a nicer apartment and furnishing it heavily with a nice couch and fancy throw pillows, though they, like me, were only home to sleep. What was all of this about?

The bottom dropped out of my tiny world, and I staggered out of the housekeeping office, up the stairs to the employee exit, and back around to the garage. I sat myself on a bench in the porte cochere and stared at the white marble fountain, trying to calm my erratic breathing. I thought about happiness, about what would make me happy. Not working so much. Travel. There it was: travel. For a man like me, someone who made friends in fifth grade only to lose them in sixth grade and, in another state, make new ones to lose in seventh grade, I could no longer deny my addiction to relocation. I wondered how I'd even lasted so long in New Orleans. But then, as I said, this business is like a methadone clinic for the travel addicted. I changed everything by simply moving departments, and no matter what, in whatever department, the guests were always changing. But that wasn't traveling: it was like watching the Travel Channel. And I didn't have much hope that West Virginia would feel like an adventure. That would feel like erasure. I needed a solid hit to the vein. I had to move and I had to move now and I had to move someplace absolutely crazy.

"Damn, son. Looking all fucked-up, you. And sitting on a bench like he a guest. Stand on up, Tommy. Let's take a break real quick, heard? Get up, let's go."

"Where we going?"

"To a bar, ma'fucker. Stand up."

Perry walked me to the Alibi and sat me down on a stool. I tried to order a whiskey, but he forced me to drink a Heineken with him. Nobody forced me to drink the next three, though.

"Virginia? *Please.* What you gonna do in Virginia?"

"West Virginia. Work, I guess. Opening a

hotel . . . that'll probably be sixteen-hour days."

"How's the money?"

"Prolly not that good."

"Damn. You trying to be a GM, Tommy?"

"Shouldn't I?"

"You *too cool* to be a GM. Anyway, they look happy to you?"

"They look paid."

"You wanna get paid, go be a bellman. Now, those dudes get paid and don't do shit."

"I need a change, Perry. I have to go someplace new."

"What's wrong with New Orleans? Best city in the world."

"You been around enough to know?"

"Tommy, I ain't even been to Houston, Texas. That don't make me wrong, though."

The next morning I gave my two weeks' notice at the hotel. I'd saved fifteen thousand dollars, and my top was ready to spin. I was going to get rid of all my useless throw pillows, pack one single bag, and move to Europe.

That should do it. Right in the vein.

I told the ladies the following day at the 8:30 a.m. meeting. Some of them actually cried. The housemen were all happy for me. Roy labored up and put his hand out for me to shake. He moved it up and down awkwardly and then teared up, and I started to get emotional. Nancy waited her turn to speak to me and said protective, motherly phrases: to make sure I eat enough and be careful over there. Terrance, of course, interrupted the flurry of positive humanity to tell the ladies to get upstairs and remind them that their jobs were "Very. Easy."

There is *nothing* easy about housekeeping. There is nothing *easy* about dealing with other people's filth and having to get on your knees to do it. There is nothing easy about scouring and spraying and polishing and getting on all fours to make sure there isn't a porno mag under the bed skirt (previously, I didn't even know what a bed skirt *was* much less how surprisingly *not easy* it is to make it hang perfectly). There is nothing easy about being sexually harassed by guests. There is nothing easy about scrubbing a toilet on Christmas morning, believe me. And there is certainly nothing easy about hearing your boss tell you every morning that your job is very easy when it motherfucking *isn't*.

"Just tell me why, Tommy?"

"Well, Mr. Daniels, I've never been to Europe, and I plan to move there. To Paris."

"You're going to move to Paris? To work?"

"No, just spend the money I've saved, get an apartment, read novels, maybe write one, drink, travel. See some of the Continent if I can."

"Well," he whispered and looked down at his desk. "I've heard plenty of reasons for leaving this gig. Mostly, someone wants to whack out a kid. But I'll tell you one thing. I like your reason." He paused and pointed a finger at me. "Your reason has balls. Get over there and sop it up."

"Do what?"

"Yeah, that sounded disgusting, sorry. What I mean is this: Usually I would try to talk someone out of leaving. I might offer more money or give them a paid vacation to one of our other properties so they can press the reset button. But in this case, I think you know exactly what you're doing here. Go do it. You call me if you ever need anything. Anything at all."

That was the last time I ever spoke to Mr. Daniels.

The day after I wrapped up my two weeks, Perry drove over to my apartment in his brand-new truck. It was a calm Saturday morning. Before heading out, we sat in the sun on the lowered back tailgate and drank beer from the side coolers built into the car, over the wheel well. I think the side coolers were for, I don't know, *fishing bait,* but Perry always had them full of ice and beer. The radio was on nice and loud. We had ourselves a few and listened to Trick Daddy, watching the uptown morning come on.

In the cab of the truck was a bottle of Crown Royal. We started tipping that up and rolling back to his side of town because Perry said he needed a fresh cut. The barbershop was, essentially, a shotgun apartment, and the barber chairs were just regular banquet chairs (probably even stolen from a hotel). It was like a house party inside. One dude kept falling asleep in his chair, like a crackhead (because he actually *was* a crackhead), messing up his own haircut every time he nodded out, his beer drooping dangerously between his knees. They gave us some free barbecue ribs, and we kept on hitting the Crown, sharing some with Perry's barber, Henry, who looked drunk already. Henry kept pausing the haircut to talk about how every man needs a wife, a boo, and a freak.

"Wife, you got that for life. Never let that woman leave you. She raising your children. The boo, she talk all day, maybe you leave some clothes over at her apartment, maybe put in some toward rent, and she'll talk shit all day about you leaving your wife, but you and she both know that shit won't *never happen.* Now, the freak? She don't say nothing. You don't buy her nothing. You just get in there, get your dick sucked, and get out. But the wife, you cherish that. Still and all, though, a man needs all three, yerd me?"

We stopped by the dry cleaner, picking up two shirts — one for me and one for Perry. My shirt, extremely oversized, was brown silk with a teddy bear DJ airbrushed on it, his teddy bear paws scratching some turntables, his teddy bear eyes bloodshot, from teddy bear marijuana, I presumed.

"Where I'm taking you, Tommy, you got to look a certain way. Otherwise those ma'fuckers'll put a bullet in your white ass."

We both laughed hard as I buttoned it up, too drunk to care how ridiculous I looked, plus it was already dark, and we got back in the truck. We drove farther away from anything I'd seen, and the bottle of Crown was finished by the time we made it to the club, where most of the valet department, all of the housemen, and more than half of the housekeeping ladies were already inside drinking and dancing. We drank thug passions (Alizé and champagne; classy as fuck, basically), and there was even a cake for me, which read, "Bon Voyage Mr. Tommy," the "Mr." coupled with my first name being a common form of respect in New Orleans (Ms. Trish, Mr. Terrance, and so on). It was so sweet and crazy, and all the ladies had their hair done and wore the same club clothes they always wore to work. I danced and said good-bye to everyone, giving and getting sweaty hugs, and some people got sick in the bathroom or outside the club but still came back in and kept going.

It was five in the morning when Perry drove me home. We each had one more cold beer pinched between our legs, taking slow and unwanted sips.

It was really quiet in the car and really sad. I left New Orleans the next day, flew to Atlanta, and boarded a plane to London.

Chapter Five

What can be said about the following year in my life? Very little about hotels. Quite a bit about hostels. The word "hostel" is just one *s* away from "hotel." And that *s* has got to stand for *"sharing."*

First night in London, on my way to Paris, I stayed at a massive shithole with the welcoming name of the *Generator.* The only thing that building could generate was bedbugs and STDs. No room keys, just combination codes for the door locks, and when I opened my door, I found my allocated bed, one of six in the room, occupied by a passed-out young lady. Back to the desk, only to be informed that I should wake her and ask her to move. I told him no, give me another bed, and he did. Then off to Paris, where I checked into a tiny shithole with the American-friendly name the *Woodstock Hostel.*

It was a terrible time to be an American

abroad. Bush had invaded Iraq, thoroughly displeasing the French, who only grew more indignant as American idiots started ordering freedom toast and freedom fries at Denny's and Waffle Houses across the United States. Trying to find an apartment in Paris was near impossible as an American, even as one who could pay six months' rent *in advance.* The benefit of getting all the money up front did not seem to outweigh the fact that I was born in the United States of Assholes. So they hung up the phone in my face. Finally, I secured a small apartment in the third arrondissement from an *incroyably* drunk landlady who *did* understand the benefit of money up front. I spent half a year walking the city and being roundly ignored by the locals. After an extended trip through Europe, even getting over to Russia, I returned to Paris, immediately repacked my (still just one) suitcase, and moved to Copenhagen, Denmark, a town I had fallen in love with during a brief two-day visit.

I spent that long summer in Denmark. Though in winter it approaches permanent night (the sky only growing mouse gray for a two-hour span before plunging back into darkness), in the summer the sun sets at 11:30 p.m., only to rise again at 1:30 in the morning. My friends and I (six months in Paris = zero friends / six hours in Copenhagen = ten lifelong friends) would lie in the park, often smoking spliffs or straight hash, and play backgammon until the unbelievably long and luxurious afternoon faded. Then we'd mount our bicycles and ride to the Søerne (the Lakes) to watch the sun rise again, the occasion normally calling for another spliff. We went on and on like this. Every afternoon (and it was *always* afternoon) we splayed out in some sunshiny park drinking Tuborg beer and rolling in the grass, pawing at the earth, not doing a damn thing. Because there was a national focus on recycling, each beer bottle could be returned for a substantial refund, which in turn created a job for people who'd simply tour the park and, after asking politely, remove your empty bottles for you. Aware that they were, in effect, taking your refund, they would also remove all trash, including bottle caps and cigarette butts, which they got on their knees to pick up. All of this created a wonderful side effect: the parks were always *immaculate*. The whole town was immaculate. I saw a production of *Hamlet* put on for free at the foot of a Danish castle. There is nothing rotten in the state of Denmark. Well, the winter, the winter is pretty rotten.

And then the money, as it has a tendency to do, ran the fuck out. I had reserved enough for a plane ticket to America and some funds to get back on my feet, but certainly my time overseas, along with my traveler's visa nine months ago, had expired. I couldn't conceive of returning to New Orleans. It would feel like reversing the tape, rewinding the video, as if it would erase all the places I'd seen and the people I'd met. I sat for a long while at the Nyhavn canal, also called the longest bar in the world (where Hans Christian Andersen lived), and got Euro drunk, staring at the colorful spectrum of shoulder-to-shoulder buildings, thinking about what exactly I wanted. And where exactly I wanted to get it.

New York. New York City. There was an option that tightened the sack. Despite all my adolescent relocation, we never moved to any major East Coast hub. Though when I was seventeen, long before I'd moved to New Orleans, I visited New York on a tryst with my first love. We'd driven up from North Carolina, where my family was "stationed" at the time, and stayed exclusively in Times Square, magnetically trans-fixed to the area by all the lights and movement, neon and action.

I remember checking into the Hotel Edison. While I was asking about the elevators, my bag was basically shoplifted off my shoulder. When I turned to investigate, I was face-to-face with a New York City bellman, who was already talking. He fast-talked us into the elevator, his jaw moving with that New York rhythm and speed, just on and on about whatever, while the two of us, just kids really, held hands in fear and stared up at his square jaw opening crookedly to speak and, above that, his wide, pale forehead corrugated with massive pulsing veins, responsible for pumping the blood necessary to keep the jaw working, veins that went straight up to the top of his skull, where they were covered by a prickly gray crew cut. He chased us into the room with his talking, and I remember the end of his long speech was incredibly abrupt and almost exactly like this: "But, you guys, at least, you know, came here to the city and got to meet a character like me."

And then the deafening silence of the room. The kind of sound vacuum only a hotel room can provide. It was like listening to the mounting hiss of cicadas instantly halt, the kind of smack in the face caused by an explosion of silence.

He was staring right at me, those forehead veins deflating.

Oh, I thought, he wants something from me. Oh! A tip! The moment my wallet came out, it was as if his face switched back on, and he started jawing again. I ripped opened my Velcro wallet and handed him a few ones. Instantly, we were alone in the hotel room, our bags by the door.

I never forgot him. No idea who he was, but now I know who he *is.* He used the shock of silence to make it clear to a young person, who normally has no idea what to do in that situation (and neither do some adults in fact), that it was time to tip. That, dear guests, is a true New York City bellman. All over the world, bellmen are serious about a dollar, but in New York *everyone is serious about a dollar,* so that makes the bellmen absolutely psychotic about a dollar.

I lifted myself up off the Nyhavn canal ledge, gave all my empties to the nearest bottle collector, and jumped on a plane to New York City. After a sleepless flight, I found myself entering that city once again. Immediately, one single issue stood out, glaring and omnipresent. I would come to find out that this particular concern, the same one referenced above, was to wake me up in the mornings and put me down at night.

Money.

Money concerns.

Specifically, the lack of it.

I secured a bedroom in a four-room apartment in Brooklyn, in an area then called Bushwick. My rent, though already disgustingly high, was soon to rise when they started calling the neighborhood East Williamsburg and then Williamsburg proper. This was even before the 1980s came back to Williamsburg, when men still wore men's pants. But it was all coming: Style was in the air. Style and bullshit. And rent was always due. First month, I had it. Second month, well, I didn't. I borrowed money from my family and went smoothly into debt. It seemed as if New York *adored* poverty because everyone did it so well.

Trust me, I was looking for work. But not hotel work. I had been fast-tracked for a career in hospitality but went AWOL. And though my résumé displayed little else, I continued to feel moving on was the right decision, a bullet dodged. Now here I was in New York, and I had my pick of careers. So for three months I tried getting a job doing anything else. *Anything.* I thought now was the time to parlay whatever I'd learned into another direction, another career.

Wait. What exactly had I learned?

During this time I was truly scared. Just deep down scared. I felt, though time had certainly *passed,* I'd gained nothing. I had a philosophy degree that didn't apply to any job, and I'm not even certain the education itself affected me in any real way. (That's not true: it made me smart as fuck.) But what of actual value had I accomplished since I turned sixteen? Well, I'd done seen some shit: Europe, strip clubs, bar bathrooms, coke parties, a dead homeless man scooped off the street like a hardened piece of dog shit, a knife fight, the backstage area, a roulette game in Russia, the hood, the basement, the penthouse, uptown, downtown, and everywhere else. But what was all that? And now here I was in a huge apocalyptic city that certainly failed to notice my arrival and promised to be uninformed of my departure, whether it be by bus or death.

All of that big pile of nothing and still I had to get a damn job.

I led a full-on attack on the publishing business. Here were all the publishing houses, encased in huge fortresses all over Manhattan. Surely some of my experience, added to my long-standing love of books, made me an asset to any publishing house. Apparently not. I couldn't even get interviews. I couldn't even get responses that said they didn't want to interview me. I couldn't even get inside the buildings. But sometimes I would stand outside in the cold and look in. That, they allowed me to do.

I was still holed up in the four-bedroom apartment, in what was now officially Williamsburg, Brooklyn, with three female roommates, none of whom I was banging, and as it stood then, I didn't have last, this, or next month's rent, it was dead-cold winter, and I was drinking myself homeless on 99-cent, 24-oz. Coors Original cans.

I would stand at the big front window, like some broke-ass Gatsby, and look down into the building's internal courtyard, not that it was used as a courtyard, more like a trash dump and Grand Central Station for huge city rats. But all of that nastiness was being covered by a thick blanket of white snow, the fat flakes still falling and resting, building. My roommates, to their unmistakable exasperation, could always find me in the large communal loft space, playing a record, drinking from those tall sickly yellow Coors cans, my forehead pressed against the snowy window, a paper bag filled with empanadas on the couch next to me, the only food in the area I could afford. At first, the dollar-empanada man, operating out of a shitty food cart parked next to a shitty dollar store, did not recognize me. Then, as my visits grew more frequent, he would reluctantly acknowledge my existence. Later, as it became clear his empanadas were the only thing keeping me alive, well, he felt pity for me, which came out in the form of irritation and then a determined refusal to recognize me once again. Still, God bless him. He came out even in a blizzard, and he is still there, on the corner of Grand and Humboldt. After eight years he has only raised his prices by a single quarter.

"We'll give you fifteen days to make rent, otherwise you don't get your deposit back and you're out."

This little pay-or-you're-out pep talk was administered by the apartment's ringleader. She was sitting inside a fully erected two-man tent she'd recently set up in the apartment's ample front loft space. I had to bend down and peer into the tent to receive this information.

"I don't care what your deal is. Fifteen days or you're out. Totally. Fucking. Out."

Jyll. Jyll with a *y*. We never got along. She wore all the latest fashions (which, coincidentally, were the latest fashions from two decades ago), and her boyfriend, though older than I, dressed, for some reason, like a British schoolboy with bow ties, sport coats with elbow patches, and khaki shorts above beige socks inside brown wing tips. I disliked her quite a bit, which I also found to be a ubiquitous attitude in New York. In New Orleans people made a determined effort to get along, to find common ground and enjoy each other's company. Here (and, man, would I get good at this) it was easier to just go ahead and, you know, *hate*.

"Can I use the fax machine again, Jyll?"

"No, because it's in my *roooom*. Ugh. Fine. Two faxes only. Let's go," she said, shimmying out of the tent.

At that moment, the empanada bag almost transparent from grease, the last sip of my tall boy warm and nauseatingly flat, snow still pounding down on the city, I broke. I broke like a little bitch.

Two faxes. Faxed to, yes indeed, two luxury hotels.

Two days later, two interviews.

Once a hotel whore, always a hotel whore.

I had been like some prostitute trying to get a secretarial position, only to have the interviewer come around the desk, get uncomfortably close, maybe lay an inappropriate hand on my knee, and say, "Look.

You're a whore. You're a *good* whore. Why don't you stop messing around and get back to working the corner, huh? Come on, baby, it can't be that bad, can it?"

CHAPTER SIX

The first hotel was a Historic Hotels of America member. That meant it was un-renovated. And that meant it was beat to shit. I was interviewed in a basement office with a yellow flickering light.

Though the ad in the paper was not clear, it turned out to be a housekeeping manager position: running the boards every morning and all of *that* mess. My lack of enthusiasm was, even in the buttery flickering light, all over my face. I didn't want the job. The old man slowly administering the interview didn't seem to care if he filled the position either.

"Okay, son, the pay is not good. And it won't get better. But at least things aren't too serious here, you know? Long hours, though. You want the gig?"

No.

In fact, since neither of us seemed to give a shit, I told him I couldn't be in at 7:00

every morning. Plus, I asked for five thousand more.

"But maybe I could roll in around 11:00 a.m.?"

"We can't even give you five *dollars* more, son, and how do you plan to run the boards at eleven?"

"So then . . . no?"

No.

Because it was for a larger hotel, the second interview was quite a bit more professional. I actually had my initial interview at the hotel's corporate office on First Avenue. It took place, strangely, in the building's large airy lobby, the walls covered in enormous, terrible pop art. I was interviewed by an insanely hyperactive Korean-American woman who couldn't stop smiling and talking and certainly couldn't stop shaking her crazy knee up and down as if voltage were tearing through it. We were sitting on a modern, almost abstract couch together, the sitting angles a bit too creative, which was awkward. After I dazzled her with my experience and dusted off my luxury phrases ("guest loyalty," "exceptional service," "empathize and react," "attention to detail," "Very. Easy," "blah blah bullshit"), she cooed in delight and directed me to the hotel where I would be working.

I took the subway, then walked to Ninth Avenue, right near the heart of . . . (Lord Jesus Christ, protect me!) midtown. The hotel was two avenues west of Times Square, but two avenues weren't enough. Despite the winter weather, the sidewalks and delis were filled with tourists, cameras flopping, maps unfurled in the icy wind, bundled children attached to those human leashes, just an incredible hustle and bustle of visitors, surrounded on every side by the thousands of service industry employees necessary to keep this tourism machine churning. Either you were a tourist or you had a name tag; that was my first impression of midtown.

I walked into the warm lobby of the hotel, and before I asked for the HR department, I took a little stroll, cruising by the front desk to the right of the revolving doors. I noticed their uniforms were a bit shabby; some of the men's black suit coats were flat and shiny from years of washing. The whole environment was a little worn: The decor was dark brown marble and yellows, essentially the same color scheme as a microwavable meal of Salisbury steak with buttered mashed potatoes. The couches were from the 1980s and sagging as if they were trying to take a nap. The front wall, which was the first thing you saw upon entering the lobby, had a large, silver-framed antique mirror hung too high to reflect anything but the dirty crown molding above the entrance behind you. Below the mirror, one tiny flower arrangement sat on a useless table. I saw the restaurant to the left (same frozen-dinner color scheme) almost vacant, though I assumed lunch would be in full swing. Walking past the front desk on the right, I found the elevator banks, and with the exception of a tiny hole in the wall that I thought was a coat check but turned out to be the concierge desk, three of them packed in there and banging shoulders like a bunch of windup toys in a small box, there was nothing else to the lobby. Front desk to the right of the entrance, front wall displaying flowers of about the same mass and quality I'd bring to a dinner party at a friend of a friend's co-worker's house, that crazy use-less mirror, sleepy couches hoping to crack a leg and die, dead restaurant to the left, and, down a hallway past the desk, the elevators and concierge rat hole. That was it.

Nice.

Let's call the hotel, for various reasons soon to be obvious, the Bellevue Hotel.

Welcome to the Bellevue.

After my secret tour, everything accelerated into hyper-speed. They shuffled me
through the system so fast I was pissing into
a drug-test cup before I asked exactly what
position I had qualified for.

"Position? Oh, front desk. Already got a
uniform suit for you, too. Last guy, well, he
no longer lives in New York. He no longer
lives, actually. Just kidding. Good news is
he was just about your size. Any surprises
with that drug test?"

"No, sir."

"You took one of those detox teas? Just
messing with you. I hope you did, though.
Anyway, okay, so, uh, what's the name on
the name tag?"

So, what's the name on the name tag? It
was like a warden asking me what number I
wanted on my orange jumper. But I needed
the money, and even though it was just a
front desk gig, I couldn't believe the hourly
they were offering. Not that I was incredibly surprised; the hotel business has a very
competitive starting wage. If hotels didn't
keep a high starting wage, they would have
the same turnover as McDonald's. You'll
notice McDonald's isn't really known for
customer service. You have to pay a little
more if you expect someone to train properly, stick around, care *at all,* and, you know,

not sort through luggage looking for iPods to steal.

So, what was the name on the name tag? It was time for a change.

"Employee X958B27."

"What?"

"Tom."

"Oh, Tom. T . . . O . . . M. Got it."

I looked at my new boss ("Same as the old boss." — The Who), and he looked at me.

"Well . . . welcome aboard."

Does every new boss in every new job say this? Or just hotel gigs? Welcome aboard. As if getting hired were similar to stepping onto a yacht, which it isn't (unless you're boarding the yacht to clean the toilets).

Well, I was aboard. Three months of searching for any other kind of profession and nothing. After I broke down, it took forty-eight hours before someone was already carving me a name tag in the hotel business. Fine. Whatever. Sure. Fine. Whatever. I needed to make rent. Whatever. Thanks, New York.

Jyll was actually disappointed. I believe she wanted to keep my deposit and have her ridiculously dressed boyfriend move in.

After getting the job, I stayed up all night pounding Coors after Coors and staring out the window again, waiting for day to break. I was so far from everyone I'd ever known. My family was scattered across the country. My friends, all those I left behind, perhaps no longer retained a memory of our acquaintance. Only a handful of people in New Orleans would remain my friends, and certainly, as I sank into this city, they might soon forget me. Now here I was, drinking alone in an apartment with three strangers who only wanted my rent and my absence. I stayed awake until the sky above the city grew felt gray before locking myself in my bedroom to sleep the entire day away. I had to. I started my overnight shift that night.

There I was, name-tagged up again, pinned down, literally. It's standard procedure to start on the overnight shift and work your way up. Even beyond the fact that most people can't stand working the graveyard shift, so the new hire must slug it out until there is a change in the regiment above (a.k.a. someone gets fired), it also happens to be an ideal shift to train on. The desk is dead. Plenty of time to struggle with the new system and be ignorant about your own property. People don't expect crazy quality from front desk agents at 3:00 a.m. They just expect them not to be totally crazy.

So I set myself to the task of learning a

new property, getting a headache from the new PMS (forgive me), and locking down the answers to the questions I was going to be asked over and over and over again, beginning at the beginning. For example: "Where is the bathroom?" Well, where the hell is the bathroom? What are the gym hours, cost of continental breakfast, do we have the Golf Channel, how does one dial out internationally, where the fuck are the ice machines, how do I lock the in-room safe, who makes our pillows because they are *fab*ulous, how do you get rid of the blinking light on the phone, where is the closest place to buy cuff links, what's the fax number, is the room available that has the tub and two twin beds facing north at the end of the hall with double sinks in the bathroom and one of the desks against the window so you can look out over the Hudson River while you surf porn on the free wireless? I'm sorry, sir, that room is a fantasy that only exists in your frequent-traveler brain. And wireless is not free, it's $9.95 for a twenty-four-hour period.

While getting up to speed on the system and hotel info, I was also going slightly mental. Living the vampire lifestyle is taxing in more ways than you can imagine. You can't sleep properly, you can't eat properly, you can't even get drunk properly. It is quite possible to spend week after week being *confused*. Just generally *bewildered*, as if you took a blow to the head. But some people love the graveyard shift. That's what a property really wants, dedicated overnight agents. Maybe the agents are going to school during the day and can't afford to miss classes. Maybe they have children, and working overnight alleviates the need for babysitters (though husband and wife never see each other). Maybe they are just crazy, scary, freaky night people. Whatever their reason, they are a godsend to any hotel. Most commonly, hotels get stuck with an agent who is forced into the shift and always calls in sick on the Friday overnight, causing the poor Friday late shift to stay and cover (the Friday late shift being just slightly more desirable than overnight and usually an agent's next rung on the shift ladder).

I was dependable, though. Always on time, I clocked in at 11:00 every night (even getting in a little early on Fridays to relieve the evening desk workers; those guys are ready to get the hell out as fast as possible). I wavered behind my terminal, bewildered, bracing myself on the desk at 2:00 a.m., splashing water on my face at 3:00 a.m., eating a chocolate bar and drinking a Red

Bull at 4:00 a.m., popping into the back office to slap myself *hard* in the *face* at 5:00 a.m., greeting the early-riser guests and beginning to check out rooms at 6:00 a.m., my mouth tasting like the smell coming from the wilting and unchanged flower display at 6:05 a.m., counting the minutes at 6:06 a.m., feeling as if I've ruined my whole life at 6:21 a.m., dreaming about dreaming at 6:32 a.m., squinting with hatred at the sun sliding into the lobby at 6:43 a.m., thinking about absolutely nothing, my head sort of rolling around, eyes twitching and staring down the hallway at 6:51 a.m., at the end of which, next to the elevators, is the door that leads to the employee locker rooms, where my relief, hopefully, is on time and changing into uniform, then stumbling downstairs at 7:01 a.m. and fighting with everything I have, mustering all the strength and stamina and intelligence left in my sizzled brain, focusing and concentrating on one solitary task, determined not to let it break me — untying the double knot on my right dress shoe, which always seems to get stuck, picking at the knot with blurry fingers that seem to be made of string — then taking the train home to lie in my bed, the bed I've been absolutely fantasizing about all night, only to find the sun painting yellow neon on my closed eyelids and my body waking up for some reason, wanting now to move and be active, but I put a pillow over my face and take deep, deep breaths until I fall into a hot, twitchy sleep that lasts no more than three hours.

I might have been confused (all the time), but I could already tell something was wrong with the overnight manager. His name was Julio, and though the policy in almost every hotel is to remain clean shaven (with the exception, absurdly, of allowing mustaches), he kept it Latin-style scruffy. I also noticed, during certain interactions with late-night guests, he would throw me a cautious look and then escort them to a saggy couch to finish discussing his business in private. These were guests who paid cash, guests who were accompanied by prostitutes or who would be shortly once they wrapped up this shady business deal with Julio. We talked very little (his choice), and he was often absent from the lobby for hours at a time.

There was definitely something wrong with the overnight bellman. But his something wrong I liked. He was flat-out manic and, as if he were born for this shift, full of energy. I don't know what his fuel was. It seemed like cocaine. But it wasn't. He was clean. His name was Filipe, but everyone called him *El Salvaje* (the Savage). Even his hair, black and wild, had too much energy. Most of the time he expended his energy lamenting the Mets and attacking the desk and marble walls with huge shoulder checks, constantly in need of releasing the gigantic surplus of frantic energy he was packed with. We got along extremely well. If I was dealing with drunk guests who were slurring and swaying (most guests who drop by the desk after 2:00 a.m. are drunk), *El Salvaje* would come behind them and do a mock impression, wiping his mouth and rocking side to side to match their rhythm. Usually, I could hold it together, meaning refrain from laughing right in the guests' faces, and finish the transaction. Not to mention drunk guests aren't particularly aware of what's taking place before them, much less behind their backs.

Though once, dealing not with an intoxicated guest but with a German traveler who took the red-eye, I lost it. In this particular situation the gentleman had failed to book his reservation correctly for his purposes. He arrived, exhausted, around 4:00 a.m. and found no room available for him. So he started to scream at me.

Before describing the circumstances that

caused me to laugh in this poor man's face, I should explain a bit about what generally happens to a hotel system when *today* becomes *tomorrow.*

Somewhere around 2:00 a.m. the front desk will temporarily shut down the PMS and then "flip the system." Once the PMS is back up, three things have happened. One: the system will now reflect tomorrow's date. Two: all occupied reservations will have been auto-charged the room and tax. Three: all unclaimed reservations due to arrive earlier that night will be canceled and marked as a no-show.

If one plans to arrive after 3:00 a.m. and expect a room (as was the case with my exhausted German traveler), there are several things to know. The only way to absolutely guarantee that you will have a fresh, clean room waiting for you after a red-eye is to book it for the night before. Period. What's more, unless you want to be considered a no-show, you will also need to ensure that your reservation is pre-registered, or pre-reged, meaning checked in prior to your arrival. This is accomplished by you (or, you know, your assistant) calling in advance and informing us of the situation. The hotel will check you in the night before to a VC (or Vacant Clean, as opposed to VD, Vacant Dirty) room and add the term "pre-reged" after your name in the system. Though you are arriving early in the morning, you will be charged the previous night's room and tax, charged for the privilege of having a room waiting for you.

My German guest got it all wrong. He booked it for Saturday, which was, technically, the date he would arrive. Unfortunately (for both of us), we had no room available that early in the morning. Essentially, he was eleven hours early for his Saturday check-in. This made him, well, angry. Irate. He started making these sharp hand-chop movements while spitting out threats, trying to convince me I was in the wrong, the hotel was in the wrong. *El Salvaje,* hearing the commotion from the back office, popped out his wild finger-in-the-socket head of hair and then crept up behind the guest, who was loudly letting me have it. From behind this man's frame *El Salvaje* kept leaning over and popping his head out from one side, then the other, his elbows out, like some sort of synchronized dance. That was fine. I could handle that move. But when he started popping out and rotating his fists at the corner of each eye, making the international sign for crybaby, then, well, my mouth kind of exploded. I laughed so hard and so unexpectedly that spittle flew at the guest, my lips buzzed trying to hold it in, and I bent over, grabbing at my mouth. Having no plan for this kind of situation, I ran off the desk, pushing quickly through the door into the back office to calm myself.

I could now hear him speaking to *El Salvaje,* and clearly he picked up on the fact that what had happened was not an explosion of illness but instead violent and unexpected laughter, and certainly at his expense. We called the manager on his cell phone, something I had rarely done, and Julio came down coked to the gills. I mean, he must have taken two fat rails immediately before rushing down to the lobby from whatever housekeeping storage closet he was partying in. The guest's anger was, in an unexpected way, no match for Julio's nonstop talking-jag energy, his accelerated apologies and tweaky explanations. Julio, in a rather brilliant move, scanned the in-house list (as in the list of rooms already checked in) for a reservation with the "pre-reg" tag, as I mentioned before. Finding one, he checked that guest out, who was only "due to arrive," and quickly, raining a downpour of heavy coke-fueled typing into the keyboard, checked the German guest into the now Vacant Clean suite and sent him on his way. Julio turned to us, his face jumping around like an agitated bunny, and then hopped off again, heading to the elevators without a word. A brilliant move, though. That is unless the pre-reged guest who had his room stolen arrived before housekeeping had time to come in and flip another room for him. Which, of course, he did. To deal with that situation, Julio simply lied to the guest, said that his reservation had been made for the previous night but, since there was no indication that he was arriving the following morning, it had been canceled and sold to a walk-in arrival at 5:00 a.m. The guest cursed his poor assistant, who'd actually done her job properly, and apologized for his attitude. Julio bought him breakfast, and the guest wandered off way more pleased with the hotel than he should have been. And we made it through another goddamn night.

Early-morning arrivals don't always have to be so complicated. My advice, after seeing it all play out a thousand times, is this: If you simply *must* have a room at 7:00 a.m., then you *must* book the night before and pre-register yourself. However, if you want to take a risk and possibly save an entire night's room and tax, call the property and find out the occupancy for the night before. If the hotel is running at 65 percent, then 35 percent of the rooms might be Vacant Clean and ready to check in, even at 4:00 or 5:00 a.m. (excluding those rooms that have been "dropped" and left dirty). Therefore, if the occupancy is low the night before, you can potentially roll on up and have an insanely early check-in. Requesting early arrival isn't enough. The *best possible move* is to call the property directly the morning you're scheduled to arrive and let the agent know you are on your way. Tell the hotel 7:00 a.m., even if you know your train doesn't hit Penn Station till 11:00 a.m., and ask to be pre-reged into a Vacant Clean suite. If the hotel has it sitting there and you call for it, it will be pre-reged and waiting for you when you arrive. Even if you have to call from the airport at 6:00 a.m. before you even *board the plane* and ask to be pre-reged, it's your best possible assurance that when you roll into the lobby and everyone in front of you is getting their luggage stored and waiting for an afternoon check-in, your reservation will have been checked in and waiting since 6:00 a.m.

Two nights after the German debacle, I came into work, passing through security on my way to change for a shift, and both security guards were staring at the monitors, too engrossed to even throw me a glance. This isn't particularly unusual, because there can be some high-quality viewing material on those monitors. I've since seen tapes of midnight sex sessions in the public business center, two guests getting oral on top of the pay-to-play fax machine. I've seen footage of close-packed fistfights in a rising elevator (fights in an elevator are incredibly confined and extremely interesting to watch, especially if there are unrelated people along for the ride, backs pushed against the wall and hands protectively raised before their faces). And, of course, drunk guests staggering down a hallway and bouncing from wall to wall like a bowling ball thrown down a lane with gutter bumpers. The video they were replaying that night was very similar to the last situation; however, it wasn't a guest. It was Julio the manager. He was walking crookedly down a hallway, his arms cradled against his chest, hands full of something.

"What's he got there?"

"Look at *this* motherfucker. Those are minibar bottles, Tom. What a moron. Keep watching, though, keep watching. It gets better."

Julio ran his shoulders along the wall,

bouncing off door moldings, until he reached the emergency stairs and pushed the door open.

"Okay, okay. Now we cue up the other camera on this monitor. Check it out, check it out."

On a second monitor, filming the stairwell, the video looked frozen or paused until the door to the hallway pushed open and Julio walked through, bending down to set the minibar bottles against the wall and take a seat on the stairs. Leonard, the overnight security guard who was queuing up the videos, put it into fast-forward, creating a comical little vignette of Julio drinking bottle after bottle at hyper-speed, his head bouncing up and down like a bobble head. The whole scene looked sort of jolly until he slowed it back down to normal speed and I saw immediately just how depressing it actually was.

"Here he go. Here he go."

Julio lifted himself up, spilling and rolling minibar bottles everywhere, used a palm to brace himself against the wall, and started urinating on, actually *on*, the stairs.

"What!? Are you kidding me?"

"Believe that? Look, *look*, it's rolling back down onto *his own shoes*. What a dumb, crazy, *nasty* motherfucker."

Let me take a moment here: Coming from a true luxury hotel in New Orleans, I was certainly *not used to this.* I was shocked. What in César Ritz's name was going on here? Was it like this everywhere in New York? Or was this hotel just cursed? It was interesting, no doubt, but I kept reminding myself that I wasn't a part of this. I wasn't a part of this. I was just picking up checks until I could pay off my debts, get a little money in savings, and then look for other work elsewhere. I also promised myself I would keep up the high standards I'd been raised on. This hotel might be filled with criminals and drug addicts, but that didn't mean I had to stop saying "my pleasure," "good evening," and slopping out incredible service.

Despite my dedication to excellence, though, when management wasn't looking, I did tend to enjoy myself a little more than proper, and during the overnight shifts management was never looking. For three nights in a row, *El Salvaje* and I had taken a geriatric power scooter, on hold for a guest arriving next week, up to the sales office hallways on our 3:00 a.m. break. After attaching a rolling office chair to the back of the scooter, tied to it with a bedsheet, *El Salvaje* and I would take turns gunning the life out of the scooter and dragging each other behind on the rolling chair, careening around corners, slamming into walls, and inevitably smashing into the back of the scooter after a hard stop. At least *El Sal vaje*'s hair acted as a helmet. I was going raw.

We would have had a fourth night of action if Julio hadn't pissed all over his own shoes. But that night we had a new manager. The hotel shifted one of the day managers to cover until a replacement could be found.

"Who the fuck are you?" he asked me, as a sort of hello.

"I'm Tom," I said, tapping at my name tag.

"Fucking new guy. Listen to me, FNG, run the reports and flip this bitch into tomorrow. Something explodes, call me in room 1402. I'm gonna throw a juke, watch *SportsCenter,* and pass out. This is bullshit."

I didn't even know what throwing a juke meant (now I know it's not performed while watching *SportsCenter,* oh no). And nothing ever exploded. Just a few "late night" women limping out of the hotel, exhausted looking, avoiding eye contact with everyone, and hurrying back out into the streets.

Like milk and cereal: whores and hotels.

William Faulkner, in his 1956 *Paris Re-*

view interview, stated: "The best job that was ever offered to me was to become a landlord in a brothel. In my opinion it's the perfect milieu for an artist to work in. It gives him perfect economic freedom; he's free of fear and hunger; he has a roof over his head and nothing whatever to do . . . The place is quiet during the morning hours, which is the best time of the day to work. There's enough social life in the evening, if he wishes to participate, to keep him from being bored; it gives him a certain standing in his society."

Hotels are the brothels of today. You rent a bed, and you're allotted a certain amount of hours. But now it's just BYOW (the *W* stands for "prostitute"). And there I was, the midnight landlord, watching the cumings and goings. The whole process is amazingly discreet. There are women who *look* like prostitutes but are *not* (they are actually gold diggers). And there are women who look like business execs; however, beneath that beige, it's all black lace. Professionals never stop by the desk, or at least they shouldn't. I see them strut into the lobby already glancing at their cell phones, referencing the only piece of info they need: a room number. Then they look up, and there I am, the landlord, throwing a finger to indicate the elevator banks. Off she goes.

One particularly busy Friday night, women constantly streaming in and out of the hotel, I took a few notes, cataloging the attire and times of arrival so I could cross-check them with the time of departure and then estimate length of service. But, you see, again, you never know. Some people rent a woman just to talk. Some of them could be married women stopping by to see their lovers. You never really know, and, believe me, never really knowing is how *everyone wants it.*

Faulkner wasn't the only writer to man a front desk, bordello or otherwise. Nathanael West worked the overnight shift at a failing Manhattan hotel while completing *Miss Lonelyhearts* and even offered up free lodging to his writer friends, like Dashiell Hammett and Edmund Wilson. In return they helped promote his work, providing blurbs in lieu of paying room and tax. That was the 1930s, though. On my overnights I wasn't even allowed to offer *myself* a goddamn *stool* to sit on.

Two months on the graveyard shift and one night an Ecuadorian comes in and stands next to me, wearing the same uniform suit, same uniform tie.

"Who are you?"

"Hector," he said, taking off his name tag and putting it on the desk in front of us. We both looked down at it.

"What are you doing here?"

"I'm jew. Jew going to deys, mang."

"I'm going to the day shift?"

"Jew didn't know? They never tell people shit, mang. It's like the fucking army."

CHAPTER SEVEN

The bellmen were the first to intimidate.

"Listen very closely to me, FNG. I see you handing guests their own keys, I'll stab you. I hear you asking them if they need help with their luggage, I'll stab you. You don't ask them shit. You call 'front' and hand the keys to a bellman. Let them tell me to my face they can take their own luggage and my baby girl has to starve. I catch *you* handing them keys, I figure *you're* the one who wants my baby girl to starve. In which case I will find out what train you take home and collapse your throat as soon as you step into your borough."

New York pep talk number two! The first, from my roommate in Brooklyn, promising to throw me out if I didn't make rent, seemed like a pillow fight in comparison. Jyll's verbal "encouragement," which forced me to unwillingly reinsert myself into the hotel business, had, in turn, led me to *this* pep talk, administered by a bellman exactly one minute into my first evening shift. Three of them had pulled me to a corner of the lobby, and while the pack leader gave me the rundown, the others stood at each flank and nodded in affirmation. The head of the triangle, according to his name tag, was Ben. Ben the bellman. I know now he was just trying to be helpful.

"I hope for your sake you don't fuck this up," he concluded and all three dispersed.

That's how I was welcomed to my new 4:00 p.m. to midnight schedule, the evening shift, the major leagues, the show. The overnight shifts had been a sobering return to the business: the echoing emptiness of a 3:00 a.m. lobby, layered by the low drone of a vacuum, punctuated by the rattling cough of a hooker returning to the streets and the sound of my own thoughts as I stood behind a front desk again, alone for eight hours.

Alone no more. I returned to the desk, a little off balance from the attack, weaving my way through a line of waiting guests. No one had "assigned" me to someone or asked me to "shadow an agent" as they had in New Orleans. In New York, management didn't even bother to check and see if I showed up.

But once I was on deck, logged in, and

ready to work, I calmed down. After all, I'm a veteran desk jockey: I can sling keys like a motherfucker.

It was immediately clear that one factor was of the utmost importance in this new environment: SPEED. In New Orleans, it was like living in syrup; no one was in a rush. The pace of a Manhattan evening shift is four finger lines of cocaine dumped into a five-hour energy drink. After a week of shifts I began to triple and quadruple task. I realized that while the credit card (or CC, we don't even have time to say "credit card") is authorizing, it's best to utilize those five seconds to write the room number on the key packet, confirm the rate, or start running down the list of mandatory information I was responsible for covering during every check-in process. In New Orleans, the one thing I might *utilize a whole five seconds to do* was, maybe: Take another sip of my Heineken? Or smile for Christ's sake? You stand on the island of Manhattan and smile while the CC is authorizing, just waiting around for five seconds smiling? That makes you a moron.

The evening shift also acquainted me with the Bellevue's place in the Manhattan hotel scene. It had a good reputation. Unfortunately, that reputation was ten years old. We had a few working-class celebrities, nice guys like Tony Danza who stuck it out Bellevue-style because the bellmen here weren't afraid to scream, "Ayo, Toneee," when he would swagger into the lobby and, you could tell, Danza *loved that shit.* Business travel put a lot of heads in beds too, and the clientele was extremely international. Truly a fresh joy of the New York hotel business, something not present in New Orleans, was the multiculturalism: Australians who flew in from South Africa to take the *Queen Mary* to England. Jews from Catalonia who needed a non-Jewish escort for Shabbat: someone to press the elevator button, open the electronic door lock, and maybe, just maybe, turn on *Sports-Center* before inching back out of that holy hotel room. As well as a huge Japanese clientele who all wanted two twin beds to avoid sleeping next to their wives, bathtubs, and ample space to bow. (The average Japanese businessman bows more than five hundred times a day. He even bows on the phone.)

And it just kept coming with these damn bellmen. Well after my two-week anniversary on the evening shift, they continued to rattle me: at least twice a day I had to dramatically jump out of a bellman's rolling luggage path to avoid getting a Samsonite to the balls. But as time passed, I grew sympathetic to their plight.

Nature's bellman: an anachronistic, virtually obsolete animal. People drag their luggage through their own house, down the driveway, into their car, up to the airline desk, off the luggage carousel, into the back of a taxi, through the revolving doors, up to the desk, and now, *now* some guy with a crew cut wants to help? You've taken it twenty-five hundred miles, and this dude wearing gloves wants to jump in for the last twenty feet and get tipped for it? "No thanks, I don't need any help."

Hence Ben the bellman's "I hope for your sake you don't fuck this up" speech. Now, the princess of Abu Dhabi, she has a fourteen-piece luggage set, more bags than her well-dressed bodyguards can handle . . . she'll need some help. I'm not saying she's going to tip, but she'll need some help. And so will the family of seven who all brought their own pillows. (In case you didn't know: hotels provide pillows. It's a standard hotel worker pet peeve to see BYOP guests. This is a hotel, not summer camp.) However, the other 98 percent of travelers would gladly refuse help, and a bellman cannot survive with a 2 percent kill ratio. Therefore, as I learned at my new perch, he uses two tools to maximize his percentage: guilt and fear. If I ask the guests "Do you want help?" the answer's going to be no. Every time: no. But if I signal a bellman silently or with the code word "front," put the keys into his hand, and then lay a strong declarative sentence on the guests, such as "The bellman will take you to your room," the kill ratio goes way up. You can see the guilt and fear well up in their eyes. They feel cheap about not taking the help, and they are terrified of telling the bellman (who has their keys in one hand and the other aggressively gripping their luggage) that they can do it themselves. Often they were so afraid of the bellman they would turn to *me* and say, "Um, you know, it's okay really, I can take it." I love that. A real "Please, sir, please!! Call off your dogs!!!" moment. I'll benevolently nod at the bellman, and he'll relinquish his hold on the guest's throat and sink back into the woods to wait for another kill. I actually invented the mind-controlling declarative sentence and later added, "This is my good friend, Ben. Ben will take you to your room," bringing the bellman's life into reality, and hence bringing the guilt to the next level. Eventually, I began to throw in "This is my good friend Ben, godfather to my child and confidant to my wife," but only if they were real-deal Japanese and wouldn't understand a word I was saying anyway. But Ben grew to love that line. It won't get him a "front," but it sounds so damn suspicious we can't get enough of it. *Confidant to my wife.*

Now, the doormen, they get to touch every bag. The cabbies pop the trunk right when they pull up. Hence, the car isn't even in park before the doorman has touched your personals, like it or not. If he just applies a little guilt and fear, you'll pay him to stop uncomfortably lurking just outside your personal space. Bellmen have to do a lot more hunting.

It's a tough world out there. Am I suggesting you always take help and always tip? Yes. I suggest you do that. However, in reality, there are times when guests don't want to be escorted by a gloved chatterbox. Maybe your life is falling apart, and you've no interest in telling a stranger "where you came in from." The best way to get back the keys to your room (and your freedom) from "the gloved hand" is to say, "I can go up alone, but thanks anyways." "No thank you, but I appreciate it." "I think I would rather just go up alone, if that's okay."

Of course it's okay. Just be polite about it.

I even once saw a guest tell a bellman, "No worries, but thank you," and still give him two dollars, just for *not* helping. The rest of his stay that guy was famous. Like a guru. There goes that guy who gave Ben two dollars because he didn't need the help. It was almost more effective than if he had taken the help and dropped a twenty in the room.

Unfortunately, it wasn't just the bellmen and the doormen I had to contend with: the Bellevue's regular guests were giving me the business as well. I had opened the hotel in New Orleans: we all started together from the beginning, both guests and employees. At the Bell it would take me years before I knew as much about the hotel as some of the guests. Mr. Sandbourg, who'd stayed here three nights a week for fifteen years running, had no patience for the new guy pretending to know about the hotel. Sandbourg has stayed in every room, *literally every room,* and eventually I took to listing room numbers, offering potential options for his current stay, and letting him shake them off like a pitcher on the mound. Room 1503? No. Room 702? No. Room 4104? No. How about a goddamn fastball?

Another frequent guest refused to stay in any room where the digits didn't add up to nine. It said that on his profile: "Room digits must add up to nine." That meant I had to do math. If I had maff skillz, I wouldn't be a key monkey, so . . . this was difficult for me. Plus, he's a light sleeper (one of many psychological problems, I'm guessing), which means nothing close to the elevator. Room 1503? Room 702? Room 4104? Curveball?

My new co-workers often tried to help me out, warning me about our guests' idiosyncrasies, oftentimes right in front of the guest. Kayla, an early-thirties Colombian with wonderful black curly hair, called me over to her terminal during a particularly difficult check-in, saying, "Hey, Tom, come see if you want to give her this room." Her manicured index finger was indicating the space where you enter and search for a guest name. On the screen she had typed: "Don't sweat this hag, she only complains at the desk, tell her you love this room, any room, and get her out of the lobby. She won't come down to complain." We would often use that space on the screen to type messages to each other, most of them tactical communiqués designed to stealthily discuss a guest issue within the guest's hearing range. But also some that said things like, "Will you ask your guest if she'll let me put it in her mouth?" After you read a message like that, it's a pretty fun game to look up, a weird smile on your face, and go back to assisting your guest as if nothing happened.

The first time Kayla utilized this technique, I picked up the game pretty quickly.

"Oh, perfect. Mrs. Lansing, you are going to *love* this room. I promise. *Front.* This is my good friend Ben. He will take you upstairs."

"I better love this room. And I don't need a bellman," she said with palpable disgust. "It's on wheels."

Bernard Sadow: the man all bellmen hate, though they've never heard his name. In 1970 he invented the wheeled suitcase, the bane of the bellman's existence. Before that the bellman was a necessity, a provider of ease and comfort, a useful member of society. After Sadow sold his first prototype to Macy's in October 1970, he instigated a catastrophic change in the hospitality environment, causing the once noble species to retreat, rethink, and reemerge as a hustler fighting for survival. Sadow might as well have invented the phrase no bellman wants to hear, the phrase that leaves bills unpaid and ruins Christmas: "No thanks, I got it."

Or that surprisingly prevalent and ignorant phrase: "I don't want to bother him." Don't want to bother him? The man has a family. No one is getting bothered here.

So, these poor anachronistic hunters roam the plains of lobbies across the world, starving for a kill. And just as any predator must adapt to a more savvy, conveniently wheeled prey, each bellman develops his own hustle, his own style. I studied Alan, bellman at the Bellevue for nineteen years, second in seniority. I watched his interactions until I finally realized his angle. Fifty-something with a salt-and-pepper crew cut and silver-framed glasses (incredibly reminiscent of the bellman I met on my first visit to New York), Alan will squat down and make your children love him. He will high-five them and ask them what game they got going on their handheld, tell the little girls how "Manhattan stylish" they look, ask the kids if they are going to get some famous New York cupcakes, and stuff like that. If Alan checks in your family on Friday, then on Saturday your kids will be running through the lobby to get one of Al's high fives and tell him all about "wha, wha happen did last night and, um, um, um."

Just when the parents are marveling at what a wonderful man, and probably what a wonderful father he is (because you best *believe* he's already told you about *his* children), he will cut the parents off cold and stare them into shock through those ice-framed glasses. They had not even considered that this wonderful bellman should be *compensated* for the unique and memorable experience he is providing. Alan has now turned to them with a look full of meaning and power. He will nonverbally make them understand that he should be tipped for this level of service: all of a sudden he has placed a check on the table for services rendered. Someone might take that opportunity to ask if there is an ATM on property. Alan will entertain your children while you go withdraw some cash.

They call him the Gray Wolf.

New York City bellmen build houses and create college funds, all out of ones and fives. This kind of life, lived on a constantly fluctuating scale of cash, comes to define their entire world. I offer an example. Let's call it *Doorman in the Mist: The Hundred-Dollar-Bill Challenge*.

"Don't act like you don't feel it, Tom," Alan says to me.

"What is it? Like a mystical attachment? The hundred-dollar bill has its own energy?"

I've got a good three months on the evening shift behind me, and my interactions with the locals are starting to loosen up and become natural. Alan is leaning on the front desk, his right hand holding a stack of ones the size of a Carnegie Deli sandwich. "Now count this stack up. I'm clocking out."

I lower my head and start laying the bills on the desk, one by one, trying to get it done without being interrupted. Turning the Gray Wolf's small bills into hundreds isn't really my job. If any guest walks up, I have to stop counting, handle it, and then start the count over. "Forty-seven, forty-eight, forty-nine."

"How come no one showed you how to count a stack? You keep it folded in half and slide your thumb —"

"Sixty-two, sixty-three — Shut YOUR MOUTH — sixty-four, sixty-five."

This daily little cash transaction is a big moment for any bellman or doorman. Consider the fact that a top earner, a real hustling bullshit artist, can make well over a hundred thousand dollars a year and all that money is in cash, and all that cash is in small denominations. You think they keep trash bags bulging with ones and fives in every corner of their tiny outer-borough apartments? So the hundred-dollar bill is the mark, the quintessential nugget of their existence. They stack hundreds. Want to rob a bellman? Don't even consider identity theft: follow him home and find his stack. (WARNING: I do not advise this. Bellmen are like grizzly bears; if you get between them and their tips, even a five-dollar bill, they will bleed you out from the throat, laugh over your corpse, and then go pound beers.)

"Ninety-eight, ninety-nine, and a hundo."

"Nice," Al croons and jiggles his "fuck you, pay me" fingers. I hand him a hundred, and he sucks his teeth. "Look at this sad, sad bill. Save that for a guest. Got anything crisp or what?"

So here we go. This is an absolute fetish with these guys. I lay out five sample bills and let him pick. You should see his face, excitedly peering through his glasses at the selection of hundreds like an eight-year-old at a pastry shop.

"That's my hundo right there. Seriously, you can't feel the power emanating from this bill? You know where they get crisp hundred-dollar bills, kid?"

"Where?"

"They slice 'em right off God's back."

"Jesus."

"I'm serious. I jab my hand in a bag of bills, I'll pull out the hundreds based on power alone. Ain't no way I can't find the hundo in a sad bag of ones, even blind-folded."

"That," I say, "is some bullshit."

"Sure about that? Care to put some money on it?" Alan asks, staring King Benjamin in the face.

"Here's what we're going to do," I say, removing five ones and five hundreds from my hotel-issued two-thousand-dollar bank. "I got twenty says I blindfold you, hand you one of each, and you tell me which bill is the hundred. Three out of five, and my twenty is your twenty."

"Kid's going for the hundred-dollar-bill challenge? I was just waiting for the offer. But it ain't gonna be me with the blindfold. I'm staking Jay the doorman."

Five minutes later Jay walks along the meandering path carved through the sea of stored luggage, like a jungle path through high grass, and enters the back office. The Gray Wolf has the bills on the manager's desk. I've taken off my tie and am holding it taut in front of me, as if I'd choke Jay with it.

"Fuck is this about? I'm missing money outside."

"Calm down, Jay, you're making money in here," Alan says soothingly. As with a grizzly and her cubs, even getting between a doorman and money he *could be making* can be dangerous. And Jay is a goddamn grizzly: tall, handsome, big American chin, and intimidating as all hell.

I slowly approach him with the tie at neck level. "Go easy now, big fella."

"Come on, Jay, sit your postal ass in this chair, and here's how it goes. Your boy here is going to blindfold you, got it? Then into each hand you're getting a bill, one a dollar and the other a brick. You pick out the brick, you win the round. Three rounds out of five and we split a twenty spot."

"You're a sweetheart, Wolf. Tie me up, Tommy. We're doing this quickly."

"The kid actually thought up this one himself," Alan says, laying a fatherly hand on my shoulder.

I secure my tie over his eyes, and we start round one, which is a randomly selected bill from each category.

Watch him now, watch how the grizzly, stripped of sight, uses all of his natural instincts. See how his head tips back and the nostrils flare. He takes one of the bills in his paw and brings it to his face, sniffing, crinkling, nuzzling the bill.

"This is the brick."

"What the hell?" I yell. "You didn't even spend time with the other bill."

"HEY," Jay says, rolling his head around like blindfolded people do, "it spoke to me. Next."

For round two we've gone crisp. Both bills sliced off a godly back, the one-dollar bill just off some lesser, pathetic god.

Oh, the grizzly likes this challenge. The crispness of the bills has excited him into a near frenzy. He is snorting and his head is shaking, crunching both bills right below his nose, mashing them up like lettuce. He freezes, as if a twig has snapped far off in the forest, lowers each hand slowly, and lets the bill in his right hand fall to the ground. "Brick," he says, lifting the hundo back to his nose and taking a deep, primal breath.

"Really? Am I being set up? This is bullshit."

"I told you," Alan says consolingly. "I told you it could be done."

"Not done yet. Round three. Good luck to you, Jay, you greedy, money-loving gorilla. Begin."

For round three Al and I have crumpled the bills into mush. We've rolled them, crushed them, flattened them, and smashed them until they are soft to the touch. I close my eyes, and, I *swear* to you, they both feel the same.

The grizzly does not like what he has been handed. The abused state of the hundred, whichever bill it may be, has angered him. But look, his head is wavering from side to side; he's been thrown off the track! He sniffs each bill and each time rejects the scent with a snort, unpleased. But now his jaw tightens, and he starts to rub at the surface of the bills, scrubbing each one simultaneously with the hairless pads of his thumbs. He's as still as a mountain, in a state of complete concentration, communing with God.

Jay blindly begins to straighten out one of the bills, lovingly molding it back into shape on his knee. It's the dollar bill, and I look at Alan, who is shaking his head. After flattening out the one, he lays it on the manager's desk, then closes his fists tightly around the other bill and thrusts his hands in the air.

"The bill of the fucking GODS!" he bellows.

The back office door flies open, and Kelly Madison, a front desk manager, surveys the situation: Alan and me in the throes of victory and defeat, Jay blindfolded with my work tie and holding his clenched fists aloft, as if signaling to begin the human sacrifice

191

ceremony.

"What the hell is this?! There are people outside who need cabs and a line at the desk. You left your co-worker alone out there for Christ's sake? You, take the tie off your face. You, put that tie back ON, and CHECK PEOPLE IN LIKE YOU ARE PAID TO DO! What the shit are you guys doing?! GODDAMN IT!"

Jay stands and pulls the tie off his face. He glances at the crushed hundred in his palm, making sure he'd been right, and then shoots a look of psychotic fire into Kelly's eyeholes. She takes a big step back.

Jay walks out.

Kelly looks at Al, and then Al looks at me. Kelly stops looking at Al and looks at me too. I'm looking out the door into the lobby, where I can see the check-in line backed up almost to the revolving doors.

"Where the fuck is Jay going with my hundred-dollar bill?"

While we are on the subject, here's a few other names I learned for hundreds: *nugget, money shot, redhead, dirty dancer, hundo, hunnert, brick, leaf, ben, benny,* and basically any word that is used correctly at the moment a hundred-dollar bill is explicitly implied in the context. As in: "Imma take these five twenties and get myself a bobo."

■ ■ ■ ■

So, victim to the hustle, indoctrinated into the vocabulary, I started to settle in nicely. The bellmen were slowly coming to my side. My money troubles had quickly evaporated. I'd cleared up my late-rent issue, and things were running smoothly across the river in Brooklyn. Starting pay was twice what I made in New Orleans, and overtime was rampant. One co-worker, a lobby porter (whose duties include fax delivery, polishing the bell carts, hitting on the housekeepers when they go out back to smoke on the loading dock, cleaning dog shit off the lobby floor, late-night condom runs, napping on top of FedEx packages, and so much more), tied together a consecutive thirty-two-hour shift. I came in fresh at 4:00 p.m. and saw him wavering behind a bell cart, one eye closed, the other staring at me.

"Who are you?"

"I'm Tom. We've met. I've been here about five mon—"

"SHUT THE FUCK UP."

"My bad," I said.

"What did you say?"

"Nothing."

"Nice to meet you," he said, gripping the

bell cart for support.

"We've met. No worries."

So, obviously, it took some time to get to know my co-workers. In general, the best way to get to know any hospitality crew is to follow them to the bar after work and kill a few bottles together. In this high-stress business, just like the restaurant industry, there is ample and nightly opportunity for this. Let's not forget it was Sanford the doorman in New Orleans who poured me back into the bottle in the first place. But in New York, drinking with my co-workers, I didn't always like what I learned. Kelly Madison, the manager who had soured the ending of our hundred-dollar-bill challenge, runs on stress, even outside work. It was immediately clear from my first overnight manager that if it wasn't one affliction, it was another with these "managers." Either stress or drugs. Drugs or theft. Drugs or more drugs.

Okay, so, management: twisted. And as far as my co-workers, once they opened up to me, I couldn't believe the kind of shit these people were getting into, the kind of daily hustle I was surrounded by.

Most companies that book room blocks at hotels will cover room and tax but won't reimburse for incidental charges (movies, minibar, and such), and so, more often than not, guests will close out that portion of their bill in cash. I noticed my co-workers, prior to posting the cash payment, consistently asking guests if they would need a receipt for the "incidental" account. If they got a definitive no, I watched them give exact change, say good-bye to the guest, and, once the yellow cab had pulled off toward Newark, simply remove the charges, type in "guest dispute," and put the cash, change and all, right into their purses and pockets. Considering, as I explained before, that movie and minibar are the most frequently disputed charges, no one is going to follow up when those charges are voided off a bill. But voiding off a *valid* charge and pocketing the cash? What a hustle. Any cash payment where the guest does not require a receipt is open for this move. This hustle is called *stealing*.

It was all part of my new home, the New York environment. When you struggle for every dollar, not getting that dollar can collapse your local economy. Bellmen feel this with every transaction, every front, so should they be "stiffed" (the term for "goddamn working for goddamn free"), it's only natural they would find a way to lash out at the guest.

Now, the kind of person liable to slam the door in a bellman's face while the poor guy is politely lingering about for a crummy two-dollar tip, that kind of person? He shouldn't use his toothbrush that night (or ever again, really). And that 3:00 a.m. call he got when someone confidently whispered "I'm banging your wife while you're out of town" into the phone receiver? Well, sometimes a wrong number isn't a wrong number.

"How you take your coffee, Tommy?" Trey the bellman asked me. "Light and sweet?"

"Light and sweet": a wonderful New Yorkism for coffee with lotta milk, lotta sugar. Another one of my favorites from New York is the term "brick," as it applies to weather. Basically, it means extremely cold. In context: "Fuck me, it's goddamn *brick* outside."

"You making a coffee run?" I asked, reaching for my wallet.

"It's on me. All the boys know you're doing a good job here. Don't think we haven't noticed. Listen . . . that new girl, with the ass, you think you can train her? You know, about calling, 'Front'? Even teach her the 'this is my good friend Trey' line. She's still asking guests if they need help, and it's cutting into our money."

"Sure, Trey, no problem. I'll handle it."

"You're a good kid."

"Your mother on all fours."

"Damn, *Tommy.* I'm getting you a dough-nut, too."

I just got a free doughnut for verbally putting someone's mother into a doggy-style position. Well on my way from clown status to New York City status. In retrospect, it felt like catching a prison sentence and carving out your place in the cell block. I kept my head down, ate alone in the cafeteria for a while, took a huge amount of shit, but stood up for myself when it counted. After a few months, when I walked into the prison yard, it was daps all around, and my fellow inmates were now joking with me, including *me* in the excluding of *others.*

People had settled in here; they were lifers. Trey the bellman had met his wife in house-keeping. It was a Bellevue wedding of a Bellevue couple attended by Bellevue employees. Now they had three kids, and everyone watched them grow up. It felt good to be accepted, slowly and by degrees, into their lives.

It was a full eight months after the hundred-dollar-bill challenge before Ben the bellman straightened me out.

Turns out those new, big-faced hundreds have an additional security feature. In the bottom right corner there is a color-shifting 100 that turns from green to copper when rotated in the light. And guess what? It's also *textured* and *raised,* meaning all that money-loving gorilla had to do was simply check the corners for a raised texture, something lacking on the one-dollar bill, and he had the bobo identified. What a show he put on.

After Ben was nice enough to explain it to me, I approached the Gray Wolf for a full debriefing.

"Al, why didn't you just run the hustle alone? Keep the twenty for yourself?"

"Well, Tom," he said, looking at me over the rims of his silver frames, "as you get older, you realize life is best shared with others. You were so new, kid, so ripe, and I just couldn't run it on you without someone else to share in the joy of it, you see?"

"Okay. Why Jay then?"

"Oh. Two reasons. One, I knew he would play the part extremely well. You were paying twenty for the show, and I wanted a quality performance. Two, well, he was sore for years after I ran it on him in '97. He lost a whole redhead on the challenge and was pretty torn up about it all the way into '99. I thought he'd like to make a little bit back."

You see the kindness? The camaraderie? With my own family so far away, Alan would become my father figure at the Bellevue, the guy I'd bring my girl troubles to, and I'd help him figure out how to use that new cell phone he was peering at with a bewildered look. Ben would become my brother, drinking buddy, and the man who'd tell me, if I ever complained about the New York City winters, to shove a mitten up my vagina.

In many ways, bellmen *are* the hotel. Owners come and go, managers come and go, carpets come and go. Bellmen create the permanent face of a property. They come with the land. And I already felt lucky to be surrounded by such an interesting and, in some ways, loving crew. Changes were coming, big dangerous shifts in the Bellevue's framework, and it was guys like that who would make it all bearable.

Not Jay. That motherfucker is dangerous.

CHAPTER EIGHT

Every day of the week operated on a sort of template.

Monday it's almost all business travelers checking in for the week. Some of them even have houses in Connecticut less than an hour train ride away, but they book a room for five days starting Monday, allowing them to avoid their families and accomplish another ninety-five-hour workweek that they've convinced themselves they don't hate. Mr. Hockstein, a longtime Bellevue guest, checked in every Monday with minimal luggage and popped in and out randomly all week. Hockstein was quiet, uncomfortable, and never interested in talking. Other business guests were more open. I personally got to know the CFO of a gigantic cable company because he checked in every single Monday between 8:15 and 8:30 p.m., sent his luggage upstairs, always ordered the same meal from the pub across the street, and brought it to his room to eat. If I was working a double shift, I'd see him head out for the day at 7:35 a.m. on the dot and return at 8:00 p.m. with the same meal from the same pub. Despite being the head of a huge corporation, this man never once complained and never demanded upgrades or attention or amenities. Because of that, we always gave him upgrades and attention and amenities. When I finally got it out of him that he liked to drink a Bud Light, just *one,* at the end of the night, I started having a bottle for each night of his stay waiting on ice in the room for him.

Tuesday you get more businesspeople and the occasional Euro traveler or Euro tour.

Wednesday it's less business travelers and maybe some midwesterners who've come to drop their jaws in Times Square, booking midweek trips to save money.

Thursday the tourists with long stays start to arrive and business-people start to disappear.

Friday it's straight tourism and Jersey douche bags wearing Ed Hardy trying to placate their fake-breasted wives with a New York trip so they can continue discreetly banging their secretary at the construction company the rest of the week.

Saturday more tourists and the occasional

New York couple having a staycation or renting a room to cheat on their spouses.

Sunday morning everyone checks out and the luggage storage room fills up to capacity, often pouring out into the lobby, which security surrounds with a red velvet rope, to give an edge of safety to the exposed luggage. After everyone clears out all at once, we flip the whole hotel and get ready for the next business week.

Sunday can be a mess for the bellmen when the afternoon comes on. As I mentioned, all morning guests are storing all their possessions, checking every bag they can find. Come 3:00 p.m., they all want them back, and they want them back fast. I saw Trey, working alone one Sunday afternoon, trying to work down a cloud of checked-out guests who all had their claim checks waving in the air and cabs to catch five minutes ago. Trey comes out with two bags, a middle-aged woman snatches them and runs out to get a cab, stiffing him. The next guest, like a clone, pulls the same move: another snatch and stiff. After the third stiff, Trey, who's about five feet nothing but has the intimidation potential of a foamy-jawed Doberman, stops cold and looks out at the rest of the cloud, all the guests wondering why he's not hurriedly grabbing at the next set of claim checks. Just as the guest who figures he's next is about to open his mouth, Trey tilts back his head and snorts.

"Another goddamn stiff. I'm batting a thousand. I am working for goddamn free out here."

He said those words at a volume that was, let's say, *extremely audible.* Then I said, less audibly, in fact under my breath, "Oh, shit."

After Trey calmly took the following guest's tickets and returned to the back to get the bags, I kept an eye on the cloud. It was as if his attack had morphed them into a solid unit, and they shook their heads at each other in amazement and said things like, "The gall!" "Can you believe that?" And even an old-fashioned "I *never.*"

Just as they were getting comfortable sharing their indignation, Trey burst out from the back, pulling two big-ass rolling hard shells behind him with carry-ons stacked on top of each and a backpack strapped right to the front of his damn chest.

Like a blown-out candle, the huffing and puffing stopped, and every single one of those guests, even the ones at the end of the line, pulled out their wallets and brought some green into the lobby. Following the lead of that first guest, they were all planning on stiffing him, but Trey had flipped them all, like a slick casino dealer drawing an ace over a spread deck and inverting every card. Now they were all faceup, ass out, ready to tip and shut up.

That, again, dear guests, is a New York City bellman.

But during the slower desk shifts, the Tuesdays and the Wednesdays, Kayla and I would amuse ourselves by pretending to verbally critique everyone who wandered into our lobby. I had her down to a science. All I had to do to make her laugh was point out anyone (that was the funny part, that it wasn't personal, it could be *anyone*) who came into the lobby, and I'd say, "Look at *this* guy." And then on and on like that: "Now, wait, oh, wait, look at *this* guy, Je*sus*," and then, "Whoa, look at *this* fucking guy, you believe *this* fucking guy?" until she had to go sit in the back and calm down before she peed herself.

Clearly, the relaxed atmosphere of the Bellevue was beginning to take a firm hold. There was no focus on verbiage here, not even a focus on AAA.

AAA are the bastards who hand out the diamond ratings. There was the Mobil "star" rating as well, but no one in the heads-in-beds game really paid the stars any mind, and now it's defunct. But for a luxury property, that fifth and final diamond is elusive and very celebrated. It can drive in tons of new business and create a huge jump in RevPAR (meaning revenue per available room. Basically, you take the average daily room rate, or ADR, and multiply it by rooms occupied that given night or month, and then, like, *whatever,* you can totally figure out how much money you're making). They would torture us weekly in New Orleans, warning us that the AAA inspector was coming, unannounced of course, and management would try to guess which potential arrivals it might be, using various telltale clues: usually a two-to-three-night stay, booked through the property (not Hotels.com or Expedia, since the reservations agents are on the chopping block as well), most likely it will be the first time the guest's name will appear in the system, with perhaps a dinner reservation already booked in the restaurant. Some guests got treated like the king of Persia only because they had "POSSIBLE AAA INSPECTOR" tattooed all over their reservations. Inspectors always take a bellman and always order room service and usually complain about the first room and so on, always taking names. Upon departure, once the agent hands the inspector a final check-out folio, he will do a cute little move where he walks away and then walks right back, hits you with that AAA business card, and requests to see the GM. At this point, it's basically as if a bomb siren goes off in the building: people start to go *ape shit*. The inspector will then take a tour of up to five random Vacant Clean rooms, with the GM in tow, slobbering to kiss ass and internally shitting himself, while playing it cool, even though every time he slides a key into a vacant he is terrified there will be a fatally wounded hooker bleeding on the duvet or a minibar mole enjoying consensual sex with a housekeeper.

A few weeks after the AAA visit, the inspector will send a *detailed* report on his stay, with names and, if you can believe it, even bits of dialogue between him and various members of the staff (as if he's William fucking ShAAAkespeare). All it takes is one housekeeper on a cell phone or one call to the desk where the guest's name wasn't used to blow the whole thing, and then everyone knows exactly who let the team down. You can lose it by setting the inspector's CC or folio on the desk for him to pick up, instead of placing it directly into his hands. You've got to put everything right into his hands. That is stress you can *taste*.

But the Bellevue? This hotel couldn't seem to be bothered. First of all, let's be honest, the place was worn down. We didn't even have Wi-Fi in the rooms yet. You had to request a room with a DSL cable installed, and then there was an accompanying charge. Even cheap roadside motels were boasting that every room had comp Wi-Fi. You could already bring your laptop into any McDonald's and surf the Net in the dirty bathrooms if, you know, you *wanted* to.

I recall checking in a famous musician, a true innovator of punk and hardcore, very respected in his own community and beyond, though as far as celebrity status he might have slipped by. But I caught him and immediately upgraded him to a room with a view of Central Park (oh yeah, we got those, and later, for me, they will come in handy). He seemed as grateful as I could expect. However, he came down five minutes later and said he must have Internet. I told him about the park view and that if I moved him to DSL it would not have that view.

"I need Internet," he said.

"Understood. And, hey, you can also just go to www dot central park dot com and check out the view on the Web site. It's just as good, right?" Dead silence on that joke.

Lotta punk. Lotta hardcore. Not a lot of giggling.

In the Bellevue's defense, there were many reasons it needn't bother to troll like a whore for that fifth diamond. A suspicious lack of Internet was just the beginning. The Bellevue, actually giving it a leg up on the majority of New York hotels, did in fact *have* a swimming pool. There's a long list of necessary features to achieve that fifth diamond, and a swimming pool is one of them. However, full spa on premises is another requirement. That we didn't have. And the requirements only get more absurd from there (including a minimum allowed size for both the television and, insanely, the length of the dead bolt). I suppose that was one reason why the staff was so lax. *That* and the fact that it seemed the management company was done with the hotel. They were not spending dollar one on renovation, and the clientele was starting to notice. Our TV screens were, frankly, just not flat enough.

That's what allowed Kayla and me to prop our elbows up on the desk and say, "Fucking look at this fucking guy right *here*. Fuck."

No one seemed to bother themselves

about anything, not even our GM. His name was Shawn Reed, and, as Ben put it, "The man is a filthy alcoholic. Filthy," and then, after his typical reassuring hand motion, like a horizontal karate chop, "Great guy, though."

Reed only asked me one question. Not that he only spoke to me once, but he only asked me just the one question and would ask it every time I saw him. He'd careen down the hallway connecting the elevators to the lobby, his body at a full fast tilt, his hair greased and dyed space black (earning him the nickname "Just for Men"), right hand always in right pocket, and, you know, drunk. He would touch his free left hand on the desk, like a bird landing briefly on a branch, and clear his throat to quickly ask the same thing every time: "So, hem, what's the occupancy tonight?"

"Running at 73 percent, sir."

Another clearing of the throat or some pressurized release of air, like a bus settling to a stop, then his hand would take off again, fly back into a pocket, and he'd beeline to the lobby bar.

"Right to the booze," Ben said.

"He might be asking about business in there, Ben. Like, how many bookings for lunch."

"Tom, he's asking for scotch on the rocks in a to-go coffee cup. Look, there, he's got it."

I suppose it could have been coffee. But it wasn't.

"This place is a mess," I concluded.

The Gray Wolf looked up while wrapping claim checks around a cartful of luggage and came over to the desk quickly.

"Judge him all day, Tom. But, Ben, you remember Just for Men during the black-out? I stopped judging him after that."

"What happened?"

"He handled business," Ben said. "The minute the city lost power, that man dove headfirst into action. He issued flashlights to all the staff, sent us off to help guests walk down or up the stairs, brought blankets and rollaways down to the lobby, served coffee and orange juice, called the hotel across the street and demanded they open their loading dock and turn on the generator lights, which flooded our lobby with light. He took care of everything."

"You guys stayed at the hotel?"

"Damn right we did. Remember, Wolf? We slept in the lobby and escorted guests up and down sixty flights of stairs using flashlights. Reed was in control the entire time, nice and lubricated. He never left the lobby, and he never slept. *El Salvaje* slept, though. You remember him snoring that night? The guests who felt better sleeping on rollaways in the lobby couldn't believe the sound of it. He didn't even have a cot or blankets; he just rolled up against the front desk like a fat homeless man and passed out snoring."

At this point a busload of Italians started pouring into the lobby, gesticulating and bellowing to each other while the tour operator tried to gesticulate and bellow louder, herding them toward the front desk.

Eduardo the doorman pushed his way into the lobby. He had a thing for tourists: one night I showed up late to the pub, and two minutes earlier Eduardo had knocked out a tourist with a napkin dispenser. As I walked in, the whole hotel crew was being ejected from the pub.

"What'd I miss? What'd I miss?" I asked.

"Everything," Ben said, emptying the rest of his pint glass and slamming it down on the bar.

But now, as Eduardo walked up to my desk, his mustachioed face was strained with irritation, which in his case looked like an insane smile. Basically, all of his expressions (sad, bitter, happy, distressed, confused) looked like a psychotic smile. His accent, because of the growl, was on the far border of understandable, and for some reason his hands were always dirty, fingernails bruised black and rimmed with irritated red.

"This group here, anyone say about this group? That bus is blocking my street. Where is the GM?"

Eduardo always threatened to take his troubles all the way to the top. Even *he* knew it was hilarious. If there were no cups by the watercooler, he would say, "You know, this is bullshit. I will have a serious talk with the GM. No cups." He would say this with a smile, the same full-on crazy smile he would give to guests while he waited for a tip, leaning his thick black mustache actually *into* their conversation and grinning like a madman until they grew so uncomfortable they would tip him just to make him go back outside. Then the guests would turn to me and complain about his insistence. Complain to me! I loved Eddie. I worked with him every day, and I was going to see this guest for another thirty seconds and then probably never again. Of course, I wanted the guest to be comfortable, and often, when an employee lingers for a tip, *everyone* gets uncomfortable. But I had watched Eddie load up that cart, heaving to get the final hard shell tucked tight, and it's fine if a guest doesn't want to tip, but why turn to me as if I'll agree? I don't agree. I think Eddie deserved a tip. Or at least a thank-you, an acknowledgment. Instead, some guests try to pretend he doesn't even exist. That's why he'll jam his mustache into your conversation: to make you acknowledge his existence, if only with a thank-you.

"No cups, Tom? Are we dogs? I should use my hands to drink?"

"Don't drink from your hands, Eddie, please. Not your hands. It's not safe."

But now he was furious about this pop-up group, a busload of Italians with a busload of luggage that had to be tagged and stored in the lobby until the bellmen could sort through it and deliver the bags. These guests would never tip, but that wasn't actually a problem, because porterage was included, usually three to five dollars a bag, both going in and going out, split among all the bellmen and doormen equally. Maybe Reed had even seen the bus pull up and eject a stream of Italians. He probably raised a space-black eyebrow, took a pull from his to-go scotch, and got the hell out of midtown. But it certainly would have helped if the staff had been made aware of the Italian assault. The other doorman working with

Eddie was at the pub next door, "taking a union break," and it was just Kayla and I at the desk, no manager. Kayla's attention was usurped by her computer, which was illegally logged in to a Web site called Mi Gente, or *"My People,"* basically the Hispanic Facebook.

This wasn't New Orleans. This wasn't a delicate situation. I put my fists on the desk and shouted: "I need CREDIT CARDS. People, put your PASSPORTS AWAY. This is not *CUSTOMS.* Credit cards ONLY." The whole lobby was a sea of red passports, and technically I was obligated to check an ID with every CC transaction, but in this case I knew the best course of action, even if management didn't agree, was to get the group out of the damn lobby immediately. Clear the room. Any guests who walked in during the onslaught would feel as if they were in a Rome train station, not a luxury property.

To be honest, I never check IDs. But it's policy. Another policy is to research if guests have had previous bookings and, if so, "welcome them back." These two policies working together at the same time killed me. The hotel wanted me to say "Welcome back!! It's a pleasure to have you with us again!!" and then, just as that warm feeling of being recognized spreads over the guest's face, I was supposed to demand identification like some hard-ass cop. I thought that kind of spoiled the soup, and though credit card fraud is a viable concern, I personally decided that if out of 100,000 guests whom I made feel welcome there came one credit card fraud, I felt it was still landing in favor of the hotel and our customers. Plus checking IDs slows down the check-in process. And also it's annoying, and I don't want to do it.

So Kayla and I banged out the Italians, doling out all of our least desirable rooms to the group because the language barrier would obliterate 97 percent of the guests' ability to complain effectively — a great way to get rid of the smoking rooms and the noisy rooms next to the elevators and ice machines. Often, as was the case here, the worst rooms are given to very specific guests for very specific reasons. There are larger factors, such as being part of a huge faceless group, that might make a guest more likely to receive one of the poorer rooms. Reservations made through Internet discount sites are almost always slated for our worst rooms. Wondering why? Does this seem unfair? Let me try to explain this decision from a hotelier's point of view. First of all, we cull the least amount of profit from these reservations. In a capitalistic business environment, that should be explanation enough. The guest pays the Internet site a specific rate, and then the hotel charges the Internet company an even lower rate. Here is a possible price breakdown: We, the hotel, are selling at $500. Expedia is offering a rate at our property online (which it reserves in bulk) for $399, which the guest books and prepays. When the guest arrives, he will never see a rate on his folio, because we are going to charge Expedia directly, which is a low, low rate of $199. Why would we sell so cheap in bulk? No matter what, it does benefit the hotel to put a head in every bed, despite a deep discount, since, first of all, $199 is better than a vacant room and, second of all, we are counting on guests dining at the property, ordering late-night room service, minibar, movies, and drinks in the lounge. So less profit equals less priority. But why do we then slate Expedia guests for our worst rooms? Well, honestly, those guests didn't really *choose* our property based on quality; they chose based on *value.* We were at the top of a list sorted by price. They were instructed to book here. But the guest behind them in line, the one with a heavy $500 rate, she *selected* this hotel.

When she comes to New York, she goes onto *our* Web site to see what's available, as opposed to a cheap rate being pushed in her face and all of a sudden she finds herself in some random hotel in Tribeca with a discounted rate. So, since we have no reason to assume Internet guests will ever book with us again, unless our discount is presented to them, it truly makes business sense to save our best rooms for guests who book here of their own volition.

And there is always, *always* a better room.

Am I suggesting that every time you book through Hotels.com or Expedia you will get a bad room? Certainly not. But your chances are increased. Are there ways to separate yourself from the discount pack and ensure a good room? Yes! The first step would be to call the property directly once the booking has been made and speak to a front desk agent. Immediately, you are no longer part of the discount-seeking masses. You are now the person on the phone who is coming in next week and wants to know what type of room you have booked. The agent can preassign you a nice room, and you can be confident that due attention has been paid. But, a word of warning, that is one week out, and as your special day arrives, VIPs and full-rate guests are also looking for good rooms, and if one is not immediately available, it can and *will* be taken from you. So now what, eh? That's where it comes down to your direct interaction with your personal front desk agent at check in. Kindness, being polite, and expressing a positive desire for a nice room can once again shift your crappy discount reservation into a corner suite, and off you go.

Not good at being kind, polite, and expressing positivity? You don't have to do that either.

Just hand over a twenty at check-in and say, "Give me something nice."

But after the Italians ran their surprise attack, all we had *left* that night were the good rooms. And soon the lobby was quiet once more, the bellmen organizing the luggage according to a rooming list I printed and over-packing the bell carts like slave mules.

All this we did without the knowledge or assistance of management. A fifty-room group? The sales department might have *informed* front desk about the bus arrival so we could staff properly. The direct sales contact might have even *visited the lobby* to ensure his or her group got in smoothly. Something was truly wrong here, and the disease ran very deep. The Bellevue was the hotel that service forgot, and like a termite infestation the damage was extensive. Nothing less than ripping out the entire foundation would do. The staff consistently set the bar so low that just showing up to work (not even on time) was good enough.

Just when I thought we couldn't be more secure in our laziness, Orianna, part of the "business center" staff, caught me unawares. She snuck up and scared the life out of me. In the men's room.

Orianna was heading the campaign to turn our humble front desk, which included the business center, into union positions. And she was dead serious. She, above everyone else, had two reasons to be. First, her position as "Queen of the Copy Machine" was in danger. Management was sniffing around and realizing they needn't pay someone to sit in the business center all damn day when, for the cost of one month's salary, they could install a credit-card-operated copier for the guests to handle their own business and draw in a nice profit on top. Her second reason was infinitely more serious. The full nature of that reason I did not discover until much later.

She followed me like a silent ninja into the men's room, and I jumped, turning to face her, my finger holding my zipper (which was already down). In her hand was a little yellow card, and in her mouth was the word "union."

Why the bathroom? Well, anyone caught trying to form a union on company time or company property was volunteering for instantaneous termination. That was it for you. Get out. However, if, by whatever means inside or outside work, you could get more than 51 percent of the staff to sign a union card, then the union, by law, was able to come inside, right through the lobby doors, and legally protect our right to unionize.

In New Orleans no one was union. Not so in New York. Housekeeping was union. Bellmen and doormen were union. Minibar was union. Room service was union. What did that mean? First of all, no favors. Whereas I was able to beg and plead for extra rooms from my New Orleans housekeeping staff, even pay them cash for the assistance, that was illegal here at the Bell. Management needed more rooms cleaned? Take someone off layoff and bring her in. No one on layoff? Hire another housekeeper, thus bumping everyone up in seniority and making room for another lady to have Christmas off. Not even union members could do favors for other union members. My previous company touted the policy that each one of us worked in every department. Water on the lobby floor? Mop it up. A room service tray sitting in the hallway, the hollandaise sauce starting to congeal and smell like a dead bird? Take it to the service landing. But not here. Even if a fellow union member from another department was caught moving a room service tray, there were serious consequences. Even if *a guest* came out into the hall, stood there with arms crossed, and asked me to remove it: I could not touch it. I could only promise to have someone come take care of it. But then, my promise was worth jack shit if the man working that floor was on his union-mandated break. I saw all of that as pure nonsense. A license for laziness. Nonsense.

"Sign this," Orianna demanded and handed me a yellow card.

"Hey. I was going to urinate right now but . . ."

"What are you, ten? You can't hold it? Sign this first."

"Well, I'm just not sure about a union, you know? Doesn't it breed laziness?"

"Only if you define laziness as job security."

"That's what I mean. People are so secure in their positions that no one has to do anything."

"Is that an argument against the union? Job security and no one has to do anything. Sounds great. Sign it."

"Aren't unions bad for luxury service?" I asked.

Oh, God, listen to me go! That company Kool-Aid done fucked up my brain juice! I was still putting the hotel first. Which is fine, if the hotel turns around and puts you first. I was pretty certain that wasn't the case here.

"Look, they are going to eliminate my position, Tom. If we go union quickly, they will have to find another job for me, even at the desk. Or they have to buy me out based on years worked. I've got plenty of years here, and they won't be able to afford that. Do you want to guess what my rights are when they eliminate my position and I have no union?"

I signed it.

After I took a leak.

"Here you go," I said and handed it to her. "I just hope that —"

"It's signed? Good. Shut your mouth. That's 60 percent of the staff. *Mañana comenzamos la revolución.* Congratulations, white boy."

"Thank you."

Sometimes people force you to do the

right thing.

For many reasons, joining the union proved incredibly wise. One reason: the economy, years later, would turn to a bag of shit. Prior to America's coming recession, hotel job turnover was legendary. It almost wasn't worth shaking a new hand; the person would be a no-call/no-show a week later, just disappear, and someone new would be wearing his or her name tag. I had friends who picked up a desk job only to work a week's worth of overnights. They were just after that *one check,* and then they'd go gamble it away like idiots in Atlantic City. But once CNN started telling everyone there was no money, no jobs, no hope, and we should praise Jesus every day for our shoe-shine positions, our staff hardened up like the marble lobby floor. And our new union kept it solid.

Extreme job turnover never occurs at the bell stand, union or no union. When you are hired as a bellman (unless you can't stomach the position), you go nowhere. You hold down that gig forever, slowly crawling up the ranks to better shifts as older, ancient, sage-like bellmen wander off into the woods to die. Ask a bellman how much he makes a year, just try to get an answer. You won't. Not even their wives know the kind of cash these guys pull in yearly. *Not even their wives.* Actually, *especially not their wives.* ("I keep all my big bills, give my wifey the ones." — 50 Cent.) I've been friends with bellmen, eaten Thanksgiving dinner with their families, done a bit of jail time with them for smoking a blunt on an Upper West Side street, and you think I know exactly how much cash they clock a year? They roll like doctors, and not just because they wear gloves.

Speaking of doctors, with the union we now had free health care. That is not a situation most people (well, *Americans*) experience in their lives. That was, coincidentally, Orianna's second reason for pushing so hard for the union: the health care. She had been trying, unsuccessfully, to get pregnant, and she and her husband had reached a dead end. They tried pills, banging around in funny positions, and timing sex to death. The last option was in vitro fertilization. And that ain't cheap. It's also not guaranteed to take hold, and they don't exactly offer refunds or consolation prizes. However, under the umbrella of the union health care, it was completely covered. Something that would have cost her over a third of her yearly salary now came free with union dues. Soon enough, she had a beautiful baby girl.

That's a union baby.

Everything was free. For the cost of the weekly union dues (same price as a Long Island Iced Tea in a midtown bar) I could roll into any union clinic (one for every borough), without an appointment, and see a doctor: get blood work, get scanned, poked, pressed, and comforted without even showing identification. Just rattle off my Social and away I went to the land of free health care. The only time I ever opened my wallet was for medications, and the total never exceeded five dollars.

Despite all of this, another class of employee wasn't interested in joining the union one bit. If anyone in the hotel business is arrogant enough to pretend they are not in the hotel business, it's the people who work the concierge desk. Now, I've met a few good ones in my time, but most of them? Free meals at the finest restaurants, comp tickets to everything, heavy cash kickbacks for booking tours, free limos, open-bar invitations: if you mix these up into one cocktail and make someone drink it, well, eventually it turns that person into an arrogant, shitty elitist. The concierges just kept strutting around in their tiny rat hole, feeling superior to the employees, superior to the guests, even superior to each other. The union umbrella now covered almost the whole lobby, with the exception of their desk by the elevators. Why would *they* need a union? They had the keys to the city! That gaggle of idiots would soon learn a serious lesson.

Unioned up and settled in, just when I thought everything was close to perfect, I was pulled aside by Eduardo the doorman, who laid a dirty hand on my shoulder. "Tommy, you seen the news?" he asked, giving me that bristly mustache smile, this one apparently intended to express concern. "Your town, New Orleans, it flooded, man."

I walked off the desk and headed down to the employee cafeteria. Everyone was watching the news. Everyone. And in a New York hotel that means representatives from every country in the world. The cafeteria is like the UN, languages flying everywhere, a small pocket of Nigerians next to a pocket of Turks. Chinese at the same table as a pair of Bangladeshis. Russians trying to talk louder than the two French cooks across from them. Usually, everyone's at their tables, talking their own languages, but that day everyone was standing, and they were all staring at the impact of Hurricane Katrina. Later we'd watch the tsunami coverage with Indonesians and the earthquake with the Japanese. But right now we were watching New Orleans, and New Orleans was underwater.

I hadn't been concerned about all the warnings. During my residency there I had been evacuated over five times, and nothing ever seemed to happen. The twisting top of the storm would always seem to do less damage than predicted or at least veer, like a badly rolled bowling ball, into Texas or Florida. This time it went right down the middle, and all my friends were there or, God willing, evacuated, and I watched the news for weeks, even though it really didn't help. It certainly felt as if there was nothing I could do to help.

CHAPTER NINE

"I am so excited to stay here!" she said.

"One night, checking out tomorrow."

"It's my birthday!"

"Nonsmoking, king bed. I just need a credit card."

"Is it a good room?"

"Yes. How many keys?"

"Can I have four? Hey, Thomas," the guest said, squeezing her tits together and leaning over the desk. I had recently gotten a new name tag because I had recently and deliberately lost my old name tag. So, technically, I stole it, took the old one home to add to my collection. Not that expanding my tag collection was a supreme joy, but I wanted to force them to carve me a new one. It was time for another change. After all these years on the Bellevue's desk, I requested a tag that read "Thomas." Why? A couple of super-great reasons. First of all, I was tired of guests rattling off my name as if we were friends. Hey, Tom, listen, Tom, I meant to ask you, Tom, would you mind, Tom, good to see you, Tom, I would like to speak to your manager, Tom. They don't know me, even though they love to read off my name as if that makes us friends. Which it doesn't. And no one in my life has ever called me Thomas, not even my mother. So the name tag forced the formality and made them call me Thomas, which I decided was a form of respect. "That's right, guests, it's *Thomas* to you." Also, on a parallel note, it helped me determine which managers truly knew me and which ones were just reading the tag. If I corrected you and told you to call me Tom, we became closer. If I told you to call me Tom and you continued to call me Thomas, we became co-workers. If I never bothered to correct you and just let you call me Thomas, I never liked you.

The name tag wasn't the only change. With the union backing me up, I'd been front desk long enough to learn a bit about the hustle. I began to notice the cash game and study it, see how it was played. They hired another FNG, a Cuban named Dante, who'd recently been catching some evening shifts. He was new to the Bellevue but clearly not new to the game. He actually brought clients *with* him to our hotel. A front desk agent that brings his own guests? Say what?

The second shift we worked together, he left me alone with a line of guests. While doing all the work myself, I watched him round the desk and pass a set of keys to a shady individual with a disgusting mustache who was lurking in the corner. Then I saw the handshake, a money shake, like a drug handoff in Tompkins Square Park. I could tell Dante was some kind of sick pro because, while slowly walking back to his terminal, he never even looked into his palm, never checked the bill. Then, when he saw me clocking him, he smiled and made a show of adjusting his tie, straightening the knot, using the motion as cover to slip the bill into his inner coat pocket.

You see something like that, you start taking notes. I would discover later that acting as a guest's single point of contact could be very profitable. Making all future reservations, preassigning the best rooms, supervising the bill, and essentially being a private concierge could put you where Dante was: in the corner getting tipped for services no one had even seen him perform.

There was cash floating around out there, and I was trying to learn how to float some of it into my pocket. I certainly wasn't a pro yet.

And it wasn't just the desk agents on the hustle; it was the guests, too. They complained, tried to name-drop, brought down roaches in Ziploc bags, roaches that looked brittle and five years old, and a thousand other techniques to get upgrades or comps. People who bring down forensic evidence in a Ziploc product make me angry.

So this birthday girl with the breasts: I figured that's what she was about, cajoling, not cash, and she was getting nowhere. It might not even be her damn birthday! Faking a birthday or anniversary is another popular guest hustle. So she could be running the birthday hustle and coupling it with the most transparent of techniques: a woman flirting to get an upgrade. I work for cash, not nipple-slips. She might be pretty, I honestly hadn't even looked, but I knew for certain there would be no money, and I wasn't interested in anything else she was claiming to offer.

"Thomas, it's a big birthday for me, please," she squeezed, "anything you can do."

It was my birthday last week. I turned thirty years old. Where were you and your breasts on *my* birthday?

"It's my thirtieth," she said. I looked up from my terminal, and she was smiling. Okay, it was a pretty smile, very sweet. And we both just turned thirty. That's truly what softened me up. I decided to take care of her.

After all, my thirtieth birthday was horrible. I had just returned from a short vacation with a bunch of the bellmen, a few lobby porters, and one concierge (who the hell invited him?). We'd taken a trip up to the Poconos to stay at Trey's cabin. Of course it's the pale, scrappy, five-foot-nothing New Yorker who has a big cabin with a breakfast nook, vaulted ceilings, and heated marble floors. We drank beer for breakfast, vodka for lunch, and whiskey for dinner. As soon as it was over and we hit the Holland Tunnel, it felt as if my body started to shut down. My kidneys were clearly disappointed in me. My kidneys were very, very angry. Irate even. Now, three days before my big thirty, I was suffering intense pain on the desk. I scheduled a doctor's appointment and was referred to an outside medical agency to scan me up (also free!!). Unfortunately, I had just received word the appointment was scheduled to take place *on* my thirtieth birthday. *That* was depressing, turning thirty and the only present I could count on was a free scan and the definitive knowledge that I was weakening, starting to die. Obviously, I was working the desk with a solid grimace. It felt as if someone had stabbed two spoons into either side of my lower back, right up into the kidneys, and at timed intervals this bastard was pushing down on the protruding handles, leaning down on them, scooping up chunks of my body and compacting them into my ribs. I was finding it hard to provide any kind of service with that kind of pain. So, of course, while at my weakest, I was approached by a monster of our modern age. Something had happened to her face, something unfortunate. She had poisoned herself with Botox. She looked positively simian. But she didn't seem to mind that her face frightened most of the world. She *did* seem to mind that her reservation had not been upgraded. She parted her hideous lips and said, "Ugh. I never get upgraded. It's my fifty-third birthday. I have a black card. Give me an upgrade."

The Bellevue had recently started a partnership with AmEx, and we were now included in their Fine Hotels and Resorts program. The FHR program (also short for Frequently Hostile and Rude) was only accessible to members with platinum and black cards. To qualify for the black card, you have to spend $250,000 every year on your AmEx. But wait! There's also a $7,500 membership fee! The black card, though I doubt this perk is specifically indicated in the brochure, allows you to be an asshole at every property you visit* (*including restaurants!). I assumed this woman easily reached her quarter-million-dollar quota with visits to Dr. Puff and Stuff.

"Give me an upgrade. I want an upgrade. You better or I want to see a manager." I was partially worried that the spittle flying off her stiff lips might be poisonous acid. Is that possible? "You give it to me. I want an upgrade now. It's my fifty-third birthday. Give me the upgrade, or I want to see a manager."

And that's when I broke. Someone leaned down hard on the spoons in my back and whispered in my ear, "This is where you are now, Tommy. You're turning thirty, and your body is dying. You're a key monkey, and you have no other options. You're a lifer here. Give this rich woman exactly what she wants. Now. It's your job."

Those who *do not have* will always serve *those who do.*

I passed the check-in to a co-worker and

walked off the desk before the tears came. Oh yes, I wanted to cry, wicked bad. I hurried to the second-floor storage room, where the hotel holds long-term luggage and larger items like cribs and bicycles. In long-term storage, the possibility of a bellman coming to bother me was remote, and I often came here during my break to read. *El Salvaje* came here on the overnights to throw jukes. He was kind enough to keep it to the same corner, indicated by a sign with a veiled reference to a jukebox. But in the other corner, behind the shelf, there was a cache of stolen minibar items for us to enjoy.

I took a Hershey's bar, sat down in the sea of luggage, and cried like a little bitch, biting off big pieces of chocolate and letting the tears fly. It was one of those unforgettable, pivotal moments in my life.

Why was I so sad about everything? I didn't have money problems. Didn't have kids. But nothing was changing for me. I couldn't afford to leave my position, and where would I go? Another hotel? Perhaps this hotel alone was the source of my pain? That's absurd. First of all, I know for a fact that another hotel would be the same shit, different toilet. Plus, changing properties would not only drop me back down to starting wage but cause me to lose all my shift seniority and throw me on the overnights again for an untold amount of time, and, again, for *less money.* No way. Leave the business altogether? I was even less qualified than when I arrived in this city. And New York had already changed me. Being surrounded by so much wealth, so much potential, eventually made me want it all. I wanted to have a black card. I wanted to see Broadway plays. *I* wanted to speak to a manager.

I had no interest in joining our management staff. The hours here at the Bellevue were even longer than at other properties because the hotel couldn't seem to keep a manager in-house for more than six months. In New Orleans the managers *cared.* They would work extra hours to help out the overnight manager on a busy night. They would sacrifice a day off because a pop-up group of a hundred businessmen rerouted their conference from Las Vegas to New Orleans at the last minute. They would take you aside and ask you how you were doing. At the Bellevue they would call in sick, just like the employees, an hour before their shift from some bar in Queens, screwing the current manager into working a last-minute double. Then the manager they screwed would do the same thing to the next manager to keep it, you know, fair. Bellevue managers got fired for doing drugs or getting a front desk agent pregnant or stealing money from their banks or pissing on the stairs, and the ones who did stick around all of a sudden had to cover those extra shifts. Plus, I was getting paid more than they were. I couldn't conceive of making that move to madness, especially as I grew more proficient at the cash game. But what did I have to be proud of? Nothing. Job security. Shift seniority. Fuck all.

I had that candy bar, though. I ate the rest of it slowly and cried until I couldn't cry anymore. Then I walked back down to the desk and finished my shift.

And then, because I had to at that point, I turned thirty.

And now, a week later, here was another guest asking for special birthday treatment. But, you know, she didn't look ostentatiously wealthy, and she wasn't being rude. And we both just turned thirty. So I took care of her.

"Understood," I said to her breasts. After ten short seconds of typing, I'd upgraded her to a Central Park view and reissued her keys. "Park view and I'll send some red wine. Enjoy. Next guest please?"

"Thank you. My name is Julie," she said.

"*Feliz cumpleaños.* Next guest please?"

Five minutes later Kayla told me room 3618 was holding for me.

"Good evening, thank you for calling the front desk. This is Thomas, how may I assist you?" (There is that phrase chunk again!)

"Hey, it's Julie. Thank you so much. I LOVE IT!"

So this one was really sweet. It was clear how happy she was. Hearing her yell about the room made me a little warm inside.

"Great. I'm glad."

"I'm having some friends over, all girls, and if they come to the desk, will you send them up, please?"

"Sure. I'll put you down on our event sheet, just in case they come to another agent."

"Thank you again. I really, really love it."

"I'm really, really glad," I said, actually smiling.

An hour later, another call on hold.

"Thank you for calling the front desk, this is . . ." *I am a robot, I am a robot.*

"Hey, Thomas, it's me."

"Need something?"

"Can you come up?"

"Excuse me?"

"Can you come up here for a little bit, to visit?"

"I can't do that."

"It's a lingerie party, Thomas. There are eight girls up here in their underwear and —"

"I really can't be —"

"Hold on, let me finish. And we have champagne and chocolate-covered strawberries. Eight girls in expensive lingerie, Thomas."

"Listen, I work here. I can't hang out in the rooms."

"When you get off then?"

"No. I can never, ever party at my own hotel."

"Oh. Well, that just makes me sad."

I put the receiver back on the cradle. Ben the bellman walked up.

"Fuck's wrong with you?"

"Eight girls in panties, Ben. Room 3618, eight girls in panties."

"That's what's up. I'll go knock and see if they need ice cubes. You know, for their nipples."

Three hours later I was counting my bank in the back office, done with my shift. Dante informed me I had another call on hold from room 3618. I told him to say I'd gone home.

"What did they want?" I asked.

"Wondering if we had Bibles."

"They wanted a Bible?"

"That's what they asked for, chief."

"Now, what exactly is *that* about?" I asked.

"Prayer meeting maybe? Though it sounded like a goddamn girl-on-girl party up there."

Next day I had an envelope waiting. No money inside, just a phone number. Fair enough. I called, she asked me out, and on the first date I brought up the Bible request. They just wanted to roll a joint, simple as that.

There are no Bibles in the Bellevue Hotel.

I ended up seeing Julie on and off for the next few years. Her life was very different from mine. She'd come to New York to live the posh life and had, after securing a good position in the financial industry, essentially succeeded. She dined at the best restaurants and saw every play. She was invited to open-bar events at MoMA and went to Kentucky Derby parties on the Upper East Side where people wore ragtime hats and drank side-cars. She hired limos. She drank champagne.

"I only drink champagne, and I don't wait for anyone." That's a direct quote.

We got along very well, though. She didn't

come from money and therefore had the ability to forgive me for not having enough of it. It gave her pleasure to make me her proverbial "plus one," and we had sex in public places, like freight elevators and once in a Michelin-starred restaurant's vanilla-scented bathroom.

"What is your natural hair color?" I would ask. I loved asking her that. "Seriously, what color is it really?"

Her pretty face would bunch up in anger, and she'd point a finger at her head. "This color."

That seemed so indicative of New York City. It didn't matter where you came from or what kind of person you originally thought you had to be. Here you could be a pill junkie, drag queen, singer-songwriter, cowboy, hip-hop head, painter, anything.

What kind of person are you really? Just point at your own head and say: "This person."

What kind of person was I? A servant to the rich! And an increasingly unsatisfactory servant as well! After spending years around my fellow agents, I had started picking up their habits. I called in sick to work (to "bang out" in the parlance of the bag jockeys). I even started banging out two consecutive days in a row, which, according to union rules, only counted as one sick day, one sickness. Then I grew even more bold and started banging out the two days before my weekend and then the two days afterward, calling it two different sicknesses and essentially ripping a six-day vacation out of thin air, whenever I wished. For this I received my first piece of documentation, my first piece of disciplinary paperwork. Management listed it as calling out "in a pattern." I was taking six-day vacays all over the damn place, and it was undeniably a pattern. But union strong, I had to go to almost insurmountable lengths to be fired. Dante, beyond hustling every guest he touched, also clocked a record-shattering forty-five bang-outs in his first year. Was he fired? No. Therefore a precedent had been established, the bar had been lowered all the way down to the basement, and we could all attempt to achieve that impressive number and be certain to receive no more documentation than he had.

We were running around wild, the weeks smearing together, only punctuated by a few outstanding occurrences.

Por ejemplo: One afternoon, I checked in the Who's Roger Daltrey, and the transaction went down like a coke deal. He came in, eyeing me sideways, and moved his face a bit closer to mention his pseudonym.

Here's a list of a few of my favorite celeb pseudonyms:

Doug Graves
Dick Shunairy
Tim Tation

And a tricky one, perhaps the best, popular with rock bass players for some reason:

Saul Goode

So Daltrey hit me with his pseudo, and I kept leaning forward to confirm info into his suspicious side eye. I slipped him his keys as if room 4202 might have three kilos of Colombian hidden under the bed skirt. He ducked his head and crept away to the elevators. The following day, after the Who performed at Madison Square Garden, a weirdo with a swollen man-child look bumbled through the revolving doors, crying so hard his tears were hitting the lobby floor. He headed to the concierge desk, and I must admit I was thoroughly entertained watching him sob it up over there while he passed across an envelope.

Ten minutes later, a concierge, a new girl named Annie who hadn't yet had the time to evolve into an arrogant elitist, brought over the tearstained envelope and asked me for advice.

"Listen, did you see that chubby guy crying all over the place?"

"I did. What's the story there?"

"Well, apparently he has 'the bone' for Roger Daltrey and somehow knows for a fact that Daltrey's here. He passed me this envelope and made me swear I'd forward it along."

"He knew the pseudonym?"

"Of course not," she said. Then, looking down at the envelope, she continued, "I almost want to pass it on, though. He was really upset. What do we do?"

I took it from her hand and said, "We *read it* is what we *do.*" I slipped it into my pocket, and then, as if to test my resolve, Roger came slinking up sideways to the desk, sliding his keys over like a secret.

"Been a pleasure having you, Mr. Daltrey, and we hope to see you again."

Right after he hit the limo, we ripped into the letter. Window to a freak show. Apparently, the man had attended the concert, and during one of Daltrey's rock moves where he grabs the mic by the cord and swings it around like a propeller, the mic unsnapped from the cord and flew into the crowd like some kind of Mongolian field weapon. It had "brazed" the man's shoulder, and "after an initial feeling of elation" he "could visibly see how disturbed Roger was, how deeply concerned Roger was for the fans in the center area." He had then immediately regretted that "initial feeling of elation" and was "ashamed by personal selfishness and devastated that Roger had saffered all that drama [yeah, *sic*]." That night he cried and cried for Roger, knowing he must be concerned for the fans, and now, as any weirdo might, he absolutely had to tell Roger that no one was harmed and that he loved him very, very much and please, Roger, please respond to this and let me know when we can meet to talk about it. He apparently didn't plan to stop crying until this was resolved. The closing sentiments included eight separate pieces of contact information. Two phone numbers, three e-mails, two street addresses, and one P.O. box.

"Oh my God," Annie said.

"This letter is the shit!"

"That guy has some serious mental issues."

"Best. Letter. Everrrrr."

"That was the right move, not passing it on."

"Sure was. Daltrey acted like I was going

to arrest him at check-in, so I'm sure this letter wouldn't have sat well in his stomach."

"Now what do we do with the letter?"

I took a moment to consider. "We respond?"

Just then, Dante wrapped up a long, tedious phone call trying to ensure a dubious guest that, yes, he swears, we have valet parking, he *promises,* and her vehicle will be taken care of. He slammed down the receiver in mock frustration and said he loved my idea. We didn't need to fill him in on the public display of crying or the contents of the letter, because while hammering the same point home fifty times with the guest on the phone, he had also been listening intently to our conversation. In this way, front desk agents are like bartenders. I can simultaneously and effectively call housekeeping for a rollaway while signaling for a bellman, while authorizing a credit card, while fielding questions about the equipment in the health club and *still* keep an ear on Kayla's phone argument with her husband next to me, listening closely to her responses because when she hangs up, she'll want me to have heard it all so I can assure her she was being reasonable, even though she wasn't. We hear and see everything going on at all times in our lobbies. It's part of the job. It's not even hard. It's just a self-generating skill, like how a basketball player can spin a ball on his finger: you don't need that move to play the game, but it develops anyway.

"We respond," Dante seconded. "We mail him a handwritten letter from 'Roger' himself, inviting him to London for a private concert, right? All of the details and flight info are included in the letter. All he has to do is show up at JFK at the appointed hour, and his guide and ticket will be waiting. He's going to pack a bag, crying from joy, then head out to the airport only to wait around to have his dreams slowly crushed! Either that, or we write a letter where 'Roger' expresses reluctance at not having aimed better and smashed the mic right into his face. We could close that letter with 'Fuck You, Fanboy. The Rog.' "

In the end we decided the last one was funnier.

Then we decided they were both unforgivably cruel. Plus, maybe that's the kind of joke that upgrades a stalker from Class A to Class KILL.

Soon after Roger-gate, I was lucky enough to meet the Beach Boys' Brian Wilson. I wasn't initially a huge fan, you know, just the hits please, and only when I was drunk and needed some happy music. But there he was, looking seven feet tall, wearing track pants, and hunching his shoulders like a teen at a dance. I wasn't checking him in, unfortunately. I was checking in an older lady who had the contents of her mildewy purse dumped all over my desk, all crumpled tissues and hard-shell cases for her spectacles. She was rummaging for what I've described as a "method of payment," and in fact Brian Wilson wasn't checking himself in either. Two comfortably dressed gentlemen were negotiating his situation with Kayla, who, even if I took the time with her to outline Brian Wilson and the Beach Boys' impact on popular music, couldn't care less.

"Yeah, but why does he stand there all stupid and shit? Reminds me of my uncle Ramón, used to stop dancing and stand there just like that, same look on his face, because he just pissed himself from being such a *borracho.*"

Like a seven-year-old at a museum, my man Brian was playing it cool. Not touching anything, just sort of rocking back and forth, his expression timid, his face saggy. The old lady in front of me had finally succeeded in peeling all the wet tissues off her Wells Fargo debit card, and I'd managed to conclude our relationship, save for me essentially *forcing* her to take help with her luggage, calling a bellman with our code word "front" so she doesn't get wind that some dude wearing gloves is going to rip the suitcase from her feeble hand and then, once in the room, pretty much demand she give him money. And not 1920s money, not jingle-jangle quarters the bellman can two-step back down the hallway with like some happy-go-lucky shoe-shine boy, no. That kind of coin tip gets left right outside your door for you to find on your way out, supposedly working on that "you need it more than I do (you cheap piece of shit)" theory. (Tipping change is bad luck, people. If you can't round your generosity up to a whole dollar, then just embrace your cheapness. Don't try to pay off your own guilty conscience with quarters.)

Anyway, so I rip out a huge "FRONT!" because these bellmen are half-drunk from last night, showing each other cell phone video of some sexual act they recorded, or busy counting up their ones. Plus, it was hectic in the lobby, and I had to make myself heard. So I roar out a nice "FRONT!" and the *F* alone caused my man Brian to pop about two feet into the air, landing back down with a look of sheer terror on his face, *terror,* his eyes reddening as if he might cry.

"Oh, God, I'm so sorry, Mr. Wilson," I said, inching over, my hands leveled out there with reassurance, as if he might sniff them and learn to trust me. "I really am sorry, sir. It's a pleasure to have you here," I concluded, giving a business smile to his two handlers. I'm always throwing out a heavily loaded "pleasure to have you" when it comes to celebrities, or a rare "an honor to have you," but only if it actually *is* an honor, and in truth it never comes off well anyway.

Mr. Wilson made our hotel his New York home for the next several years. I came to realize his true condition and repeatedly observed that he was never alone, always had no fewer than two male handlers with him, and never spoke to anyone, just hunched off to the side, usually in track pants and not always unhappy. His moods were leveled out, like a big lake with only the occasional ripple (unless of course he was startled by anything, in which case: TERROR).

One beautiful spring day, I caught Brian and his boys coming out of the elevator, the two handlers walking up ahead and Bry Guy sort of bounding behind them, a nice lift to his step, his big hands swinging like pendulums, and I heard him: he was humming, a strong little tune, all over the place, but clearly, for him, it was exploding in his head and giving him the crazy positives. I followed as long as I could, listening to his humming, through the lobby and even outside through the revolving doors, snapping off my name tag just in case one of the handlers realized Brian had picked up a tail. Though over the years those casually dressed gentlemen had gotten to recognize me as a "sympathetic," or maybe the only one who knew how important their client was, or at least someone who knew who the hell he was at all. Plus, in the intervening years, Annie, who became a good friend of mine at the concierge desk — yes, a good concierge friend ("If I can change and you can change, everybody can change." — *Rocky IV*) — had taught me to love and respect the Beach Boys music, just before she was fired.

(This particular firing was memorable and eventually became *historic.* It occurred one morning following a huge snowstorm. In the event of a snowstorm — or, as before, a blackout — a hotel will offer any unoccupied rooms to the staff, ensuring we stay in the building ready to work should huge chunks of the scheduled staff become unable to make it in due to weather and train shutdowns. So what does the staff do after their shifts, up in our own hotel rooms? We party, brah. We fill the ice buckets with ice and jam forties of Budweiser into them. We put fresh towels under the doors and spark joints. What did my friend Annie from the concierge desk do? She called for a coke delivery at 4:00 a.m., and the dealer walked up to the desk, looking pretty much exactly like a coke dealer, and started asking for Annie. The dealer didn't even know her last name. The following morning, and this is when it gets historic, Annie, who stayed up inhaling line after line — apparently listening to *Ride of the Valkyries,* she told me later — then had an emotional breakdown and banged out of work. She banged out of work ten minutes before her shift. She banged out of work from the room phone. She banged out of work five floors above her own desk. Sadly, for me, but not unreasonably, she was "let go.")

Prior to her firing, though, Annie had burned me several albums, *Friends, 20/20, Wild Honey,* and *Smiley Smile,* all of which I shuffled on my iPod for sixty days straight and almost went insane with a dark, crazy breed of happiness. And I mean it, Brian

Wilson is special and a genius and he paid the price.

I kind of feel as if Brian Wilson died for our sins.

It was amazing to interact with a man whom I'd come to admire so much. Soon I'd get to interact with many celebrities I admired. Also celebs I didn't admire. Also celebs I had never even heard of but could cause a lobby full of teenage girls to scream.

And all of that begins now.

CHAPTER TEN

Ben the bellman walked up to the desk. The hotel was as dead as ever, so I was busy creating some new OSA, or Office Supply Art. Last week I'd made a triptych of panels on the thick-papered checkout folio sleeves. I dismantled blue and black pens, cutting the tops off the ink tubes, then dipped an unfolded paper clip into the heavy ink. Folding the folio envelope around the paper-clip "brush," I would draw out the ink-slathered tip, leaving harsh branch-like cuts on the panel. Then, after meticulously and irreparably destroying a highlighter and using the inner spongy mess to smear bright color over the severe ink streaks, I tempered the entire project by squirting hand sanitizer on the still-wet ink, rolling the empty highlighter tube over the hand sani, which was already breaking up and bubbling the ink, creating mixed and blended circles of paint over the dark ink branches. After I finished the triptychs with an emotional splattering of Wite-Out, the pieces looked like the work of a mental patient. Or, I guess, synonymously, the work of a front desk agent. But that doesn't mean they weren't also, you know, gorgeous. I even sold one to a rooms control agent for five dollars. ("Every day I'm hustling." — Rick Ross.)

But today's OSA project was completely different, more of a crafts piece: I was using a personal sewing kit amenity to make an embroidered pillow out of two napkins, with tissues for stuffing. I used every thread in the kit to decorate the top of the paper pillow, and it was looking pretty colorful.

That's when Ben the bellman disturbed the artist at work.

"You hear the news, shit-throat?"

Ben calls me "shit-throat" because we are close friends now. With New Yorkers, the more they love you, the more they insult you. Briefly we had a manager from Japan who, every shift, would shake in frustration and say, "For one day can't we get along and be nice and stop insulting each other?" The whole back office, in the middle of loudly insulting each other, tried to explain that we were actually having a *great* time and getting along splendidly.

"The news about what?" I asked, testing

the softness of my fragile paper pillow.

"What's that? A pillow for your tiny dick?"

"Hah. Well, my dick needs a lot of rest after spending all night —"

"Don't do it, Tom."

"— *fucking your mother.*"

"AYO, he did it. Anyway, you hear the hotel's been sold? Seriously."

"What? Who bought it?"

"A private equity firm," Ben said mysteriously. "Whatever the fuck that is."

Hotels and restaurants are alike in one way: news travels at the speed of heroin in the vein. One person knows, and everyone knows. Doesn't matter if it's about a manager impregnating a room service dispatcher or someone getting suspended. We talk endlessly about everything that happens to everyone because we are bored out of our goddamn minds (see also: Office Supply Art).

Guest gossip is also open for discussion and can be some of the juiciest stories. I, personally, never minded pleasantly diverting myself with gossip, so they started calling me Tom Jennings.

"Dante, you hear about Mr. Hockstein?"

"Do dah do do do dah do do do. Tom Jennings reporting to you live from the helm of the Bellevue. I swear, my man, you are always talking shit."

"I am the editor in chief of the *Bellevue Observer,* am I not? This just in from our man covering the bar scene: Front Office Manager Kelly Madison; another mouth herpes outbreak? Details at lunch."

Mr. Hockstein, as I mentioned before, had been a guest at the Bellevue since before I could have orgasms. About as tall as a trash can with meticulously parted, heavily pomaded black hair, he spoke to no one, not even the bellmen, who were masters at breaking down walls, since once the wall is down, it's easier to hand over a tip. Hockstein usually checked in on a Monday with little or no luggage and checked out sometime on Friday, often without even stopping at the desk, in which case we would auto-check him out to the card on file, and then the following Monday his secretary would call to have his bill faxed. After a year or two I started to recognize him and decided to treat him as I felt he should be treated: preferentially. Guys like that use the same business CC every week, and so, if there was a line at the desk and he was at the back of it, I would pull up his reservation, telling the family in front of me to give me a moment, explaining I was trying to find them the best possible suite (LIE), which bought me enough time to copy and paste Hock-stein's CC info, check him into a nice room, and burn the keys.

"Excuse me one moment, Mr. Whatever-thefuck, let me just confer with the bellman about the room I have for you and your family. Let me make certain it's the biggest room possible." Mr. Whateverthefuck was impressed, even though I was doing exactly zero work for him, but not as impressed as I figure Hockstein's going to be when I slide up to him at the end of the long check-in line and slip him his keys.

"I just ran your card from last week, sir. You're too loyal to wait in line with all these tourists. Enjoy your stay."

Did I get a smile? No. He snatched the keys, grabbed the stapled-closed shopping bag at his feet, turned his back to me, and headed to the elevator. What was that about? That's the kind of service you *read* about. That would make some old ladies have a huge, wet servicegasm. But he, apparently, couldn't give a shit.

"I was correct, Mr. Whateverthefuck! Your family is going to love this room." I screamed across the lobby to Ben, who was scratching at a new Yankees tattoo he got on his wrist. "Ben, thank you for the invaluable advice!" Ben looked up, completely unaware of what the hell I was on about. "Mr. What-everthefuck, Ben is the bellman who told me about your suite here! Give him a wave, Whateverthefuck family!" The whole family turned and waved. Once they were focused back on the desk, Ben gave me the finger, but he couldn't help but laugh. Plus, he's up for the front, and though I have done exactly NOTHING for Mr. Whateverthe-fuck, he already feels grateful to Ben, which should translate to an increase in tip.

But what about Hockstein? Ice-cold! I decided at that moment I was going to continue to give him super service, start upgrading him, pre-reg him every time, and keep his keys in my suit coat pocket so that when I saw him spurt through the lobby door, I could pass the keys off like some clairvoyant key-genie. Who wouldn't like that? He didn't seem to want to make any connection with people, so you'd think he'd appreciate how I'd whisk him through the lobby faster than a Japanese businessman late for a meeting.

Soon enough, regarding his attitude, I found out the why-for. The next Thursday, Terrell, the Bell's laundry guy, came into the lobby to pick up some dry cleaning and leaned over my desk with a wide smile.

"What up, pimpin'? How you live? Dig

this, Tommy, guest in 3215 left a bag in the room, right? Shopping bag was the only thing in there, and when the housekeeper threw it in the trash, guess what was in there? Sex toys. *Dildos,* dog. Even one of them blow-up dolls! *Whoo!* You white people crazy! Nothing but supa freaks in this building."

Before he was halfway through his story, I was already pulling up room 3215.

Oh, dear. Hockstein, Hockstein, Hockstein. *Cock*stein. See: it had already begun.

"Yo, Terrell, I *know* that dude. He never talks to anyone. Next time I see him . . . damn."

Then, like hotel magic, Hockstein shoved through the revolving door, not using the push bar, just putting his hand flat on the glass, which annoys me because now my boy Tanglet has to clean it again. Plus, there's no telling what's on that man's hand. (See? It's begun, and now it's getting worse.) He kept his face pointed down at the floor, tearing toward the elevator.

"Oh no," I said.

"What up?"

"There he goes now."

"Dildo man? He going back to his room? *Oh no.* Hell with this. I am out of here. I gotta go iron me a shirt or something."

Five minutes later Hockstein was at the back of the line, his face on fire, veins pulsing, hands clenching, lips mashed so tight he looked like a fish in the wind.

"What can I do for you, sir?" I instinctively knew it was not a good time to use his name.

"WHERE ARE MY PERSONAL ITEMS? WHY HAVE THEY BEEN REMOVED FROM MY ROOM?" he said in a psychotic explosion. I thought his head was going to blast off.

"Sorry, sir?"

"I LEFT A SHOPPING BAG IN MY ROOM, JUST ONE BAG, AND SOMEONE HAS BEEN IN MY ROOM AND REMOVED MY BAG. I DO NOT CHECK OUT UNTIL TOMORROW."

This was a perfect opportunity for him to throw some four-letter words at me. Somehow, it was even more terrifying that he didn't. This guy was going to lose it, bigtime. I could hear his teeth grinding.

"Well, sir, perhaps if there was just one shopping bag in the room, the housekeeper assumed you had departed and was attempting to save you from accruing tonight's unneeded room and tax."

"I stay every week until Friday, and I keep my suits at my office. Where," he hissed, and I thought I heard a tooth snap, *"are the items I left in my room?"*

"Most likely they tossed the shopping bag directly in the trash, sir."

Looking me right in the eyes, he was starting to calm down now. He began taking deep breaths, reassuring himself that perhaps they had not looked in the bag and, even if they did, no one would connect the contents to him, at least visually. Meanwhile, the story was already public domain. Across the lobby, I could see Dante telling it to Trey. Dante bent over one of those hard-shell Euro suitcases in profile, and Trey began to mime a hotel umbrella in and out of Dante's ass.

Jesus Christ. I never broke into laughter anymore, though. Now I was a pro: all day long I could laugh on the inside, even if guests were SCREAMING at me, showing their ass, and saying ludicrously funny shit, I could hold it all in. I was *always* laughing on the inside these days. (When I wasn't crying in long-term storage, I guess.)

Dante walked back behind the desk, sort of saddle-walking as if he had ass trauma.

"I apologize again, sir," I said loud enough for Dante to hear. Then I really took it to the next level of brilliance. I picked up a notepad and poised my pen for action: "If you'll provide me with a detailed list of the bag's contents, sir, we will replace the items within the hour." This was some classic shit.

Hockstein was now eyeing Dante, aware the conversation had gained a new member. "No, fine. Don't do anything. Just put a note to never check me out early ever again. *Perhaps I'll find a new hotel,*" he said and walked off.

He never did. He continued to stay at the Bellevue. And no one ever made him feel uncomfortable again. We never thought less of him. But that's the point about hotels. Everyone knows everything. He assumed we never found out, and meanwhile people started calling him Cockstein or Anal-Block-Stein, which everyone generally thought was funnier (you win, Jay). Later that day Terrell returned to the desk to inform us that the blow-up doll had been sanitized, dressed in a housekeeper's uniform, and was now located in the tenth-floor storage closet, available for viewing. Or use.

So, still holding the napkin pillow in my hand, I knew I wasn't the first person to hear about a private equity firm buying the Bellevue, and best believe, within five minutes everyone knew. We just didn't know what any of it meant for us.

Three weeks later we began to grasp the full extent of the change this would bring.

Just for Men looked heartbroken. Reed would walk into the lobby, nowhere near the same energy, nowhere near as drunk as he should have been. It was as if he were too sad to be an alcoholic anymore. I could have hugged the guy.

They shut down the lobby on a Monday afternoon. Now, normally, if a hotel goes through renovations, it's done a few floors at a time. Perhaps the hotel shuts down 20 to 22 for remodeling, along with 19 and 23 for a sound buffer. Impossible in this case because the private equity firm was planning a full-scale gutting: with the exception of the name, everything was to be ripped up and thrown out on the street (some said perhaps the employees as well). A normal move might have been to put us all on unemployment, board up the doors, renovate, and reopen as fast as possible. Not this company. These motherfuckers (excuse me, these asshole motherfuckers) were about one thing: the bottom line. That was it for them. This company was a machine that ran on money and did not consider the people affected as human, be they employees *or,* and here's when it gets absurd, even the guests.

They shut down the restaurant. They shut down the bar. They shut down room service.

They shut down internal laundry service. They shut down the goddamn lobby.

What is a hotel without the above really? Just the room. Which is why you'd think they'd have closed the doors, but they had a better idea for the bottom line.

Eventually, I figured it out. They knew one fact: once the doors reopened, the rate was going to double. What once cost $299 was now going to cost $599. Planning on such a dramatic rate hike, they assumed, correctly, it would come with a new clientele. All those businessmen and family travelers who'd been supporting the Bell for twenty years would find themselves priced out and searching for another property in their fiscal range. When calling for a reservation in the future and handed a double rate, they would say, "Excuse me? But I always pay half that. That rate is higher than my company allows for business travel. I simply cannot stay at the Bellevue for that rate. Can you help me?"

No.

Fine. That's fair enough. The world moves on, hotels renovate, rates skyrocket, and people change properties. However, prior to relaunching the hotel, when the staff was crippled with layoffs and you couldn't even order fries in the building, the private equity firm, working on the knowledge that soon enough the clientele would change, did not feel it was necessary to inform guests making reservations what state the hotel would be in.

"Yes, we have your usual rate available, sir. See you next week."

The guests pushed through the revolving door into a construction hallway, plywood ceiling and everything, like a fun-house tunnel through the lobby, the surrounding sound of hacksaws and drilling adding to the fun-house vibe. Then they took the elevators to the second-floor meeting spaces, and there in the back was our makeshift front desk, a tiny desk in the middle of nowhere. No couches, no music, no art, nothing. A conference room with a lone desk agent staring out the window onto Ninth Avenue. It was sad as hell. And it got worse from there.

"This is the lobby?"

"Yes, sir."

"So you have no lobby."

"No, sir."

"No restaurant or bar?"

"No, sir."

"I assume the fitness center is still open."

"Oh . . . yeah. No, sir."

Now the guests would start to take it

personally. "Why was I not informed of this? Why is my rate still the same? Nothing was mentioned when I booked my reservation. Who is going to answer for this? I would like to make management aware that I will never stay here again in my life."

Oh, they were aware. That was the point. They assumed the guests would be priced out anyway, so why not suck out that very last room and tax from them. Then they can feel free to, you know, *fuck off.*

It was not easy to man the desk during that time. I had grown familiar and friendly with many of the repeat guests, and it hurt me to see them screwed over, hustled, and treated so poorly. It wasn't fair. And then it got unfairer.

At 6:00 a.m.

When the goddamn drilling started.

It sounded like Beirut.

In truth, conversely, I dealt with fewer complaints. This was due solely to the fact that our guests didn't pass by the front desk when exiting the building, just straight from the elevators into the fun-house tunnel. I would estimate that 90 percent of all complaints are "Oh, well, I might as well bitch in person" decisions made while passing the front desk. You can see them throw a look at the desk, and then their walk will sort of run out of batteries before they whip a 180, put a finger in the air, and say, "You know, I wasn't going to mention it, but . . ."

We stood in our conference room lobby, free from what are commonly called lobby lizards, guests who seem to spend all day sitting in the lobby, ostensibly waiting for someone who never shows, just rattling a newspaper, listening to our private discussions, and occasionally talking a bellman's ear off about some New York topic they actually know nothing about.

"It's the most famous pizza place in Brooklyn, called Grimomo's. It's, if I remember, on Madison and Thirty-First Street. Oh, I know Brooklyn."

Now, since we were in a converted conference room, we had a huge wall of a window overlooking the street, and I would spend whole hours staring down into the passing madness. I started to notice the same homeless man, sporting the classic fat-dirty-Jesus look, dragging a black trash bag westward around noon and back east after 2:00 p.m. Across the street was a parking garage, and an old Hispanic man inched his feet out into traffic every day for hours on end and waved an orange flag at approaching vehicles, trying to shoo them into spending twenty dollars an hour for parking. At the end of a long day you could see his lack of enthusiasm translated directly into his flag waving, no longer whipping it around, just sort of lifting it up and down. Watching that used to really give me the sadness for some reason.

So I continued to forge ahead on my Office Supply Art projects and even developed a bowling game, using upended matchbooks for bowling pins and arranging them at the end of the window's long marble sill. If you took a room key card and polished it enough on your suit coat, it would do that wonderful air hockey type of float, with zero resistance over the marble. So a polished key card was the bowling ball, and we took turns sliding it down the long sill, hopefully straight enough so it would slice right into the arranged matchbooks, causing screams of joy. Match bowling became popular with the bellmen, and of course they started to put money on the games.

Bellmen certainly had time to kill. They had time to murder slowly, in fact. What with the extremely limited number of rooms available for occupancy, arrivals on any given day could be fewer than fifty. And forty of those would refuse help. And five of the remaining ten would refuse to tip just based on being misinformed about the hotel's current condition.

But every day the bellmen were told to stop looking at their empty wallets and start looking toward the future. Soon the hotel would reopen, rates would skyrocket, and the clientele would be the type who couldn't distinguish a twenty from a hundred: they didn't need to.

Months later new management brought all the employees back down to the first floor and unveiled the lobby. Cool trance music seeped from recessed speakers, and we all ate cold cuts, drank non-alcoholic punch, and looked around at our new home.

Jay, who'd been at the property since it opened, who helped "lay the fuckin' bricks," as he put it, wandered up slow-sipping his punch as if he poured a little something manlier in it. He picked up a cold cut and then threw it back on the pile.

"Well, boys, it looks like they took a ten-million-dollar shit in our lobby."

It was all dark marble with red lounge lighting, slick and sexy but almost claustro-phobic. A single painting, a huge abstract monster of an image, provided the only focal point in the lobby, and though it looked like a mass of soft golden clouds, the first thing I saw was an image of a death skull in the dead center. A gold skull of death and it reminded me of money. Private equity money that cares for no one and operates on its own, for its own sake. Not money that one spends on groceries or tickets to Disneyland but Satanic Money that is never spent and just collects and collects like a yellow cloud of poison until it forms a super-scary skull and starts burning out people's eyes and starving children.

The next day the firings began. The next day the children began to starve.

The new GM arrived. Barry Tremblay came from the bowels of nowhere. Well, he must have spawned from some origin, but he was just an overweight, money-loving private equity puppet. Apparently, he had some experience in food and beverage, but that was it. We were all expecting someone slick, a smooth operator all lounge lighting and leather just like the lobby. Tremblay looked like the fat kid from middle school who spent years getting spit on and has now attained a position of power for no other reason than to put him in a situation where he can now do the spitting. He walked with his legs in front, his back curved and hanging behind as if he were being pulled forward by the knees. His suits were expensive, but I suppose there was no way to cut anything to look sharp on an eggplant.

When he spoke, it sounded as if his tongue were too swollen for his mouth, the words wet like a flopping fish.

First thing he said, apparently, was: "Fire everyone we can."

That little yellow union card, signed reluctantly next to a urinal, saved my job. All non-union positions were cleaned out immediately. The first Friday following the lobby opening, once we all moved back to the first floor, Tremblay called the entire security staff into a meeting room at 3:00 p.m. The security staff all assumed it was a meet and greet, perhaps the GM was going to introduce himself personally and make it clear how important their positions were in the property.

He fired them all, told them to get the fuck out, and handed them a check for two weeks' pay. Thank you for your twenty years of service. Here is half of next month's rent. Find a new life.

Many of them cried. Leonard, who'd shown me the tape of Julio all those years ago, had just put a down payment on a house in the Poconos. He cried. Rafael, always strong and full of pride, walked up to the new GM, shook his hand, and said, "Fuck your mother, you sad piece of shit," then escorted himself out of the building.

They all followed, and there outside, since due to fire codes a property can never be without a security department, stood their replacements, lined up along the perimeter of the building: a security company consisting of untrained eighteen-year-olds willing to do the job for eight dollars less an hour. I guess no one was tearing tickets at the Forty-Second Street movie theaters anymore; they were now loitering in our lobby, wearing oversized suits, praying for a fire-free, bomb-free life at the Bellevue.

Service-wise this made no sense. Rafael could tell you the best restaurants in a twenty-block radius, including information about each head chef, as well as interesting facts about the history of midtown. Leonard could tell the best way to get to Yankee Stadium and what view you'd have just by looking at your ticket. All that knowledge and professional service walked right out the door and was replaced by a rotating clan of frighteningly ignorant kids, a staff who'd answer any guest question with the useless and unsatisfying reply of "Wha? Oh, huh? Nah, I don't know."

No one saw any sense in this. The new managers had severed us from our security friends before we could even say good-bye, twenty years of friendship instantly washed away into Manhattan, and beyond saving money, it didn't make business sense. In the hotel game if you up the rate, you up the service. A restaurant doesn't spend thousands of dollars buying new crystal wine aerators and then fill them with grape soda. You don't build a beautiful concert hall and then fill it with stools from Walmart.

It was clear that even if they couldn't fire us, they wanted us gone. Especially the front desk. There was palpable disgust in Tremblay's black eyes. An immediate dislike for every single one of us. So we shined that light directly back in his face.

You ever met someone who makes rude jokes about your personal life the first time you meet him? You ever met a person who demands respect instead of trying to earn it?

Nothing was the same after that. It was the union versus the new management. It was a war full of hate. The new managers installed security cameras everywhere, started counting our hotel-issued banks every week. They randomly searched our lockers.

Since the only way to remove a union department was to buy out the entire staff, which involved huge severance packages based on years of service, our new management's main directive became discipline at any cost, for anything, build up records on all the workers and pin them against the wall. Make them unhappy and they will leave. They sure as hell had that wrong.

But something else changed too: our clientele. The renovated rooms had flat screens everywhere, iPod docks, double showers, plush couches, and twice the space of an average Manhattan hotel. CEOs started walking in. Celebrities started booking the penthouse. Paparazzi began to loiter outside the lobby. We often had to sign release forms because reality TV shows were blowing by the front desk, and we'd all be on next season's premiere of *Who Wants To Be the Next Whatever the Fuck.*

Behind this external success, though, morale was shattered. Managers followed you to the bathroom and stood outside in the hallway like prison guards. They timed all your breaks to the second and began taking the guests' word over the employees', breaking an unspoken commandment of the hotel business. The rule (an ancient and holy one) is this: It is *us* versus *them.* The *hotel* versus the *guests.* Not to say that providing service isn't the main focus, but a hotel is a business, and businesses must be protected. Some of these guests are here to break, devour, lie, steal, and get over in every way, and *we* are here to battle back against the masses, politely insinuate, refuse to reduce the rate, and deny all the bullshit lies some of these guests push over the desk at us. Managers know this. It is their job to back us up, apologize, hand over a business card, and get the lying masses out of the lobby. This no longer happened at the Bellevue. These managers crossed over to the other side of the desk, stood behind the guests, and massaged their shoulders while they screamed at us, whispering apologies regarding the terrible staff.

As far as the renovations, everything was a facade. The rooms were built cheaply; mirrors fell and shattered on the thin carpeting, shower handles detached themselves from the bathroom tile and smashed on guests' feet. The couches were beautiful but as stiff as a park bench. Our new uniforms frayed after a month, and we sewed them up ourselves.

No more Christmas parties, no more Employee of the Month. We were all lucky to have jobs, and if we didn't like it, we could clear the fuck out, and they would be more than happy to replace us with cheaper labor.

Dark days were upon us. Basically, all

pride in our property was gone. They'd taken our hotel right out from under us. The job became solely about the paycheck, and when that happens, service is the first sacrifice.

God bless the New York Hotel Workers' Union.

AFL-CIO, *bitch.*

We dug in, because, well . . . why should they win?

CHAPTER ELEVEN

And that is how I got my doctorate in hustling.

The Bellevue Hotel became like Rikers Island, and since no one was getting longer walks in the yard for good behavior, we figured we might as well make booze in the toilet.

There was zero reason to go "above and beyond," that sparkling ideal of customer service. Above and beyond? Never again. Management wrote me up the first week. (Definition of the term "write-up": Noun as in "I'm not signing that damn write-up"; or verb as in "You're going to write me up for *that*?" For example, to get "written up": *to receive official documentation effectively increasing a first verbal to a first written, from a first written to a second written, from a second written to a final written, from a final written to suspension pending termination. Then termination. Game over.*) The first write-up new management laid on me was because I took an extra ten minutes on my break, a ten minutes I actually spent talking to a guest who cornered me by the elevators (as guests do) while I was on my way to the employee cafeteria, complaining that she couldn't operate the iDock in the room. Someone had set an alarm for 5:00 a.m., and it went off every single morning. (How many guests prior to her had silently suffered through that? I wondered. Heroes.) I took the elevator with her to 47, navigated around her Fifth Avenue shopping bags, and after she, "on second thought," removed the diamond bracelet on the night table just in case it was "in my way," I proceeded to figure out how to operate the dock and turn off the alarm. We hadn't even been trained on the new technology. The new owners had installed touch phones as well, and we would receive calls because guests couldn't figure out how to dim the background light at night. No one at the desk had even *seen* the phone to begin with. So we said crazy shit like, "Is there maybe a button for brightness? Maybe it has a symbol of a sun on it? What happens when you press options? What does it say?" Oh YEAH! Excellent service! If you took a bit of time to enter a vacant suite and familiarize yourself with the phone, it needed to be done on your own break. I took an extra ten minutes on my break to help a guest, and my new front office manager, hired by the private equity firm, had no interest in hearing my "elaborate excuse." How kind of him. I even fought back and requested he review the security tapes, have him follow my progress from the lobby to room 4715 with a guest in tow.

"Not going to happen, Tom. Those tapes are not for your personal use. Sign here please."

I refused to sign. That was my right as a union member: a refusal to sign. The union mantra was don't sign anything but your paycheck, but it didn't matter either way. It was still going in my file, which was swelling up like a sponge, soaking up every little wrong step I took. Management filed it under work performance. To fire a union member, managers had to stack write-ups on a series of topics, and if you accrued enough in one category (is this sounding like a sick game show?), they could effectively terminate your employment. So they started calling everything "work performance." Before, if my bank was three dollars short, it would have been overlooked in the form of the auditor "going to go get a quick sip of water" before he or she counted it again, giving me enough time to settle out of pocket. If the discrepancy was too large and the auditor simply had to file a report, it would go under banking procedures, since there were a million ways to screw up your bank with over a hundred transactions a day. Not anymore. It was all "work performance," and everyone was getting buried under write-ups.

Keeping your bank tight is no easy process. You've got Germans signing over $1,000 in $25 traveler's checks, cash payouts for in-room services such as doctor visits and professional makeup sessions that last twenty minutes and cost $250, cash coming in for movies and minibar, return deposits, and maybe some criminal pays his $4,000 bill in cash. (Did you know if anyone pays more than $10,000 in cash, it must be reported to the U.S. government? I know that.) Also, you can pay your bill in euros. Or you can pay your bill in yen, in which case your total comes to 5 billion yen. So there is money coming in and money going out, and then everybody wants to break a damn $20. (There is a term that never caught on, and I want it to catch on now: "a flat." That's a super-easy way to request a ten, a five, and five ones. Give me a flat. If we can start implementing this, we will save so much breath it might positively affect climate change.)

Things started to get very dirty, very quickly. Our new clientele seemed to be in on the whole hustle. They knew a twenty at the desk could get them hundreds of dollars in upgrades and comps.

It was a guest who first showed me how easy it could be for both of us. A well-traveled businessman in an olive-green suit, without a word, handed over his platinum AmEx card to begin the check-in process. Veteran hotel guests know it's faster for both of us if I get the card right up front and simply pull the last name off the CC instead of mishearing and misspelling our whole day away.

But when the businessman in the olive-green suit handed me his card without a word, there was something wrapped around it, something covering up his name: a fifty-dollar bill. There was no mistaking this bill was for me. Some guests will put a twenty on the desk, but that could mean they were after some change. A bill around a credit card meant he was after an upgrade.

Oh, God, does this work. Let's talk about ways to get upgraded. People will *do* almost anything and *say* almost anything to get an upgrade. But words rarely work. In a hotel, money talks and bullshit gets walked (to Hotel B).

You say it's your birthday? No one gives a fuck!

First time in New York City? Who cares!

Anniversary? You're boring me.

Moving your business from another property to ours? I don't own stock.

Trying to impress your lady friend? I'm not.

So happy to be here? Write it on a postcard and send it to your mom. Maybe she's interested.

You never get upgraded? There is probably a reason for that, and it's not going to change today.

The bellmen have a Psalm for this: "You can't pay your rent with thank-yous."

Money. Cash on the *desk*. Most guests put money in the wrong hands. If you really want your stay to improve, whom do you think you should tip? The bellman? The doorman? The concierge?

If you tip any of the above, those employees will, sure enough, come directly to the front desk to ask for a favor. Why people tip the middleman is beyond me. It's a business maxim: whenever possible, bypass the middleman.

Think of it this way: Who is doing the typing? Who's assigning you a room? Who burns your keys? Who knows the availability of every room in the property today, tomorrow, and three months out? Me. Your cute little hero, the front desk agent.

We can improve your life with a keystroke. We can keep your secrets and flood your room with wine.

Guests who really know tip the desk: *nada más.*

So there you are, walking into the lobby, defenseless, a doorman hunting you down for a fiver he feels you already owe him and a bellman waiting in the jungle to get a ten. Those animals work for tips. Dropping money on them is extremely normal, so unless you make your presence felt with a brick, it's not going to elicit much more than a smile and a thank-you.

But drop a twenty, a baby brick, on a front desk agent, and something has shifted. It works because, for us, it is a commitment. We become indebted to you. That's what I learned as I unwrapped that fifty-dollar bill and slipped it casually into my back pocket. Now it was mine. The first reaction, if I may borrow a phrase, was "an initial feeling of elation." The second, surfacing a moment after, was a feeling of *obligation*. No agent will pocket a tip and just say thank you, not one who has a soul (and yes, we do have souls — except for overnight agents). We have to earn our tips. I will do whatever I can to make you happy. A bellman doesn't even have a log-in to the property management system. I have control over every charge applied to your CC, and immediately I will make it worth your while. Even if I can't find an upgrade proper, I will put you in the very best room of your category.

Here is one of the top lies that come out of a front desk agent's mouth: "All the rooms are basically the same, sir."

Bullshit. There is always a corner room, a room with a bigger flat screen, a room that, because of the building's layout, has a larger bathroom with two sinks, a room that fits two rollaways with ease, a room that, though listed as standard, actually has a partial view of the Hudson River. There is always a better room, and when I feel that twenty burning in my pocket, I will *find it for you.* And if there is nothing to be done room-wise, I have a slew of other options: late checkout, free movies, free minibar, room service amenities, and more. I will do whatever it takes to deserve the money and then a little bit more in the hope you'll hit me again.

Some people feel nervous about this

move. Please don't. It's not a drug deal. There is nothing more awkward than people who tip with a twenty folded down to the size of a Tic Tac in their palm. Just hand over the money. To everyone else it looks as if you are asking for change, that's it. And damn do we appreciate it. We are *authorized* to upgrade for special occasions. The special occasion occurring now is that I have a solid twenty to get drunk on once I snap off my name tag for the night. That's special enough for me! Having a wonderful, generous guest staying with us: clearly another special occasion, one that merits a view of Central Park in the spring with no additional rate increase.

Plus, though it really saddened me to think it, screw the Bellevue. I mean, after years of service I had come to really love the property. I might have complained before about its wildness and lax attitude toward service, but now it was as if an invading army had come to occupy our city, altering it drastically. Not only did the occupying army create a spontaneous and intense love for the city it was in the past, it made me hate what the city had become, what the new regime had made it. Why "upsell" a guest into a suite running a hundred dollars more a night when I could "personally take care of the increase in rate" and accept a twenty-dollar bill in gratitude? We blamed upgrades on keystroke errors or covered them by claiming a guest had just received a big promotion. And just like in a prison, there were too many inmates doing too much dirt to put a handle on. The minute managers started investigating upgrades, we were already comping breakfast. As soon as they cracked down on free breakfast, we started giving everyone 4:00 p.m. late checkouts. When the directive came down to kill all late checkouts, we began slicing off hundreds of dollars in minibar revenue. After they required we authorize adjustments over fifty dollars with management, we were back to comp upgrades and free breakfast.

In my own way, I reinvented the game. I stopped waiting for savvy travelers to dispense a well-directed ten into my wallet. I learned how to hustle it, how to extract it, how to make them *want* to tip me. Starting small, I utilized the whispered-upgrade technique, where I lean over the desk and whisper, "I might have something special for you," just loud enough for his trophy wife or prostitute to hear. If I can make the right guest feel the right kind of special, then out comes the money clip, the hundred peeled off cleanly and pressed into my hand. We call this "the crinkly handshake."

My skills sharpened. I realized the size of the tip given to the doorman indicated the possibility of a tip to me. If you tip the doorman large, you are here to play.

And I am here to help.

Eventually, I developed a list of regulars, a list of names, big hitters (which every bellman has as well). On top of that, I would still size up arrivals for new "generous" guests and developed an eye for potential. Wearing sunglasses in the lobby and a wife with too much Botox? Hitter. An Italian in from New Jersey just for the weekend? Hitter. The morbidly obese? For some reason, hitters.

"Never forget a twenty, Tom," the Gray Wolf said to me one day. He never did. If a bellman came up to the desk after a standard check-in and asked for the last name, writing it down in a little book he kept in his vest pocket, it meant *at least* a twenty. He would lock in that guest's name and use it as often as possible when the guest came through the lobby. Some bellmen request an arrival list every day, scan the printout against their own personal lists, and then wait for the right guests to come into the lobby so they can position themselves for a well-placed front. They even started to ask for my assistance with this. If a fifty hitter was in line to check in, I might be asked to slow down or speed up my process, essentially lining up the right bellman with the guest he had intimate knowledge of. The bellmen loved me because I would always comply. Hell, I thought it was fun. I had my average check-in time down to less than thirty seconds by this point, every single step in the process streamlined, which allowed me to speed up and slow down at will. The only time I ever mentioned the restaurant or location and hours of our gym was when I was stalling a front to let the family of five Kayla was checking in head up with Ben, setting up Trey for his regular. In addition, getting this inside information from the bellmen helped me directly. Certainly, while servicing a proven hitter, I had the opportunity to throw a little something extra in there.

"Mr. Hansen, I see this marks your fifth stay with us?" Meanwhile, Ben, since he is up for the front and wants Hansen, is giving me the hurry-up motion from across the lobby, in his case like a third-base coach waving the runner home. "Such loyalty does not go unrewarded. Not on my shift, sir." Upgrade. We share a crinkly handshake, baby brick to me. The keys go to Ben. Ben gets fifty dollars in the room.

We all worked together. "Mr. Palay, Mario the doorman put in a good word for you, asked that you be taken care of. A doorman's will be done. I've got you in a Central Park suite, and please allow me to deliver wine on Mario's behalf." The guest turns around toward the street because he doesn't know who the hell Mario *is*. But Mario knows who *he* is. Five months ago, out of nowhere and, according to Mario, for no reason, this gentleman handed him a crisp hundred-dollar bill. If Mr. Palay, the moment after handing him the bill, had taken a quick look at the doorman's face, it might have looked as if Mario were giving him an intensely focused scowl. But what Mario was *doing* was memorizing his face. Five months later that memory work was about to pay off because Mr. Palay was now looking out the window and there Mario stood, giving a knowing salute to Mr. Palay.

"Break this hundred for me."

"How would you like it, Mr. Palay?"

"Twenties. Keep one for yourself."

"Thank you, sir," I said, removing one of the five bills and handing over four. Mr. Palay, while I burned the keys, walked all the way back to the street to pop a twenty on Mario.

What's more is the Gray Wolf (*of course*) saw the whole transaction go down and approached me quickly the moment Mr. Palay walked outside to tip.

"Working with the doormen now, Tommy? You slick bastard. Hand to God, you're like a son to me. What's left?"

By this he meant what was left to offer the guest once he had him up in the room.

"Upgrade and wine done. You're a go on the late checkout, Wolf."

"Here he comes. Set me up."

"Mr. Palay, this is my colleague Alan. He will take you to your suite. I also placed my business card in your key packet. Don't hesitate to contact me if something comes up. Enjoy your stay and welcome back."

Just recalling this hustle gives me the chills.

Alan came down five minutes later smiling. He handed me a five off what I assume was a twenty, but you never know. The hustle is now complete, and that five on top is the icing. Alan was good about that, kicking back on an effective setup. Other bellmen will take your assistance, jump in on your hustle, and then come down and say, "Sorry. He stiffed me. Do you believe it?"

No, I actually don't believe it.

Does all of this seem morally corrupt? Well, consider this: the guest dropped a total of sixty dollars in ten minutes, for which he received an upgrade, wine, and a late checkout. He is more than satisfied, and of course so are we. What was in it for the hotel? Well, I'll say it again if I must: the Bellevue, well, the new Bellevue regime, could blow me. But even still, Mr. Palay will never stay anywhere else, believe me. These guests fly from hotel to hotel in Manhattan, always trying a new property and looking to find a home for their gigantic expense accounts. He has a home now. Mr. Palay will now clock over fifty nights a year with us, quite a sight more than the five bookings in the previous year. We just generated forty thousand dollars in new revenue for our property. What did it cost the hotel? An upgrade, which costs the same to clean as any other room, totaling zero dollars. A bottle of red that runs for seventy-five dollars on the room service menu but is purchased in bulk for four dollars a bottle. The late checkout jams up housekeeping but at no loss in revenue.

We turned four dollars into forty thousand dollars.

You see? We were *kind of doing our jobs.*

Mr. Palay *loves* the Bellevue. Won't stay anywhere else. Two years later we will have all met his wife *and* his kids *and* his mistress. He can't wait to come back, drop a few twenties, and talk with Mario about sports and even connect with the Gray Wolf about child rearing.

You may have noticed from my extended check-in verbiage that I'd started to take my hustle one step further. I now had a business card. Did Tremblay shell out for employee business cards to make us feel special and part of the team? Yeah, *no.* Just a blank Bellevue Hotel business card with my name, e-mail address, shift schedule, and, in some cases, cell phone number handwritten on it.

Street hustle.

Now I could remove a business card from my pocket, where I kept at least five pre-written at all times, and say, "Mr. Uzzaman, please, if you ever need anything, do not hesitate to contact me. I can even make all of your future reservations if you'd prefer, ensuring the best rates. I receive e-mails on my smart phone instantaneously, so if you find yourself having to cancel last minute or need a complimentary bottle sent up, even if I am not at work, I will handle it."

How much do you think service like that

is worth? I was getting bricks like a contractor. And it wasn't always about the money, either. I took personal care of CEOs because they were CEOs and, hey, you never know what kinds of kickbacks might come from them. My e-mail contact list was littered with leaders of industry. I would train home to Brooklyn and find a large company-logo'd box filled with hundreds of bags of potato chips waiting on my doorstep and inside a personal note from the CEO promising to ship a box like this anywhere at any time. Assorted flavors. Great for throwing a party. I even sold some at work, two bags for a dollar.

This year's Hustler of the Year Award goes to . . . Tommy "I'll personally take care of the increase in rate" Jacobs.

I was reinventing the game, attending movie premieres all over the city with tickets for the show and after party waiting for me at Will Call, placed there by my contact at Universal Pictures.

I also met some plain old normal *extremely wealthy* people. The first time I checked in the Bekkers, we became immediate friends. Two simple coincidences occurred simultaneously to spark our lasting acquaintance. First, we all loved the South. Though Mr. Bekker and his fiancée no longer live there, they met and fell in love in North Carolina, a state that, through my childhood relocations, I also share a deep love for. They now live in Cape Town, South Africa, an international city that has always intrigued me. Mr. Bekker was, in fact, born there and it lingers in his English, but his fiancée is North Carolina to the core. The second simple coincidence? He was extremely forthcoming with bobos.

Fast friends.

They would just flutter from his fingers and fly into my back pocket. Then his reservations would flutter on up to the sixtieth floor: a comp-upgrade luxury suite. Soon enough dark bottles of wine would walk themselves up to the door, surrounded by truffles and fresh fruits, and waddle their way onto the dining room table, the dining room table itself being a unique feature of the upper-floor luxury suites.

So, sure, the money certainly helped, but I grew to love those two, and they loved me. And they loved each other. Randomly one fall, I received an emergency e-mail from Mr. Bekker, requesting the recipe for a certain cocktail served in our lounge. It was an emergency because his fiancée remembered and loved the drink, and he intended to surprise her by making it the signature cocktail for their North Carolina "society wedding." He listed a few of the ingredients he remembered, and with this info I started grilling the bar about it. It was a spring cocktail and no longer on the menu. Thus, I had to wait until the following week when the mixologist returned from vacation. As soon as I saw her strut through the lobby, I laid down the ingredients and two minutes later had the full recipe on a napkin. It was even called the Belle of the Ball. Perfect. I thanked her and mentioned it would be the featured cocktail at a huge society wedding in the South, trying to explain how important those could be and the kind of news coverage they receive.

"I know. I'm from South Carolina."

That was it right there. South Carolinians can be ice-cold sometimes. She wasn't even flattered about her cocktail creating such a lasting memory. And that is her JOB. She's a mixologist. That's what she was *doing with her life.* I even promised to introduce her to the Bekkers when they returned.

"I don't care," she said.

"Well, you might. He is *very* generous and would most likely drop a hundred on you, probably more, just for creating the drink, not to mention helping him re-create it."

"It doesn't matter."

What a doll. No bother to me, though. No worry on my wallet. I e-mailed the recipe over to Cape Town and made them both very happy. After the wedding, I got a letter from the new Mrs. Bekker, on a beautiful piece of monogrammed stationery (but of *course*), thanking me for my help. Knowing my interest in South Africa, she also offered to accommodate me lavishly for as long as I should choose if I ever made the trip over the ocean. How wonderful is that? It was so sweet, and, you know, at this time I was really considering getting the hell out of town. Maybe even for good. I sent her a handwritten letter, thanking her for the offer and explaining that I might actually take them up on it. In fact, I informed them that perhaps, after saving up a bit more money, I might relocate to Cape Town, find affordable housing in the city, and burn up my savings, just as I had before in Paris and Denmark.

A month or two later (international mail is something else) I received a response: she was thrilled about the idea and would assist me in finding a place to live, and certainly they were happy to put me up while we found a place together.

Goddamn it, I love the Bekkers! They are both so sweet and wonderful.

And look at that: now I had an *escape plan.*

CHAPTER TWELVE

The paparazzi. What a ragtag bunch of idiots. They were twenty-deep outside, pushing their unshowered bodies against each other, holding cameras high overhead, hoping to get a decent shot of something.

We had celebrities running around all over the lobby. I could write another 250-page book on all the action I've seen firsthand, like listening to a young, rail-thin Nickelodeon superstar actress complain to her mom that they never feed them anything but cucumber sandwiches on a Nickelodeon set. Whoa. For reals. That girl was starving. I almost gave her a bag of chips right then and there.

And guess who stayed with us after the transition? My man Brian Wilson from the Beach Boys. Probably because he was mentally accustomed to the Bellevue and it was easier not to stress him with a change in location. I'm certain the increase in rate was not even a bother.

The hotel was at capacity because Elton John was having his sixtieth birthday party, and it promised to be a gay affair (come on, like Great Gatsby gay), and we had a large slice of the celebrities lodged in our rooms. The lobby was looking like a freaky circus as they headed out to the party. We had the D-list invitees too and also gay dudes who were not celebs but more like made men, the Velvet Mafia, I believe they are called, all of them scooting past my desk, and they all had the backs of their sport coats riddled with rhinestones: sparkly lion heads and glittery anchors.

Anyway, here comes my man Brian, utilizing his top-level invite as he damn well should, all tuxed up and looking sharp. Well, looking like a freshman on his way to prom, but he looked good, though shy, but as if some lucky girl were going to find him rocking back and forth quietly by the punch bowl and fuck his brains out in the back corner of the cafeteria. So the handlers swung Brian by the desk on the way out to get a fresh key, just in case Bry Guy had been floating his in the toilet or whatever. I was busy with another guest, so they approached my co-worker, new on the job, a guy with a sweaty-hand condition, you know, constantly wet and everything he handles at the desk develops a gritty crust all over it. You'd come back from lunch, and it seemed as if a snail had crawled all over your terminal. So, anyway, he's all, "Who? What room? What is the name registered to the room?"

What choice did I have? I left my guest standing there, halfway helped. I said, "Excuse me," and he got all huffy because he was busy grilling me about where's good to eat tonight, even though that's really not my job: that's like asking a doorman to clean a toilet. We have trained concierge elitists for that, and they get paid five dollars more an hour.

I put my guest on pause for a moment, though, mostly because Brian was looking right at me. He was sort of peering at me, like through a fog, looking all sad and cute in his tuxedo. I burned off three new keys, and I didn't need to double-check the room number, because I'd kept a protective eye on Wilson ever since noticing the last line to "I'd Love Just Once to See You," which ends with the sweet refrain "I'd love just once to see you, I'd love just once to see you . . . in . . . the . . . nude." Hilarious. So I handle the key situation quickly, and Brian was still gazing at me, as if he knew I was taking care of him.

Then it happened.

I slipped the keys in a packet and gave them to the handler, the one I recognized most, and Brian smiled at me, as if he'd seen me before, knew I'd been helping him for more than five years, and he stepped forward. His face lifted in a smiley smile above his boyish black bow tie, and he put out his big hand for me to shake, held it over the desk, like let's-be-friends. ("We've been friends now for so many years." — the Beach Boys.)

I put my hand in his, and he said, "Hi. I'm Brian Wilson."

"I know who you are, Mr. Wilson." I moved his hand up and down a little, since he was just keeping it still. "And you look sharp, my man. It's an honor to have you. I hope you have a good time at the party, Mr. Wilson," and I let his hand go. His face clouded over a bit, but his happiness remained, and I know there was music blowing up inside of him and that he felt good. The handler I recognized gave me a genuine smile and took Brian by the elbow, leading him off.

The lobby cleared out, just the over-whelming lingering odor of cologne and a few rhinestones left on the ground that the bellmen were scooping up and rocketing at each other's faces now that no one was in the lobby. One of the stones hit me hard in the throat, and I smiled at Trey. He said, "That's right, bitch. Throw it back and I'll break your left leg." I used a pen to pick it out of my keyboard, where it had lodged itself, and while staring at it, thinking, shit, maybe it's a real diamond, and I can sell it for a hundred thousand dollars, quit this shit job, and buy a mansion in South Africa. Then it hit me.

Brian hadn't recognized me at all. I thought the sad-happy fog he lives under had parted for one magical moment and he'd seen me. But no. His handlers had probably sat him down on our uncomfortable couch while tying his bow tie for him and said, hey, Brian, so tonight we are going to be around a lot of people, okay? We won't stay long, but some of these people are going to know who you are and might want to say hello. Don't worry, we'll be next to you the whole time, and all you have to do is say, "Hello. I'm Brian Wilson." Here try that once. Good. See, that's all you have to say, okay? Don't worry, we can come back soon, and we won't let anyone bother you. Can you let me hear it one more time?

"Hi. I'm Brian Wilson."

I know who you are, Brian. You were just programmed for meet-and-greet party mode, right? You are not there yet, buddy, you're still in the lobby, but I hope you had fun when you got there, and I hope everyone who shook your hand felt as honored as I felt. I'm so sorry you had to die for our sins, Brian, and thank you so much.

Two weeks after that I met Ginger Smith.

Ginger Smith. For the purposes of this book, that is a fake name *of a fake name,* meaning the name she stayed under was fake to begin with and I have altered it again. How awesome is that? Ginger, model-slim brunette, five feet ten, was always dressed in tight-fitting business attire, the kind that looks a little *too* good, something maybe for a porno. A porno set in the workplace. She was always in a hurry and always smiling.

Things were a little odd. First of all the fake name. If you asked her for an ID (you know me, I never did), she would hand you a twenty-dollar bill instead. If that didn't work, she would cancel the res and walk right back out. Shady. Sometimes she would lay down a CC, but she always paid cash at checkout, always. And if that wasn't odd enough, she always checked out the same day she came in. Up to the room around 1:00 p.m. and back at the desk at 4:00 p.m. with a stack of dirty dancers to settle up with.

She was *always* in a rush and wouldn't even wait for change. If the room and tax came to $459, she would hand over five Bennys, and the $41 on top went, without question, to the agent, since the minute an agent touched the bills, she'd say, "Thank you, sweetheart," and blow out the doors.

I once saw Ginger Smith, in an *unprecedented move,* walk right down the desk and hand every single one of the four working agents a baby brick. The classiest move I have ever seen in my life. So sexy. So beautiful and, hence, she was loved.

Ms. Smith. She was/is gorgeous. The first step with a guest of that caliber is to lock her down hard. Become her only agent, the sole recipient of her generosity. And I tried. Every time I was lucky enough to pick up her call, usually about an hour before she'd roll in, I would have everything waiting for her (including a slip of paper inside the key packet that laid out her room and tax in advance, so she could get her money in order before she came down). Plus, also inside the key packet, you guessed it, one of old Tommy Jacobs's business cards with e-mail *and* phone number, including a little note that told her to text me any day she wanted to come in and I would take care of it. For months she never utilized my personal contact info. I would bring it up, and she'd say she lost my card but, yes, agree that having a cell number she could text would be the best.

"Ms. Smith, put it in your phone right now. Tom at the Bellevue. Stand still for three seconds, and put it in right now."

She did. "Here," another twenty on top of the sixty in change she was going to leave me. "You're a sweetheart."

She was the sweetheart. And the next week I got the text.

:Coming in, darling! Around noon!:

:You got it, Ms. Smith. Rate is $429.50 after tax. I'll have the keys waiting!:

:(Smiley face):

From then on she could fly through the lobby, and I would hand the keys off like Gatorade to a marathon runner. Off she went.

"Ms. Smith was coming in today?" my co-worker Janelle asked, clearly jealous she hadn't gotten the reservation call.

"Yep."

"You always get her now. You should share."

"Yep." Not going to happen. I locked Ginger down hard. I was in love with everything about her.

Except for the fact she was a prostitute? A prostitute, right? I couldn't see it any other way and, believe me, I *wanted* to. She used the room for three hours max and paid cash (at *checkout,* even though paying up front would be more convenient, a single point of contact simultaneously beginning and ending all business with the hotel, but, prostitute-wise, she wouldn't have the cash until after the deed, feel me?). But, just like Hockstein, you never really know until you *know.* Some people blow money for no reason. Plus, I've seen my share of working girls, and they *do not* make reservations. The johns secure the room, and the pimp just points the hooker missile in the right direction.

But eventually, adding another hazy clue to the mystery, she mentioned she could use some extra amenities (razor and shaving cream, extra soap). I guess she liked to get superclean before or after whatever happened up there. So I started filling our little Bellevue gift bags with bath salts and soaps and creams and mini deodorants and lint rollers and whatever cool stuff I could find in the housekeeping closet. I would paper clip her keys to the side of the gift bag, and she would fly through the lobby, looking beautiful and talking fast, snatching the bag with a wonderfully grateful smile. These care packages ended up getting me into substantial trouble with the new director of housekeeping. Hired from some brutal land of feudal reign, our new housekeeping director fit right in. She looked like Shrek rolled in mud. As I was organizing a care package one afternoon, there she was, more than obstructing the door to the main storage closet in the housekeeping department, not allowing me to leave.

"Why are you taking this bag of items?"

"Well, it's for a frequent-stay guest. She only uses the room to freshen up but still pays full rate, so I think it's nice to make sure she has what she needs in advance so she can be in and out as fast as possible."

"There is no reason she is getting these items for free."

"Yeah, well . . . Aren't they free to all guests?"

"If they request them."

"Well, she requested them."

"No, you are stealing them. Tell her to call our department directly, and we will deliver the items."

"What? Seriously? How about you grab me a piece of paper and I'll write down every item in this bag and then you can pretend she called you directly and go ahead and deliver them up. And do me the favor of delivering them ASAP because she is on her *way*. That work for everybody?"

(Another definition of "write-up": disciplinary action issued for going above and beyond while simultaneously anticipating a guest's needs.)

That put an end to the gift bags but certainly not an end to Ginger's willingness to tip me heavily.

I owned Ms. Smith. Or, well, maybe someone else did, by the hour. After a year of working together exclusively, we started to talk a bit more at the desk, real casual and about nothing, before she flew out the door, back into Manhattan. She once claimed her apartment bathroom was being renovated so she thought it was easier to shower here. Another time, when I directly asked where she, you know, *worked,* she said for the CEO of a hedge fund and he often had her work early a.m. and then attend dinner parties, hence, rather than make her go all the way to her apartment (which was a whole twenty blocks, one mile, away, less than ten dollars in a cab), he would give her cash to throw on a room and never needed receipts. *Okay.* Why the fake name? I asked. Well, Ginger was actually her first name, but her last was so eastern bloc, she claimed, that it was more trouble to use it, what with the difficulty in spelling.

Prostitute? Right? I DON'T KNOW!! She was so very sweet and generous and . . . well. Feel free to make your own decision. But me? Why would any working girl cover the overhead of the hotel room? I've seen it all, and I still, even today, can't call it for certain.

I decided to do something really nice for her. After she left the building but before posting her rate and settling the account, I went to the front office manager and explained a little bit about Ms. Smith: her revenue stream, low-maintenance status, and how her short, three-hour stays allowed us to double dip the room. Double dipping is essentially charging two guests full rates for the same room on the same night. Usually, double dipping is illegal. *Por ejemplo:* when a group books twenty rooms, but one traveler is unavoidably delayed without enough notice for the group to avoid paying the night's rate, yet the hotel allows another guest to occupy the paid-for-but-vacant room for the night and effectively clock a double rate, that's a fat double dip. In Ginger's case, I inquired about the possibility of offering her a half-day rate, since she only occupied the room for three hours, causing minimal damage, leaving the room easy to flip and sell again.

"Go for it," the manager said.

I texted Ginger right outside the manager's office, explaining I had reduced her rate by half, hence I had $200 cash waiting for her, which I offered to hold in my bank and apply to her next stay.

:You're a sweetheart! No, no!! I insist you keep it!! It's all yours!:

Again, does that sound like a sex worker to you? Keep my $200?

And that totaled a personal take-home of $250. In one day. With Ms. Smith.

How much did I love her?

Let me count the ways: twenty, forty, sixty, eighty, BRICK.

Two weeks later she booked another room, and after she departed, I secured her another half-day rate, asking a different

manager of course. She texted back immediately.

:Keep it!:

:Fuck no. This is yours:

:Please, baby, just keep it:

:No. It will be in an envelope under your
name at the concierge desk. Not another
word about it. Buy yourself a beautiful
dress with the money!:

:How sweet of you! I will pick it up tonight:

That was that. Until I checked my phone
an hour later and saw she had texted again:

:You are so sweet. I hope you have a nice
girl who takes care of you. You deserve
one:

That stopped me right in the stairwell.
What exactly was *that about*? I didn't have a
nice girl. In fact, I had just separated from
Julie two weeks prior. We'd been seeing each
other irregularly, but in this lonely town
those infrequent dates drew us out of
obscurity, and we became dependent on
them, began to enjoy the knowledge that

there was one other person who knew what your bedroom looked like, knew where you were born and what kind of person you had become. That became a relationship to me. And it wasn't easy, the separation. I listened to Elton John and felt miserable every night. Honestly, I am *still* horribly in love with Julie. But now here was an unusual text from an unusual woman. Who hoped I had a nice girl.

:I don't anymore, Ginger. But I hope you have a nice man to take care of you:

:I don't anymore either (wink face):

I sat on the stairs before heading down to the cafeteria, which would submerge me below cell service, and waited to see if she would text again. She did.

:We should get a drink together!:

TOMMY, ASK YOURSELF: Are you certain she is not a prostitute?
I texted her back.

:Ok!!:

Indeed.

We met for drinks at Columbus Circle with a view of Central Park. I was dressed above my station, wearing the nicest clothes a front desk agent is legally allowed to wear in public. Fifteen minutes late, she flew into the bar, saw me in the corner, and hustled over. I couldn't believe she was going to sit still and talk. She was like a shark, always moving, and now here she was taking a seat next to me on the couch, her brunette hair a bit disheveled and her forehead cutely perspiring.

She was sitting still.

Then we started to drink. For every one of my Jack on the rocks, she downed a martini. She drank *seven goddamn martinis,* and I have never seen anything like it. I went to the bathroom about three hours into this drinking war, and when I returned she had paid the whole tab (and, well, I couldn't really fight that. Fourteen drinks anywhere near Columbus Circle comes to, essentially, my weekly paycheck).

Minutes later we were walking along Central Park South (she was stumbling a little, holding on to my arm) on the way to a second bar, one where we could smoke. Yes, you can legally smoke inside, and it's right there in midtown, but I will not mention where, because this bar belongs to me and not to you. I propped her up on a stool at the antique wooden bar, and all the old cigar-huffing fat cats stared at me in what I suppose was envy. Hooker envy.

She took off her diamond-bezeled Rolex and put it before me, next to my drink. "You know, I bought that because it reminds me that money doesn't mean anything. Money doesn't mean anything at all." The Rolex was all scuffed and scratched but definitely sparkled magnificently in the low light. "You take it, Tom. Take it."

"You're giving me your Rolex?"

"For a time. Just take it, okay? Wear it for a bit."

I put it on my right wrist. I was now rocking two watches. We ordered another round, and she brought out her iPhone to show me pictures of her family dog.

As she wiped a drunk finger across the screen, she slowly passed several nude photos of herself, some taken inside a tanning bed, staining her naked body with eerie yellows and greens. But, you know, they were still hot. Then she really began to open up, but not about her profession. About herself and her problems, mental problems that manifested themselves in physical ways, like a compulsion to pick at her chest with tweezers until it bled.

I have to say, at that moment, I was living the life. Whatever else I might be, I was *not bored*. This was some other, other, *other* type of shit.

So we ordered another round.

Everything else was continually escalating at work. I received almost weekly documentation for some crime, along with the rest of the desk staff, and everyone's service and commitment just got worse and worse.

All of my service training was gone. I talked fast and dirty. If you weren't tipping me, then move on. I had money to make. Want to know all about the property? Read the book in the room.

Next guest, please.

But just like drinking toilet hooch, these clandestine operations began to give me stomachaches. It was dirty money that I spent on dirty martinis to forget how terrible it felt to hustle and steal every day. This life was giving me the frowns, daily, but as the hundreds began to push my savings account higher, I started to think about a nice clean break, getting back out into the world, posting my own bail, and flying away.

Cape Town. I could go to Cape Town, strip myself to zero, and then see what I had left.

I couldn't help but think back to New Orleans. Hadn't I been happier there? I was a nicer person there, right? How come I'd even stayed this long in New York? I might have already left the city, but in a way New York put a hex on me. The gravity is so strong here, that center-of-the-world feeling, it made leaving the city unfathomable. It often made leaving my own apartment unfathomable.

And then there was the money. The number one reason any ho stays a ho: the hundos just kept flowing in, and it takes a real serious motherfucker to turn off a money valve, especially in a city that carves poverty into every line of your face. I thought about my New Orleans railroad apartment, with that backyard I never even utilized, and my spinning top started to lean, dreaming of finding a backyard somewhere else to not utilize. Center of the world, my ass. I needed to get out for a while. Get back to New Orleans.

CHAPTER FOURTEEN

(Hotels have no thirteenth floor, hence I
have no thirteenth chapter.)

The hotel wouldn't give me the time off
(shocker). But by this point my seniority
had secured me weekends off, something
essentially unheard of in the business, and
my fellow agents despised me for it. Another
reason to leave town for a while: get a break
from my co-workers. My request was
promptly denied by management. So I just
took it anyway, booking a ticket for Thursday through Tuesday and planning to double
bang before and after my two weekend days.
By this point I didn't care. They could go
ahead and write me up. And they would. I
knew I deserved it.

Immediately after touchdown in Louisiana, I felt calmer, cleaner, better. Once I
exited baggage claim, the hot puff of heat
that circled me felt like a warm, moist hug.

The taxi drove along I-10, through Metairie (Metry, brah!), and despite the devastation of the storm everything appeared fine. The French Quarter smelled the same. The locals drank the same. It was all so soft on my eyes and soothing to my heart that I started to feel concerned about the person I'd become. My humor had changed. I told my close friends to suck their mothers' dicks now, something considered hilarious up north. Not so much in New Orleans. It sounded like a pretty mean thing to say down here. And now back in this town (where I had once existed pre–cell phone) my smart phone was still surging out e-mails from New York hustles. A big-tipping adulterer asking for a day room discount. CEO of a dying video rental empire asking for a late checkout. Ginger Smith telling me she'd be in at noon (for that one I had to call the Bell and set it up; I never left Smith to fend for herself).

I turned my phone off and walked into the Alibi, and he was there waiting for me.

"That's my *boy* right there."

He stood and we shook hands, smiling and looking each other up and down.

"You ain't changed a bit, Tommy."

"Just on the inside, Perry. Just on the inside. You look healthy, my man." But he looked older now, his eyes had softened and his hair had flecks of white. He was wearing a Yankees fitted cap, something I never would have noted or associated myself with all those years ago.

"You go first," he said.

"No, you."

"Come on, Tommy, speak."

"No. Is your family okay?"

"Everyone fine. Go on."

"Go on with what, Perry? I got no story. *You've* got a story."

"Let's get some alcohol — hah?"

We moved to the bar. The bartender placed two Heinekens before Perry without asking, and he lifted his chin to me. Perry ordered me a Hennessy for some reason.

"Welcome back to New Orleans, Tommy."

"Happy to be home."

"So this your *home,* huh? Glad to hear that."

"It certainly feels like it. So your family is fine. What about everyone else from the hotel?"

"Oh. Well, now, which ones?"

"Come on, Perry. All of them. Debra?"

"She back. Lost her mother, though. Went through it with her little boy, you know her son, right? He had a bad time of it. Next."

"Roy?"

"He back too. Crazy as ever. Still in housekeeping. Got a new tattoo and everything."

"Something about the storm?"

"Nah. Dude got another gun for some reason! Right on his tiny forearm. Shit is ridiculous!"

"Sanford?"

"Oh, man, he gone."

"Where?"

"He dead, Tommy. Before the storm. Sanford got shot up on Rampart Street."

"What happened?"

"Oh, you know how it is, cops won't tell you shit. Maybe he was in on something, they say he had a gun too, but lots of people got guns, he might a just been passing through. Who knows, but he gone. Had a nice funeral, though, you should have been there. Real nice. We all danced and it was beautiful. That was all before the storm, though, but it was a real nice service. All love and everyone dancin' to a brass band. I paid for the brass band. But it was beautiful. You get good music for my funeral, you hear? You hear? That was before the storm, though."

We sat in silence for a long time. The bar wasn't empty, but it did seem quieter than I remembered. The flood had left large eddies of silence in its wake, tiny reoccurring pockets where New Orleanians would sit mute over a drink, memories rushing like a strong current through their minds before they'd blink, be back at the bar, and find their voices and drinks again, find something to say about something.

I spent the long weekend with Perry and my other friends, walking the city like a tourist but loving every bar, every pissy corner. The French architecture leaned out and over me, a strong change from the straight-cut shiny skyscrapers of New York. I found myself stepping into the street to bypass a slow-moving couple, and it wasn't until Sunday I discovered I wasn't in a rush anymore and eased up on the throttle to enjoy the hug-like heat and sweet smell of garbage and culture that fills the air in the Quarter. Though the devastation was tremendous just outside the city, downtown and uptown were perfectly intact, including a bevy of new paint jobs, mostly bold and vibrant color choices. I did hear something new for the first time in the city: Spanish. Strains of Mexican music and a new population, brought in to rebuild after the storm, added to the music and life that floated along the streets. It just made it better: another spice.

I took a bottle to the Mississippi River. Where else would I go to be alone? I sat out my final night, watching shipping boats push hard and slow against the strong brown current, heading upriver. The *Mississippi Queen* belted out a howl and departed for a river tour. The commuter ferry crossed back and forth from the Northshore, passengers leaning over the rail, happy, and they all seemed to be in love or at least drunk. The homeless walked slowly along the wooden boards that framed the river's edge and smiled at me, nodding. People biked by, and trumpeters walked along behind the benches, playing slow jazz over the lapping hiss of the dirty river, not even playing for money, but playing for themselves and this town. And me.

But I had to return to New York, didn't I? I had clients who depended on me, and my wallet depended on them. I thought fondly of Julie, missing our evenings on rooftops where the city exploded around us, keeping our feet steady while we slowly sipped twenty-three-dollar cocktails, the buildings shooting over our heads. In that way I missed New York. I knew the city was not mine forever, that I would leave it. Perhaps I should leave it. Even after the New Orleans expenses, my savings account was growing, and travel was once again an option. I felt a frantic need to return and take advantage of everything New York provided. My time up north felt as if it were coming to a quick and harsh closing, and I didn't want to miss any of it. New Orleans, the storm, Perry, the river: they all reminded me not to take anything for granted. It all washes away, and we are all washed away with it. So when the ground is steady and the sky is clear, we should breathe deep until our lungs inflate against our ribs and hold in that one breath until we are light-headed with the privilege of being alive. The absolute privilege of being human.

I began to consider, upon the thought of "permanently" relocating, everything New York had made me. When I arrived, I was like a half-carved sculpture, my personality still an undefined image. But the city wears you down, chisels away at everything you don't need, streamlines your emotions and character until you are hard cut, fully defined, and perfect like a Rodin sculpture. That is something truly wonderful, the kind of self-crystallization not available in any other city. But then, if you stay too long, it keeps on wearing you down, chipping away at traits you cherish, character that you've earned. Stay forever, and it will grind you down to nothing.

CHAPTER FIFTEEN

"Well, then, ma'am, would you like to play a game? How about this. I've got a three-digit room number put aside for you. If you can tell me which city's area code it is, then you get a free bottle of red wine. Sound good?"

"Really? Sure! Okay, I'm ready!"

"I have you in room 504."

"Um . . . I don't know. Darn it. Houston?"

"Oh! So close. Five zero four is the New Orleans area code."

"New Orleeens! I love *New Orleeens,*" she said, pronouncing it incorrectly. "But I never would have gotten it . . ."

"You love New Orleans? Well, then, I'm sending you the wine anyway! Enjoy, and welcome to the Bellevue." I passed the keys to a bellman with a smile. Ben snatched them from me with a disapproving frown.

He came right back down.

"What's the matter with you, Tom?"

"I feel good."

"Clearly. You'd better get a handle on that."

"I'm refreshed, you know? I got nice and centered down there."

"You're a real douche when you're happy."

We both had a nice laugh about that. But it wasn't long before the job started hacking at my soul, cleaving at my heart, wearing me down again. Not long as in three hours.

A guest was already attacking me.

"You think this is funny? I stay here ten times a year. That makes me one of your top guests. You'd better get me the room number I was guaranteed *right now,* or you are going to be in serious trouble."

A couple of things were dead wrong with this businessman's thinking. First of all, we never guarantee room numbers. The worst mistake an employee can make is to promise a room number. Anything can happen: extensions, flooding from the room above, a murder, someone else paid me twenty for a nice view and I already gave it away.

Second of all, ten times a year does not make anyone a top guest. We've got people who clock two hundred nights a year. Anal-Block-Stein even has that beat. This current guest's ten-night-a-year/two-grand-in-revenue was like a small black mark on the lobby floor; it doesn't mean jack shit to anyone, especially not the GM.

This guest here, Asshole A, apparently was also the type of idiot willing to take it one step further and really point out his ignorance of the situation.

"I will never stay here again, do you realize that? I will take my business to the Plaza. What do you think about that?"

Though I couldn't say it out loud, here is exactly what I thought about that: "Well, sir, I imagine it would be impossible for me to care less! *Please,* stay at the Plaza. *We* don't want low-revenue/high-entitlement guests like you pushing your way into our lobby anyway. Plus, do you think I own stock? Think of it this way: Perhaps McDonald's gets your order wrong, maybe they overcooked your fries into little black sticks. Would you attempt to use this logic on the fry cook? Promise to only eat at Burger King? No, you wouldn't. Because they are just fry cooks. They don't care about McDonald's revenue stream, sir. And here, dear guest, I am just a fry cook. Stay anywhere else, it'll only make me happy not to see you."

Threatening a front desk agent gets you nowhere. Well, that's not true. It gets you into a worse room. I have broken blocks, taken rooms from people who were even *pre-reged* into a gorgeous room just because their attitude was off. They never even knew they were originally set to see Central Park in one of the corner rooms with the big bathroom. I took it from them just because they yelled at their wives or manhandled their wives' elbows in a way I didn't appreciate.

It might not be pretty, but it's important we cover this topic. Because that's just the beginning of the ways I can and *will* punish guests. I am a god of instant karma. Instant. No waiting for it to kick in. No four to six weeks for delivery. If a guest makes a racist comment about a cabdriver, the backlash comes now. If some ignorant guest thinks it's at all appropriate to make homophobic comments to anyone around me, much less directly *to* me, I dispense justice: Harsh. Instantaneous. Justice.

Por ejemplo: Speaking of area codes, one of the most wonderful tools at my disposal is putting a guest into a certain room on the twelfth floor. What is so punishing about this room? Nothing by the look of it: a decent room by all accounts. However, if I put you in room 1212, your phone will not stop ringing with wrong numbers. Why? Well, a surprising number of guests never seem to learn that from every hotel phone you have to dial out. In general, to place any call, one must press 9 prior to dialing, local or otherwise. So all day, and believe me, all night, idiots dispersed throughout the building will pick up their phones and try to straight dial a local number, starting with 1-212. Whatever they press after that matters not because they have already dialed room 1212, and 1212's guest will constantly pick up the 3:00 a.m. call and hear the loud mashing of other numbers or some drunk guest saying, "Hello? Hello? Who is this?"

"What time is it? Why are you calling me? Who is this?"

"I'd like to order the Szechuan chicken please? Excuse me? Is this Happy Family Palace?"

All day. All night. Just like that.

As early as my second year, I invented the "key bomb," and it became instant protocol. A move someone, perhaps a bellman, could request.

"Yo, Tommy," Trey would say to me, pulling me to the side of the desk, "key bomb this dude. He called the cabbie something racist. Something I hopefully never have to hear again."

"You got it, Trey-Trey."

When I cut the keys for a bomb, I do it a little differently. Any arriving guest should receive what's referred to as "initial keys," which are programmed to reset the door lock when they are first inserted, deactivating all previous keys. Guests seem to think these locks are supercomputers, connected to the system wirelessly, hence if they check out at the desk and realize they forgot something in the safe, they ask me if their keys will still work. I inform them they certainly will. Again, they point out that I just checked them out. But, man alive, they will still work until they auto-expire at a certain date and time (designated automatically at check-in and set for 3:00 p.m. the day they depart). Not until the keys expire or a new "initial key" enters the lock will their keys fail to work.

Therefore, dear guests, if you ever extend, even if the front desk forgets to inform you (which we will), then, YES, you need new keys. (You're welcome, my front desk people! I just told everyone all at once!)

And NO they do not have your personal information on them, with credit card info, passport number, and the ages of your children. Who started that rumor, I know not. Why the hell would we put personal info on a disposable key card?

But back to the key bomb. If I wanted to, I could actually go ahead and never even program your keys, just hand you any old set and send you up to battle that red light over and over before dragging your bags back down to get new keys, keys that I could again refuse to program correctly, though it looks as if I did, since I ran them through the programmer but authorized them for the health club only. That might draw heat, though, which is why the key bomb is so gorgeous. What I do is cut one single "initial key," then start over and cut a second "initial key." Either one of them will work when you get to the room. Slide one in; you get green, and as long as you keep using the very first key you slipped in, all will be well. But chances are you'll pop in the second key at some point, and *then* the first key you used will be considered, as far as the dumb-ass lock is concerned, an old key and invalid. Without a doubt, at some point after that, you will be locked outside your room, jamming your first key into the slot, fighting that damn red light, or maybe the yellow light (whatever the yellow light means, I don't know, but it won't get you in either). And that's the key bomb. Trace that back to me? Not a chance. Trace that back to the fact you told your nine-year-old daughter to shut her mouth while harshly ripping off her tiny backpack right in front of me at check-in? Never.

I also happen to know the electronic curtains are not functioning in room 3217, and it gets loads of morning sun in there. Good luck sleeping in.

Recently, I called Perry, and he related a story told to him by a bellman friend at another property. Among all get-backs there is a king. And this might be it.

"So this ma'fucker has fourteen bags. Takes me three goddamn trips, up and down, up and down. I'm feeling lovely about it, I mean, this dude's one of the greatest athletes who ever lived, not to mention he's up in that movie money. Dude is getting *paid,* and here I am poised to pocket some trickle down. So I lay his last bag on the carpet, actually wipe some sweat from my forehead, and this dude gives me a handshake, nothing in it, just a friendly ma'fuckin' handshake and a smile. A Walt Disney zip-a-dee-doo-dah smile, and I almost lost my shit. He closed the door on me. I'd heard he was famous for being cheap, but I didn't believe it, especially not with the work I put in. So, damn, it's not like I could miss him coming out of the lobby, and it's not like I didn't know he'd be doing his thing live at the Superdome for the next four hours. So I strolled back up to his room, unlocked the door, and went into his bathroom. He'd unpacked, laid all his luggage out, and I was gonna do a couple laps with his toothbrush in my ass . . . until it hit me. Boom. I mean, the man has his own cologne, and he actually *wears* it. So I unscrew the top, pour out a bit of the bottle into the sink, and fill it back up. With my own piss. The color was a perfect match. Gave the bottle a little shaky-shake, squirted a few clouds to get it going. And then I walked on out. Felt pretty good about it too when I saw him pimp through the lobby that night on his way to some party, looking sharp and smelling like bellman piss. Professional athletes, my man. They are some cheap-ass ma'fuckers."

Tread lightly, and beware of any employees not wearing name tags. They are up to something and don't wish to be identified.

With this kind of history, it's easy to see how the floodwaters of irritation that I hoped would recede in New Orleans were quickly back to storm surge. I received immediate documentation for abusing the call-outs, which I deserved, but in addition kept getting bombarded by mean guests.

Tremblay had also implemented a wonderful new policy. In the hotel game, a gift of wine or liquor to your favorite employee is a cherished tradition. I mean, you bring a bottle to a dinner party. You hand over an expensive one on a birthday. And you give one to the front desk agent who always upgrades you and never even *hints* he knows how often you cheat on your wife. Or maybe we remembered you from your honeymoon three years ago and immediately went to work making it your second honeymoon. That deserves a bottle of white, eh? But hotels do have a general rule: you cannot take liquor out of the building that is also *sold* in the building. That would make it just too easy to, you know, lift an errant bottle from the back room and then parade it to a manager, convincingly grateful about the bottle the couple in 912 left you. That makes the gift of hard liquor difficult for a hotel worker to get out of the building and into his or her liver. If I get a bottle of Jack Daniel's, let's say, I will put it in a bag that I wrap up in a sweater that I put in another bag, that I then cover with dirty black dress socks, all of which I then put in a backpack. I'll try to fly past security as if my crosstown bus stops running in five minutes. Even if they do stop me to peek in my bag, which they are supposed to do every time, they aren't going to dig through my work socks. They will tilt their head back and say, "Get out of here. And wash those socks."

"That's the plan, boss."

But a bottle of wine shouldn't require a *Shawshank Redemption* type of operation. With so many wine varieties the possibility of matching a brand sold at a hotel is very low. Not to mention sommeliers like to order and uncork five-hundred-dollar vintage bottles, not the nasty cylinder of Yellow Tail a guest left me. With a wine bottle, we show it to our immediate manager, and he or she will get us a "red tag" signed by the director of security. You could haul a fifty-inch flat screen out through security as long as it's red tagged.

Apparently, though no official memo had surfaced, the policies had changed at the Bellevue. And I found out because Kayla was in the back office. *Crying.* This girl cries for no one. She is more liable to rip out hair and cut a bitch. But there she was, leaning against the schedule posted in the luggage storage room, crying hard. Her hands weren't even covering her face, just hanging limp at her sides, letting me see the full extent of the damage, the crushed-up cheeks and mascara and total sadness.

"Baby, oh, what's wrong? Kayla?"

"This place, Tommy. It's cursed. Sometimes, when I'm in the basement changing, I get this death feeling, like they built this hotel on an Indian burial ground."

Al flew by dragging a purple carry-on and said, "I commute here from a town called Massapequa. This whole damn country is built on an Indian burial ground."

"Good point, Wolf," I said to his back as he flew out the door to the lobby. "But, Kayla, what did they do to you, girl? They write you up?"

"Well, I also got written up, yeah. But they do that every week now. It's not that. No, they stole from me."

"An employee?"

"That's what I thought at first, but no. You know the Howells, that old white couple? Well, they never give me *anything.* But I help them *all the time,* and the wife really likes me. I mentioned about how my husband and I were having problems, you know? Since the last baby? I just mentioned it quickly to Mrs. Howell. She said there is no situation a good bottle of wine won't improve, and nothing two good bottles won't cure."

"That was cute."

"Yeah, so she brings me two bottles of wine yesterday, and I don't know, but they looked like expensive bottles. I couldn't take them home after work, because I was going to the gym because my ass is getting fat. So I put my name ALL over them and left them in the manager's office. I told my husband, for some reason, what Mrs. Howell said, and he took the day off work to stay home and cook all day. All four kids are in the Bronx with their grandma and he's cooking for me and I'm bringing the wine and we were supposed to eat and drink the bottles and then fuck. And maybe make a sex tape like we do on Valentine's Day."

"That sounds nice."

"I know." Now she started crying again. "But when I came in today, the wine was gone, and they told me the policy had changed and we can't take any more liquor out of the hotel. I even had the handwritten note from Mrs. Howell that talks about the wine, and still they wouldn't give it to me."

Something dropped in me at this point. She was really shooting out tears and still not hiding it with her hands. I hugged her, and that made her cry harder at first but then less hard. When she pulled back, I had mascara all over my white work shirt, but I didn't fucking care. I had some serious hatred spinning around in my throat.

Why doesn't she just buy another two bottles of wine? Her husband, a bellman at the DoubleTree, broke his arm a year ago. You can't sling suitcases with one arm. The doctor even told him that due to the nerve damage, since it was crushed (long story), he might never be able to do heavy lifting again. For six months he couldn't find work and then finally pulled a gig as an elevator operator, up and down all day in a building's delivery elevator, and the pay was garbage. And they have four kids. And they are now almost four months behind on bills. And that wine was special. The kindness of it, the thoughtfulness with those words of encouragement, would've given those bottles a power no other bottles could have. Why doesn't she just buy another two good bottles of wine? Open your eyes.

Before I know it, I'm on the way up to the GM's office. I was furious and shaking in the elevator, watching the numbers rise and thanking God there were no guests in there to look at me and ask me things. I found him standing in the hallway with none other than the director of security. Perfect. Our fat eggplant of a GM looked like an inner Russian doll next to the gigantic director of security, who was unaffectionately known as

Lurch. Our old DOS, before the takeover, had been about five feet four inches and an ex-cop (as basically all DOSs are). But we all loved him. As Italian as possible, loud and always accusing me of being high on coke, though I was pretty sure he knew that I, above everyone, never touched it. I used to call him "Cop Show" because everything he talked about, even if it was just the mac and cheese in the cafeteria, sounded as if he was on *CSI* or some shit. After they fired him, they brought in Lurch, who looked like two "Cop Shows" stacked on top of each other, wrapped in a crazy suit coat as big as a wind sail. No one liked this guy. He wasn't a born-and-raised New Yorker, which is a bad start for any NYC DOS. I looked way up at his pale head next to our squat fuckup of a GM and waited for one of them to open his mouth so I could cut him off.

"Is ther—"

"Why have the liquor policies changed? Since when can we not remove wine from the hotel?"

"Four months ago. Haven't you noticed? I guess you don't get a lot of gifts."

"None that you can drink, Mr. Tremblay." What a prick. But I probably shouldn't have said that. It's always best for a hustler to keep quiet. Real hustlers are never, ever flashy. ("Let them tell it, you was just another guy in the crowd." — T.I.) "Well, Kayla is currently crying on company time because she left two bottles in the manager's office and now they are gone. Care to tell me where they are?"

"You can no longer take liquor out of the hotel," Lurch said, like some big gigantic gorilla asshole.

"We covered that. My question is this: Where are the bottles now?"

"What do you mean?"

"Well," and here my emotions were burning neon bright, "have they been placed on our restaurant menu? Are you now turning a profit on gifts given to your employees? Or, and perhaps this is it, did one of you take those bottles home and drink them? Did one of you confiscate a gift, a gift accompanied by a *corroborating* note" — Cop Show would have *loved* to hear me drop that word — "a gift given to a front desk agent with ten years of service, given for no reason other than she utilized exceptional service to create customer loyalty . . . did one of you take those bottles to your own house and drink them? *Which one of you drank Kayla's wine?*"

Man alive, I was balls-out ape shit.

Tremblay was giving me a burning stare.

Say what you want, here is a man who doesn't have much fear in him. The whole hotel hated him, even the managers who kissed his ass in the staff meetings. Did being universally hated behind his back bother him? No, not really.

He began to speak and very slowly, "Well, Thomas, all bottles of wine and liquor are now disposed of in the loading dock."

"Excuse me? You are throwing out full bottles of wine?"

"No, security assures me they are uncorked and poured down the drain in the loading dock."

"You are going to look me in the eye and tell me that this guy," I said, pointing a thumb at Lurch, who was so tall it looked like a normal thumbs-up, "is uncorking bottles of wine and pouring them down the drain?"

"Yes, Thomas. That is exactly the policy." And then he smiled at me. One of those smiles that, like a magnet, can somehow cause a beer bottle to smash into it.

Here was my GM, looking me right in the eye, lying to my face, and then smiling about it.

Where have you gone, Chuck Daniels? Little Tommy Jacobs turns his lonely eyes to you.

Because what the fuck do you do with that? What would *you* do?

I walked away. I went back to the first floor, and looking up into the lobby at a line of guests, all expecting exceptional service, I logged in.

I typed in my password, pressed enter, and said, "Can I assist the next guest?"

So here is the following day in my life. But not just any day, a day that ends with me completely losing my shit in the manager's office.

I woke up hungover, out all night with a few doormen doing the passé New York club scene. Meatpacking District and all that. After the confrontation with upper management, I wanted to *get lit,* and if you want to *get lit,* you cannot beat partying with doormen. They have cash for days, huge knots thick with twenties, and usually they grew up with the club owner (or if not that, the bartender, or at *least* the guy working the door).

What's good for a hangover? I'll tell you what's *not* good: getting absolutely bombarded by checkouts. And we've got the usual complaints. I removed at least five hundred dollars in minibar charges throughout the morning, trying to ignore the guest's twenty-minute headache-inducing explanation about how she put her sister's organic wheat bars on top of the cashews so that they would be cold when she came back from getting fitted for her wedding dress in SoHo, and so why were they charged for the cashews? They never *ate* the cashews. They never *touched* the cashews. I'd removed the charges long before she started going on about wheat bars, much less the non sequitur wedding info, even attempting to cut her off to *assure* her the charges have *already* been removed, but even that won't often stop an intricate and useless story from growing more intricate and more useless.

Then an unpleasant old man interrupted me while I was in the middle of a guest checkout.

"Hello, *sir, EXCUSE ME,* I want a card for my free breakfast."

I apologized to the guest he was interrupting and told the interrupter I'd be with him in a moment.

"Breakfast ends in ten minutes, and I want my card."

The guest before me, who had waited patiently in line, tilted his head and gave me a nod with a half smile, one of those expressions that say: "Go ahead and help this jerk,

344

and also, dude, sorry your job sucks."

"Okay, sir, were you given breakfast certificates upon check-in?"

"Yes. My rate comes with breakfast. You can look it up if that's what you're *insinuating.*"

"Sir, I am not insinuating anything. However, were you not given enough certificates at check-in?"

"Look, they are up in my room, and I won't go get them. Breakfast ends in ten minutes. You are wasting my time."

In the drawer next to me, buried beneath a pile of loose staples, is a stack of breakfast certificates. The policy is, however, that we cannot hand out extra cards. He could have his daughter sitting in the lounge, who lives on the Upper East Side and is not actually staying at the hotel, hence shouldn't get a certificate. Therefore getting this extra cert from me could cost the hotel $35. But was I worried about the hotel losing money? Was I trying to follow procedures like a good little boy?

Not really. I was training an asshole that being an asshole only jams up your life. Showing fiscal responsibility and adhering to company policy: that was just the spoonful of sugar.

"I am sorry, sir. You will have to retrieve

the original certificates from your room. However, I will alert the lounge to your situation, tell them you are on your way, and make certain they wait before breaking down the buffet."

The old man gave a look to my waiting customer, trying to get him to witness and verify the terrible service I was giving. My guest pursed his lips and shook his head at the old man, who walked away, probably assuming that reaction actually confirmed I was a bad employee.

"Sorry about the delay, Mr. Peterson. Thank you for your patience."

"Hey, not to worry. You're doing a great job."

Something special happens to guests when they see another guest act like a child. If I'm at the desk getting loudly reamed, screamed at, and abused, that is the only time I can guarantee that the next guest I help, the very next guest, the one who saw the scene from an outsider's perspective, will treat me with dignity and extreme patience. If a guest sees another person publicly humiliate himself about something minor (and believe me, it's all minor), when his turn comes, I could tell him he is staying in the basement rat room for fifteen hundred dollars a night, and he would say,

"Hey, not to worry." Maybe even lean in and add a concerned, "Have a nice day, okay?"

But the guest after that? The one who failed to witness the public reaming? Watch out.

About an hour later the old man is back, again standing to the side of my line, trying to skip past everyone waiting. Just one errant second of eye contact from me was all he needed before he stepped up and pushed a breakfast certificate *right in my face.* I am talking *close to my face,* so close my release of an irritated breath rattled the card. Or maybe the card was rattling because this old man was now *livid* and his hand was shaking in anger.

"You tell me where on this card it says my room number. You tell me where on this card there is a bar code or number or anything that makes it not just a piece of paper that you could have just handed me. You tell me why you couldn't give me another one and made me walk all the way back upstairs."

Honestly, I wasn't even bothered by this. I've been rocking this desk so long I don't even pay attention when people are yelling at me. In truth, I look at their faces, distorted in anger, and think about *other things.*

("I don't get mad, I just get money." —
Young Jeezy.) Though I especially didn't like
that he was still holding that damn card up
against my face as if I were a dog that
chewed up his slipper. I'm not paid to be
abused. I'm not paid to relinquish my
personal space.

Also, I had four people waiting in line,
and it was my job to process them through
the system. That's all I wanted to do, just
get them checked into their rooms so they
could begin their New York experience. But
first I had to get this card out of my face
and this old man off my ass.

This, dear guests, is what management is
for.

"Sir, I understand you are unhappy, but I
was simply following the policies set forth
by management. I understand that you
disagree with these policies, and the best
possible course might be to express your
concerns directly to management. Would
you like to speak to a manager?"

You read that *verbiage*?! I'm like a politician! There has got to be a better job for
me somewhere, talking some official garbage
like that.

"You're goddamn right I want a manager . . . Thomas."

We all know what that means, including

my name at the end. Not my concern, though. There were now seven people in line, and number five was the tour manager for Kings of Leon, a really nice guy. But he'll definitely want the four VIP pre-reged keys for his group immediately so he can deliver them to the band, who are hiding in the tour bus so they don't get fan-fucked in the lobby. Number six is the CEO of 7-Eleven, who is also a really great guy and far too busy to wait. Number seven is just a normal guest, but she deserves efficient service like everyone else.

Sara, our newest manager, responded quickly to my phone call and took the old man (and his precious certificate) to the far corner of the lobby.

A few hours later some Jersey mafioso is fondling his roll of cash, rubbing his thumb over an amazing collection of hundos, asking if there is something special I can do for him. After my day, after my week, I could use a brick, maybe treat myself to a nice lunch and avoid the shiny, greasy meal they were serving in the employee cafeteria. I unblocked a VIP suite, held for a famous actor, who I think is a bit overrated anyway, one who thinks every role and every day is Halloween. I leaned in and whispered, giving this dude and his bankroll the full performance, authorizing a hundred-dollar-a-night upgrade for four nights, not to mention leaving the actor unblocked and roomless. As I passed him the keys, calling the Gray Wolf over to grab his luggage, he slipped the money roll back into his pocket and put out his empty hand to shake. No question about it, I could tell from the way he held out his hand that it was empty. Goddamn it. I should have seen it coming: he was fondling the money too much, too obvious. I got played. I told him if he needed anything at all to ask for Terrance (when you give a fake name, it's important to avoid names of employees currently working at the property *and* that it be a name of someone from your past whom you hate) then walked off, leaving his hand floating over the desk, unshaken, and he knew exactly why.

I took a lunch break, starting the countdown timer on my smart phone to make it back exactly on time. The managers were still tracking employees with the security cameras to crack down on extended lunches. In order to take a break, you had to call the manager's office so the manager could queue up the video monitors on the computer screen (a new feature they had installed that could be accessed from any computer, anywhere. In fact, rumor was Tremblay would watch it from home, spying, and call in various infractions).

Work Environment of the Year Award goes to . . . Hotel 1984.

After lunch I almost felt better until some seventeen-year-old trust-fund toddler in a pink polo started treating me like his pool cleaner. I had just gotten back, I looked up, and in seconds this kid was going at me hard. Apparently, reservations promised him a room with two king beds. He, or his mother, booked through Expedia and then called Expedia directly to confirm his seventeen-year-old special requests.

Outside agencies know absolutely nothing about specific properties. In fact, even if it's a large chain, it will have "central reservations," which is some remote desk in India or Canada, and the agents there generate reservations for more than five hundred properties, five hundred buildings they will never, ever see. Certainly the system lists the features, bed types, views, and other property-specific info, but it is fallible. If you truly want to know what you booked and what that means, you have to call the property itself. You have to call me at the desk, and I will tell you exactly what you're getting. In fact, especially if it's an extended stay or an important reservation, having a contact at the hotel proper is invaluable. You can even prearrange a hustle and upgrade with a simple question like, "Will you be there the day I check in? I really would like to personally thank you for taking care of me." That is code for, or should be code for, I will give you money if you stay on top of my reservation and hook me up. I've met and started long-term relationships with clients that stemmed from preemptive phone calls such as this.

But now, this kid, who confirmed his details with Expedia, a company thrice removed from us, is screaming at me, demanding to have what was promised. He wants his two king beds. We don't have rooms with two king beds, *they don't exist,* and I just wasn't strong enough to let this kid's attitude slide. Another day I might have been able to pull this one off without getting involved. But that day I slipped into "teach a lesson" mode. As I relayed the information, apologizing that Expedia misinformed him about our property and reiterating that we simply don't have that type of bed layout and can we perhaps talk about other forms of accommodation because I assure you we can find something that will satisfy blah blah blah bullshit, he cuts me off again, slapping his soft, never-worked-a-day-in-his-life hand down on the desk to silence me. Like a crazy person, he once again demands I provide him with two king beds. I looked at his mother at this point, pleading. She determinedly avoided my look.

I then proceeded to politely, oh so sarcastically, offer to *build* him a room big enough for his two king beds, if he wants to wait two months. I looked again at his mother, and, let me just say this now, she herself lived in fear of her own child. Her expression was indecipherable, but in her eyes I'm sort of sure she was apologizing to me for her son's attitude. But then this terrible teenager turned on his mother, giving her a look of control and hatred. The mother split open her face to ask for a manager. The kid crossed his arms in victory and stared at where my name tag should be. I knew what kind of day it was going to be after I chewed up that old man's slippers: it's like that sometimes, the job has a temperature, a feeling in the air, a discernible evilness. Today, sensing an evil wind was blowing, I took my name tag off immediately after dealing with that old man.

I informed them that I would absolutely call a manager and said I was sorry I couldn't assist them. It didn't even matter that I wasn't wearing a name tag, because every time I alter or touch a reservation, my personal log-in code embeds itself in the system. In this case, like a blood trail.

Sara, like a blood*hound,* happened to be approaching the desk at that very moment. I made the introductions and moved on to help the next guest, who was abreast of the whole situation and already had that facial expression I cherish: "Hey, you were in the right on that one and your job sucks, and I promise *I* won't give you a hard time."

Two hours later, I clocked out with a long sigh, slipped my ID card back into my wallet, and almost smashed into Sara. She'd only been here for two months; two months and she'd made negative-twenty friends.

There are all types of managers out there. I remember once, back in New Orleans, I found myself walking out of the building with Trish, my first FOM, the one who saw my potential in valet and invited me to the front desk. It had been a long day for both of us, and we were headed to the Alibi to drink a bit with the crew. That's how you want things to be in a hotel: everyone drinking together at the bar, planning trips to go bowling, meeting up at Jazz Fest. If you look forward to hanging out with your co-workers outside the job, then performance inside the job will be stellar. It also has the side effect of *everyone* banging *everyone,* but, you know, that builds morale in a way too, so might as well let us go at each other.

It was a warm August night, the heat close to our faces, the roaches scurrying happily from trash piles to vomit, people strolling slowly toward Bourbon Street with sweating drinks, the live music perfect for the evening, all the harsh edges of the sound mellowed and smooth. Maybe because we had walked there together, maybe that's why, but near the end of the night we met up at the edge of the bar to order our "last" drink and stayed together talking. She told me about my potential, but not in a bullshit way. She mentioned my drive and dedication, pointing out only two flaws I needed to watch out for:

One: I made too many jokes.
Two: I had a slight problem with authority.

Ha, ha, ha. *No shit.*
She then gave me a chunk of advice. "You'll be a manager soon, Tommy. Everyone likes you and believes in you. But before that happens, take the time to analyze the managers you have now. Pay attention to

the way they treat you and the rest of the staff. Are they too friendly? Not friendly enough? Are they enforcers? Company drones? Too lenient or never, ever lenient? Just keep your eye on them, watch how their attitudes either cause or eliminate problems, and then, when you get to be a manager, you can pick and choose the type of manager you want to be, the type of manager your employees will think you are. Start thinking about that now, and you'll be successful."

This new manager at the Bellevue, Sara, was an enforcer. The hotel hired her away from Trump International two months ago, and recently I had the opportunity to do some recon. Julie and I, in our meandering yet loving way, were back together. She threw herself another fancy birthday party, this time at another fancy hotel. Knowing she'd want me in attendance, she booked at the Trump, and I went with her to oversee the check-in process, make sure everything went smoothly. Then we planned to rough up the bed before her friends arrived. (We ended up roughing up the bathroom. Anyone seen the Trump bathrooms? So much marble and gold it's like banging in Versailles! I swear I heard trumpets and shit!) Sara had been with us for only one week at

that time, and so far she was all smiles, waiting to get the lay of the land, much as a
new sergeant dropped into the middle of
Vietnam might want to hang back a bit
before loading the rifle and starting to fire
at the trees.

In between dropping tens on every front
desk agent who looked my way (which got
us the larger, fuck-worthy bathroom, wine,
and, most conveniently, a late checkout), I
asked about Sara, what kind of manager she
was.

"Oh, she's wonderful! We were devastated
to lose her!"

What the hell was *this* nonsense? Had I
not mentioned I was a front desk agent?

"Yeah, yeah," I countered, leaving another
ten on the desk, "but anything to watch out
for?"

This agent gave me a psychotic smile, like
a doll smile, as if her face were going to
break. What were they doing to these
people? Did this woman have electrodes
clipped to her body that administered a hot
current of electricity every time a negative
word was uttered? I let it go because she
was frightening me.

Would we like a bellman to accompany us
to the room? Yes, we certainly *would*.

"We don't really have luggage, Thomas,"

Julie pointed out.

"I know. I'll take care of the tip. Let's just give our man here a front."

On the way to the elevator I mentioned I was front desk at the Bellevue. In the elevator up I mentioned I was union and inquired about the strength of the union here. Once we hit the floor, I asked about Sara. He gave me a flat statement about how she was fine. I gave him a twenty and said, "Hey, come on, man, just let me know. Me and the boys are getting a funny feeling. Anything to watch out for?"

He stopped pulling the cart behind him, which was light with our two small overnight bags. "Don't trust her smile. Don't trust her at all."

Yep.

And now here she was two months later, asking me to get a union delegate and come upstairs.

"Really? Why? I just clocked out, and it's my Friday."

She just kept staring at me.

"Okay. Let's go," I said.

There were two other people in the bathroom-sized manager's office, both of them pointing their much calmer gazes at me.

One: Orianna, my union delegate. Your

union delegate is your elected advocate. Your uneducated, uninterested advocate. Soon after joining the union, they held elections for the delegate position. Two kinds of people try to be delegates. The first kind are after the perks. To begin with, being a delegate always pulls you off your job, taking you down to HR to hear a case or witness a write-up. Lazy people *love* being delegates. Also, as a delegate you are essentially bulletproof. It is near impossible to fire a delegate. If one even gets suspended, anywhere in the New York Hotel Workers' Union circuit, then all the business reps (who actually work for the union) will roll out and protest. It's a mess. It's better to just set the delegate free than deal with the fallout. Beyond being bulletproof, a delegate is also unable to go on layoff. The hotel could shut down all but one goddamn room, and there would still be delegates from every department running around the property, waiting for the single guest to request some toilet paper or order a sandwich. In truth, that was what Orianna was after, since she was assimilated late into the realm of the front desk and put in the back of the line seniority-wise. She took the position to secure a paycheck and ensure the Similac kept flowing for that union baby she had.

The second type of person who goes for the delegate position is the shit-talking, fake politician. The kind of person who has little education but loves to try out big words and be in charge, know everyone's goddamn business, and write little ineffective letters asking for this and demanding that and just generally embarrassing him- or herself with an over-the-top I-am-important attitude.

Which delegate is the better of the two?

It's not much of a choice.

Perhaps the politician types will be better informed about the policies and loopholes. At least they *want* to think of themselves as good delegates. But again, they are playing a political game, and often, and this must make them so happy, they make "sacrifices," bow down to management, let employees go, just to keep up the "dialogue" and make "concessions." Games like that get good people fired.

There is actually a third kind of delegate, rare, but one that you'd actually want: a delegate who hates management. One who gets angry and thinks every single thing management does is bullshit. Those kinds of troublemakers can actually overturn a decision. They sincerely care about their people and will fight to the death, even if their union member was caught reading the *New York Times* while taking a shit in the presidential suite master bathroom.

I didn't have that kind. I had Orianna. Perks.

The second person in the room was Sara: this new manager who came in here with new plans and processes as they all do, more than ready to jump into the Bellevue's current "the flogging will not stop until morale improves" mentality. And now she was trying to discipline the white whale.

I am the white whale.

I've been here for centuries.

I came with the land.

Who does this woman think she is?

"Poor service." That's what I am being disciplined for. I can see the term traced huge on the write-up, extremely legibly. Poor service. The livid old man and that sucker-ass pussy in the polo.

I mean, eating shit is part of the job. Hell, eating shit *is* the job. And I used to have an iron stomach. But that was New Orleans. That was me *ten years ago.* This is New York. Christ, this is midtown Manhattan. Why can't I do it anymore? What really changed: I became a semiprofessional alcoholic? Sure. Retaliating against new management? Yes, please. Been working as a front desk agent so long it makes me want to shit out my heart?

Absolutely.

We discuss the events of the day. The breakfast cards. I explain how, to me, her evidence is inadmissible (look at me go, Cop Show!) because I was directly following procedures. How can I be disciplined for any anger resulting from my request that a guest retrieve his original certificates, when two weeks ago there was a memo that said all guests must use their original certificates? You say break eggs, so I break eggs. And then you accuse me of getting the kitchen all dirty and getting salmonella in your mouth. I also pointed out that if I hadn't been slightly curt with the gentleman, the line behind him would not have moved, and then we'd have guests complaining about the long wait to check in or maybe even silently deciding to find another property for any future New York City stays, one with better, more efficient service.

The kid, the seventeen-year-old. Whatever. I didn't give Sara many words about that. That kid was out of line. Can I really be responsible for the accusations of a country-club teenager? I explain that perhaps management should take into consideration that his opinion of my attitude might be swayed by the fact he just rocketed through puberty. And he was *unreasonable*. Only providing him with a *nonexistent room* would have made him happy! That is the definition of unreasonable: demanding something that isn't even possible.

"You know, Sara, I have been here for a long, long time. I may have helped 500 guests today. I may have helped 500 yesterday. I help a lot of guests. Out of today's 500, 498 were pleased or perhaps more than pleased. Now you've got an unreasonable child and a man who disagrees vehemently and *exclusively* with *hotel policy,* and you are going to write me up? One more write-up after this, and I'll be suspended pending termination. Does that seem fair to you? Orianna, does that seem fair?"

Orianna heard her name and looked up at me. Then she looked back down at her nails, enjoying the fact that it was a Friday rush down at the desk and she wasn't hustling keys.

"Tom, you need to improve your attitude at the desk. You have to make every single guest happy. We feel that you are just cruising along, not going 'above and beyond,' not even paying attention. You are cold at the desk. Uninterested. Curt. In short: rude. If you cannot do your job properly, it will be *our pleasure* to fire *you* and find someone who will."

And then it happened: I felt as if this woman grabbed my heart and rope-burned it, squeezed its pulpy flesh until blood, hot angry blood, flooded my face and my stomach and pushed the burning lava right to the tips of my fingers. I mean, I guess that's why my hands were shaking.

I slowly pulled out a stack of letters from my inner suit coat pocket. I had this plan to prove to her how well I actually do my job. On top was a letter I'd received yesterday from a guest I'd helped last month. And I remember him.

He had checked in early, alone, and wanted to get upstairs as soon as possible.

"Please," he said, "my girlfriend is taking a cab from JFK, and I want to prepare the room. I'm going to propose."

I hear this *a lot*. And honestly, it is super pleasant to deal with. The man will be all nervous and happy and tell me the situation while his soon-to-be-fiancée is helping the doorman get the bags from the car. Then she'll come inside and be all smiles because maybe she knows but probably she doesn't, and sometimes there will be notes prewritten on the res that say, "DO NOT UNBLOCK!! Special room for guest who

is proposing. DO NOT MENTION PRO-
POSAL, EITHER." You actually have to put
that last line in there because, frankly,
people are morons. I was witness to a co-
worker once reading just the "do not unblock — *proposal*" message, and she smiled
and said, "Oh my, congratulations you two!"
and the woman was confused and the man
tried to wipe the anger off his face and play
it off. Then the woman started to pick up
on it. It was pretty fucked-up.

But this guy wanted to get in early and
prep the room. "Certainly, sir. I've got
something wonderful. It's a big upgrade,
but I'll take care of the difference in price."
Okay, you got me: I'm hustling just a tiny
bit here. I am going to give it to him anyway,
so what's the harm in mentioning the price
difference? He might be feeling generous!
"So just let me free the room up. How
about you ask her with a view of Central
Park as the backdrop?" Earlier that day I'd
checked out our Central Park views. It was
fall, and the park was gorgeous, the reds
and yellows of turning foliage spreading
warmly against the long wall of Upper East
Side buildings.

"Well, here is the thing. Can I trust you?"

"I am a front desk agent, Mr. Blanchard.
You're goddamn right you can trust me."

"I need your help, then. I am going to propose *in* Central Park. I plan on taking her up to the room for a bit and settling in. I hired a photographer, and if you want to help, I'll give him your name, and he'll introduce himself. When you see us come back through the lobby, make certain the photographer sees us, and if he *doesn't,* signal him to follow us."

"This is extremely covert, sir, and frankly I am all about it."

"You see, the photographer is going to follow us and secretly take pictures when I drop my knee in the dirt. Then, on our wedding day, I'm going to give her the photos she doesn't even know were taken."

"Well, damn. That is. That is borderline . . . you know, what with the photographer in the bushes and all? But when I picture the wedding present on wedding day, it's amazing. I am your man, sir."

And that is exactly what I did. I like to think the photographer would have missed them if I hadn't been there to flail around like a maniac when the couple passed through. And after I saw the soon-to-be-groom's gigantic smile on the way back in and the woman's eyes glued to her diamond ring, I sent them wine and a personal note.

Yesterday I got a letter from him. It said

he'll never forget me. It said the Bellevue is their New York hotel for life. It said they've decided to have the honeymoon here.

Beneath that letter is one from Mr. Palay. He's the big hitter we hustled into becoming a frequent-stay guest. The letter, which came out of nowhere and included, um, a fat-ass personal check with my name on it, said he has never experienced service of this caliber before. The fact that I have given him my personal e-mail and I respond even when I'm not at work (I've helped him while I was drunk at a bar before) has convinced him my hotel is the place for his next group block. Turns out he's the president of a huge investment firm and the group totals more than 150 rooms. That's over seventy-five thousand dollars in revenue. In one night. He sent a second letter to my GM explaining the excellent service I provide, mentioning our e-mail correspondence and my twenty-four-hour service. Mr. Tremblay told the FOM to tell the assistant FOM to tell the manager on duty to tell *me* that I was no longer allowed to give out my personal e-mail to guests. Apparently, that was inappropriate. At seventy-five thousand dollars, how inappropriate can that be?

Weren't these people all about money? Was it *possible* to please them?

Another is a letter from the Bekkers. The letter where they offer to house me in their mansion while assisting me in finding adequate lodgings. The one where they thank me again for making their wedding so special and giving them a home in New York. The one where they say, again, that I should get on a plane, fly into Cape Town, and be taken care of. I received that letter a while ago but still kept it in my pocket. I really liked that letter.

All of these little pieces of proof were now in my shaking, angry hand. Sara was looking calmly at me, one hand flat on her thigh, the other softly resting on my write-up; that current write-up, plus one more, and they could fire me. Maybe Tremblay had offered a trophy for the manager who finally succeeded in terminating me. (What would that trophy look like? I wondered. A gold figure of me with a boot up my ass, probably.)

Clearly, they really, really did not want me here. But, damn it, I love this hotel. The Bellevue is my home. I love the Bellevue. I loved what it had been. It had changed now, and I was having trouble accepting that.

I'm not proud of it, but at that time, in that moment, I felt I had one move left. Apparently, that move was to snap. So I snapped.

"You want to fire me for poor service? I don't GIVE poor service. And if you need proof, read these," I said, pretty goddamn loudly, and then tossed the letters into the air.

Considering the consequences of this action, I remember it in slow motion: the letters slowly twisting in varied trajectories, unfurling, arranging themselves high in the air like leaves on an invisible tree, and then slowly, slowly falling down on all of us.

The beginning of the end.

I know I'm to blame. Because this is the goddamn hotel business. You either strap it on hard or, if you can't handle it, go wait tables. I flashed back to the image of Keith and Walter, those two valets, flopping around on the concrete, screaming, trying to choke each other to *death.* Maybe those cats had been running cars for two decades, and they'd had enough. I recalled Chip, drop-kicking those two shiny quarters, and I saw his image clearly in my mind now, specifically recalling the face he made while he executed the kick: It was furious. It was determined. It was psychotic. And behind that, it was filled with so much sadness.

Now I understood. Maybe I'd had enough.

CHAPTER SIXTEEN

I gave myself another long weekend. Even after my two days off, I called in sick Monday and Tuesday. I needed the time. I really, really needed the time. It was like self-prescribed mental leave.

I dialed Julie, whom I'd been out of touch with for a month, and she invited me out to dinner. We dined on caviar, scooping it into our mouths with tiny spoons, and drank seventeen-dollar cocktails that arrived in whatever color you wanted. I chose blue.

"Stop slumping."

"I'm depressed."

"Well, drink more, then, baby. Get another. A happier color. Get orange maybe. Orange is a power color."

"Orange? Okay."

"So you hate your job, Thomas. Be comforted by the universal truth that everyone hates their job. Or, you can change it. Get a new one."

Finding another hotel gig in New York made no sense. Beyond the fact that I would be forced back onto the overnights, I wouldn't be able to pay my rent after dropping back down to starting pay. A few years ago, feeling financially stable, I moved farther out into Brooklyn, deep into an area called Bushwick, where I could afford to live alone. Having my own apartment improved my life but doubled my rent. It was either stay at the Bellevue or clear out of the city altogether.

"Why don't we move to L.A. together, Julie?"

She set her cocktail down carefully on a napkin. Hers was yellow. It looked like urine. I wondered if urine was a power color too.

"Nonsense," she said quietly.

We'd discussed it in the past, moving away together. She could easily find work out there, and you know me: if there's a hotel, then pass me the drug-test piss cup because I start tomorrow.

"You think it's nonsense?"

"It is, Thomas." She still called me Thomas because, in a way, she was still a hotel guest. "That doesn't mean it's not a possibility, though. You know we could make each other perfectly happy."

Here I was, expecting a guest to take me away, to pay for my life. Ben the bellman, as always, had offered some sound advice on this flawed plan: "You fucking moron. Never get involved with a hotel guest. Bang 'em on the minibar, but leave it there. You'll never be on their level. Get you a nice Russian housekeeper. Russian housekeepers, Tommy, now, they know how to love."

I drank a whole rainbow that night.

Soon enough it was the following Friday, a week after the tree of letters shed its leaves down on everyone. During the intervening shifts I'd been extremely timid, almost *over* servicing the guests, earnestly trying to make up for my previous week's deficiencies. I also, in an effort to avoid confrontation with anyone about anything, handed out breakfast certificates like they were free samples.

As if stuck in a repeating pattern, I was informed that my presence was required in HR, again on a Friday after my shift, when I should be walking out of the building. I wasn't worried: I assumed Sara wanted to finish what she started last week in the company of HR, since, if I recall, I had walked out without giving her a chance to ask me to sign the write-up. Which I wouldn't have signed anyway, because we all know the union rule about not signing anything but your check. The delegate does sign it as a "witness." But we hadn't even gotten to that point.

I walked to the back office to get Orianna and bring her down there with me.

"They're calling me down to HR. What's up, you think?"

Orianna was concentrating hard on the computer screen. I should have sensed something was horribly wrong. She never concentrates hard on anything.

"Orianna?"

"I'm not involved anymore. There is a delegate down there for you," she said, picking up the phone receiver, though there was no incoming call.

"What's going on here?" I said, actually out loud, before turning and walking back through the lobby. I found Jay, the union delegate for the bellmen and doormen, and ran my situation by him. He's got the perfect kind of psycho-terror for a delegate.

"Yeah, Orianna's stepping down as delegate," he said.

"Now? She witnessed the whole thing, and she steps down now?"

"It doesn't look good for you, chief."

Downstairs I was introduced to Teo, a union delegate from housekeeping whom I had never, ever seen before: not in the halls, not in the locker room, not in the cafeteria, nowhere. One thing was clear: he didn't speak much English. But, whatever, let's get this over with, I thought. Just take my write-up and move on with my shitty little life.

The director of HR was leading the witness. She kept saying, "And then?" which made it clear to me she was hoping to fast-forward directly to the letter-throwing incident. I certainly wasn't falling for that. So I continued on my slow path, explaining the certificate policy calmly, going over all the reasons I was being punished for doing my job properly. Teo, my delegate, was struggling to keep up. It wasn't just the language barrier; there was a lot of front desk minutiae here, a lot of little policies and rules that are nowhere near his expertise. That's why you're supposed to get a delegate from your department, someone who knows what the hell you're going on about. I don't even think the director of HR was following it all.

It seemed so tedious to me, all of it.

Somehow, while continuing to explain my side of the situation, I figured out what happened with Orianna. Her husband had been walking down Queens Boulevard when a car driving down the road paddled him with the passenger side door. Which was fully opened, like a wing. I can't imagine why something like this would happen. *You* try to figure it out. No serious damage to the husband, he was out of the hospital two days later, but Orianna took advantage of the situation, as any union member would, and secured two months' Family Medical Leave to help her loved ones through this emotionally devastating incident. It was the end of the summer, so she went to the Dominican Republic, as you might do after a vehicular paddling. Last Friday marked her first day back after the two months off, the day I snapped. She came back tan, happy, relaxed, and unprepared to be thrown back into the cage-match environment of the hotel. She still had sand in her toes, and me getting loud and throwing shit was too much. Plus, she had all the seniority she needed to avoid a layoff, which was one of her initial reasons for seeking the position. So she stepped down as delegate. I was considering this fact, realizing how bad this really was for me: my union delegate stepping down implies my guilt and leaves me without a witness, without a defense.

Orianna could have said, "No, Tom never threw anything. Maybe he *tossed* them onto the table but certainly never meant to hurt anyone, and he never *threw* anything, not that I saw." Then I could say, "What she said," making it two against one, and we would walk out unscathed. I might have bought Orianna a bottle of Brugal for her trouble.

"We have testimony that you threw objects at her face."

"At her *face*? I never threw anything at her face, I —"

"Stop. Thomas, listen . . ."

Just then I was thinking: Why isn't Sara here?

The director of human resources cleared her throat. "We have decided to terminate your employment here at the hotel."

Teo heard that shit. He said, *"Ess yuse me?"*

"I'm fired?"

"Yes, Thomas, we have decided to terminate your employment. Effective immediately."

There followed a long, long silence during which all the blood in my body sank to my feet and started pooling up, filling my legs like a pitcher, leaving my face dead white.

"I've never been fired before. What do I do?"

I really sounded, and felt, like a lost little

boy at that moment.

"Get your things, turn in your bank, and leave the property."

That sounded easy. It seemed as if that's all there was to it; get your shit and go. Things went white for a while as I sat there, Teo staring at me as if we all just found out I had cancer. He looked as if he didn't even want to touch me.

Soon enough, I was helped to my feet by Mike, a big, aggressive security agent.

"Let's go, Tom. You gotta get your stuff and go."

"Am I really terminated? Can I tell people?"

"No, just get your stuff and go. Quietly."

Fuck that. I walked through the lobby with big bad Mike's hand on my elbow, telling everyone, bellmen, doormen, concierge, and guests alike. "I GOT FIRED. MY EM-PLOYMENT HAS BEEN TERMI-NATED. THEY FIRED ME."

And the strange part about it? Everyone thought I was joking. They were all smiling at me, shaking their heads like, "Oh, Tommy. He's so funny."

I told Ben in the back office while cleaning out my mailbox.

"Fired, huh? I get it. Cleaning out your mailbox, right? Your mother."

Twenty minutes later I was pushed out the back employee entrance. They had provided me with two guest laundry bags to shove all my shit in. Almost a decade's worth of detritus: letters, photographs, pins and pens, a book about Bob Dylan the Gray Wolf tried to force me to read, deodorant, a bunch of socks — a life's worth of what now looked distinctly like *garbage* stuffed into two hotel laundry bags.

It was Friday, 5:30 p.m. Happy hour.

I dragged the bags across the street to a bar on Ninth Avenue. I had passed this stupid-looking bar before and after every single shift I had ever worked at the Bellevue and never once stepped inside. We certainly drank in the area but never here because this place was for tourists. But that's where I went. Maybe because it was closest; that was definitely one alluring factor about it that afternoon. Maybe I went there because I knew, without a doubt, I wouldn't run into any co-workers. It was filled with tourists and strangers, a new environment. I took a stool at the bar, right across from the hotel, a nice view directly into the lobby, set a laundry bag on either side of the stool, and ordered a shot of tequila and a beer. Fuck me.

One tequila in me and half the beer to

wash it down. That was step one. I had to accomplish step one before even beginning step two, which was to order another round and drink that. Step three was to start thinking again, to start processing. My whole life was shifting, like a fortress coming down into the ocean, everything was sliding and cracking open, and the noise and movement was tremendous, deafening. There was a lot of dust. I poured another shot and another beer onto the dust and waited for the whole mess to slide into the ocean so I could sit in silence and figure out something, anything, get a fresh look at the new landscape.

On one side my heart grew strangely light. I thought about the depravity, the hustling, the utter childishness of the hotel, the managers, the fighting, the faxes. I was free from having to raise my hand to go to the bathroom, free from whispering to hookers and trophy wives, free from guests coming down with Ziploc bags, claiming they found a bedbug, though the only thing in the bag was a sunflower seed shell. I no longer had to wear a name tag. My name tag was somewhere at the bottom of a laundry bag. Garbage. Buried garbage.

On the other hand, despite happy hour, right off Times Square a shot and a beer came to fourteen dollars, and I'd failed to hustle any cash that Friday. I only had a five-dollar bill in my wallet. My cash-hustling days were *done.* I brought out my debit card and, shamefully, started a tab.

That was the first real ramification: some-one had poked a hole in my money balloon. It was no longer filling; it was now hissing, shrinking, floating back down to earth.

But I had plenty of escape money.

In a way, I'd mastered New York City, come here with nothing and had my way with the city, that nasty, thieving whore: I had stolen thousands from her tiny whore purse, and now it was time to move on.

I thought about Julie and Los Angeles. I thought about the Bekkers and their villa in Cape Town. I thought about Julie in Cape Town.

If I recall correctly, I hadn't wanted this job to begin with, right? Now I was forced to make a change, a good change. I had had five beers and five shots, and you know what? I felt *pretty damn good.* I brought out my phone and put it next to my beer, perhaps to browse for international flights. Maybe I was just drunk (I was absolutely drunk), but I couldn't help thinking: Even in this cold, touristy, expensive bar the sun was shining on me. Summer may be dying here in New York, and snow was on the way, but halfway across the world, on another continent, spring was approaching. Everything good was making preparations to bloom.

"WELCOME TO THE FRONT DESK: CHECKING OUT?"

Did I make it out? Am I writing this on a mosquito-netted porch while a thick red sun sets over Africa, a book on the table next to me, its pages shifting gently in the warm, fragrant jungle breeze? Sorry, dear guests. I'm in Bushwick, Brooklyn. I'm wearing a name tag while typing. I'm gonna be thirty minutes late for my morning shift.

Again, it was that damn yellow union card. All weekend, once the news circulated that I'd been fired, my phone exploded with texts and voice mails from co-workers. About 95 percent of them were total insincere horseshit. You see, I'd been holding down my seniority for years, and at the time of my firing I was almost at the very top. That gave me weekends off. That gave me Christmas off. And *that* gave me a huge target on my back from everyone below me who figured, as a single white male with zero children, I didn't deserve a goddamn *thing,* especially not Christmas off. When the news hit that the number three in seniority was gone, everyone flocked to the back office to look at the schedule, ready to pick apart my shifts like vultures, ripping at the fleshy Sundays off and screeching and pecking at my morning shifts. They called their husbands and said something wonderful had happened. Then they called me and said they couldn't believe something so terrible had happened.

But those were just the desk people. The bellmen and doormen were, if I may say, pretty unhappy about the turn of events. Some of the sentiment was based on honest friendship. But most of it was due to the fact that I was efficient and I earned for them. While other agents would take fifteen minutes for a simple check-in, irritating the guests in line, which, in turn, directly affected the size of a tip, I was handing out fronts and ushering in guests like a traffic cop, just running them through with a wave of my arm like, "Go, go, go!"

In fact, one voice mail, one of the greatest of my life, came from Mario the doorman an hour after I was fired and went pretty much like this, but, you know, in a grimy Italian New York accent: "You see what happens? You see what happens when you take twenty bucks from me? You little fuck, you. Don't worry about a thing. My boys at the union will have you back on Tuesday, kid. And don't get too whacked-out over the weekend, you little fuck, you."

Okay, so that was maybe the sweetest voice mail I'd ever received. If you don't understand at all why that voice mail is sweet, then perhaps, in a certain way, I have failed in these pages.

The comment about the twenty I allegedly took from him concerned an event that occurred a week prior to the letter incident. A rock band, as they are known to do, tipped out Mario $500 Bennys in cash, as opposed to charging it to an account where it gets taxed (imagine how much they hate *that*). It was then Mario's responsibility to divide up the cash among the bell and door staff working. He spread the hundreds out to the three working desk agents to break down and came back later to collect the twenties for the boys, just grabbing the stacks and heading back outside. As he passed them out, getting rid of more and more bills and getting it down to just his share, he found that after he paid out the last bellman, his own cut was twenty short. The math hadn't worked. First thing he did was hit up all the bellmen and doormen and see if he overpaid. He didn't. Then he came to the desk and stared us all down. One of us, he thought, shorted him on the change. How did he decide it was me? That was part of the joke. He knew I was the *only one* who would *never* cheat him.

Mario had even run tests on me during my first year. A bellman is *supposed* to be in the lobby, hence when he passes you a stack to turn into a brick he can, and certainly will, loom over you and supervise the count. Conversely, a doorman, with his big coat and silly hat, isn't really supposed to be loitering in the lobby. He's an outdoor creature. So when he wants a stack converted, he has to leave it with me and come back later to pick up the dirty dancer. The first time Mario handed me a stack to convert, my count was $105. I handed him back a brick and a fiver, and he said, "Oh, shit. Must have counted wrong." No problem, I said. Two weeks later he handed me $102 and then the next month $105 again. I always, always returned the overage and thought to myself: "This dude can't count for shit." I would never have known what he was doing if it hadn't been for the first time he handed me an even $100 and when I passed him back a crisp slice he looked me in the eye and said, "You're a good kid." All of those off counts had been a test.

So Mario knew I would never steal from him, and he chose to joke out his anger on me because all the other desk agents would take him to HR for even accusing them of stealing and then, on top of *that,* point out to HR that breaking those bills isn't a desk agent's job and his choosing to put us in that position depleted our banks and made it difficult to provide change for the customers when that's actually why we have the banks and . . . blah blah blah *bullshit.* You see how exhausting it was just reading that? Imagine a tough-ass Italian New Yorker having to sit through that childish tantrum in HR. It was just easier for him to spend the next week saying, "Tommy, you shitty little thief. I need my twenty by sundown, or I'll break your shitty little legs."

"And don't get too whacked-out over the weekend, you little fuck, you."

I failed to take his advice on that one. Those happy hour drinks propelled me back to Brooklyn, to drop off my life garbage, and then right back out the door. I suppose the Mafia tones present in his voice mail put me in the mood to walk into a Mafia bar, one close to my apartment that I'd always wanted to enter but never entered because it looks like the place they will kill you for entering. But I was drunk, so I did it.

Yeah, it was uncomfortable for the first few drinks, but since I was tipping more than properly, the bartender came over and asked me about my Friday. I said I'd been fired. He said he was real sorry, kid. I said I was a dues-paying union member.

That he liked. He said, "No shit? Well, friend, sorry about your troubles. Here's a whiskey on me, and let me know if you want to blast off, okay, friend?"

"I will, thank you," I said, taking down the whiskey. As far as "blasting off," I didn't know what the hell he was talking about.

Two more rounds and he came back and put something beside my beer. A tiny baggy. A tiny baggy filled with white powder.

Now, I know. I *know*. Never touched the stuff. Ever. Been surrounded by it plenty of times. In fact, I sat in the very back of the historic Ziegfeld Theatre in midtown with a few bellmen, watching a special screening of the New York classic *Saturday Night Fever*, and while everyone else got skied up, rubbing their noses and laughing their asses off, I just stuck to the bottle of vodka we were passing around. I had too much to lose then.

Now I had nothing to lose. I sent out a

call to Julie but, sadly, I hadn't heard a word. So I pushed back my stool and went to the bathroom.

Blast off.

Thirty-one years old and doing key bumps of coke for the first time, alone, in a Mafia bathroom. I would have done it off my hotel bank key, for style, but I had turned that in along with my bank and everything else that symbolized my entire New York life up to that point.

I looked at myself in the mirror, lowering my apartment key from my face. Even for this, *for this,* I blame the goddamn hotel business.

Next day I felt, well, horrible. My phone kept ringing with false condolences, and I wasn't picking up. I wasn't responding to anyone. The plan was currently to sit in my apartment alone and be alone and stay alone and then, way later, figure something out. Maybe in like two weeks.

"My boys at the union will have you back on Tuesday, kid."

The union didn't even wait past Monday to ruin my current plan of hiding from life. How? By fighting for my job. A union rep called me at home that Monday, where I sat wearing pajamas and a New Orleans Saints winter hat, listlessly researching Cape Town, and drinking Heineken for breakfast. I learned, squinting at the phone, that apparently I already had an appointment. I was to meet my business rep at the Bellevue, in human resources, 9:00 a.m. tomorrow. Tuesday.

The case against me turned out to be weak. First of all, my delegate stepping down, which I assumed to be a terrible turn of events, ended up altering the characters involved and turning the scene into a "he said, she said" case with no third-party witnesses. Anything that happened or didn't happen was all opinion without the corroboration of my delegate, the only other party in the room. And Orianna had refused to put her statement in writing. Good girl. Good union girl.

She *had* given verbal testimony, however. Bad girl. *Bad union girl.* But when my business rep noticed that management had handwritten her verbal testimony to make it look like written testimony, it was thrown out immediately. Suspiciously, Sara and my delegate's testimony had the same handwriting. Management had in fact put words in my delegate's mouth, incriminating words that were now unsubstantiated. Without a valid testimony they didn't have a case at all.

And just like that the gods in hell fired me another name tag.

With a few stipulations.

Clearly, as far as expressions of anger or frustration, it's a zero-tolerance situation: if I drop a pen at the desk, I better have a witness willing to testify I didn't hurl it in a rage. Further, and here is where it gets really, absurdly good, human resources threw in six months of mandatory Anger Management Group Therapy. Every Tuesday, an hour a week, for half a goddamn year, plus two private counseling sessions a month. Not to mention a general psych evaluation, which I passed with flying colors, thank you very much. They also tacked on a three-week unpaid suspension, trying to starve me out. Those three weeks were like an extended mental leave for me and, coincidentally, gave me the time to embark on this project it seems you might be enjoying, since we are quickly coming to the end.

Anger Management Group Therapy? I need *Heads in Beds II* to cover all of that.

Surprisingly, no complaints from me. You know how much a movie ticket costs in Manhattan? AMGT, that's my Emmy-winning television. The class comprised union hotel workers, only my hotel-motel-trade-union people, half of whom are in "job jeopardy," as I am, and the other half of whom are in what you might call "life jeopardy." Imagine me telling my letter-tosser story a semicircle away from the carpet cleaner who just told *his* story of . . . well, you probably couldn't even imagine. But trust me, it is *not boring.*

So this is me now, head lowered, all "yes, sir" and "no, sir," just like McMurphy in the final pages of Ken Kesey's *One Flew over the Cuckoo's Nest,* minus the friendly Native American willing to hold a pillow over my face until I stop kicking.

I float into work, friendless (my co-workers took me for terminated and had already come to expect my better shifts and holidays off; therefore, my return was unwanted. I can't really blame them for despising me, I guess). I drift into group therapy every week, where my AMGT attendance senior-ity has now garnered me some respect and the group accepts me.

Do I have increased motivation to perform with excellence at the desk? Yeah, *no.* Don't think so. My main focus is simple: *Don't get fired.*

Dead man clocking in, dead man clocking out.

Oh, hotels.

You made me a whore and then beat me for whorishness. And I cannot seem to leave the business. As I said, the reason any ho stays a ho: it takes a serious motherfucker to turn off a money valve.

And unions will not protect our pride; that we must defend on our own.

Those who *do not have* will always serve *those who do.*

Hotel employees: I did this for us.

And you, dear, sweet guests: See you at the reception desk.

(Try not to give me a hard time, okay? I got fuckin' anger issues.)

■ ■ ■ ■

APPENDIXES

■ ■ ■ ■

THINGS A GUEST SHOULD NEVER SAY

"My credit card declined? That's impossible. Run it again."

Man, don't make me run it again. If your CC declines *once,* it will, without question, decline *again.* Your card is not a crumpled old dollar, and the banking system is not a stubborn vending machine. That's not how the banking system works. You need to call your bank.

And, no, you can't use my phone.

"They told me I should ask for an upgrade."

Who the fuck is they? Oh, *they.* Well, *they* told *me* to remind *you* to tip the doorman.

"Don't you remember me?"

Let me think about this . . . average of five hundred guest interactions a day . . . it's been two years since you stayed with us. So that's a clean *quarter of a million* separate interactions between now and your last stay.

Wait . . . Wait! No. No, I don't remember
you.

*"Do I really have to show my ID? Ugh, I just
checked in an hour ago. It's not my fault you
weren't here."*
Anger rising. Need to attend Anger Management Group Therapy. How about you
*just hand over the goddamn ID anytime
anyone in the world whose job it is to ask for
an ID asks for an ID.*

THINGS A GUEST SHOULD
NEVER DO

Do not continue your phone conversation during the entire check-in.

Can you imagine how it feels, as a human, to be part of someone else's effort to multitask? While you say to the phone, "Uh-huh. Yeah. Yeah, well, I told her they wouldn't go for it. I know these people," I get the lift of an eyebrow, side-glances, brief and uninterested head nods thrown in my direction indicating your main focus remains on your call, perhaps a moment where you hold the phone slightly away from your ear to benevolently allow me 5 percent of your attention. That call will end in five minutes. But because you treated me like an automatic check-in machine, this room I'm giving you will plague your whole stay. And also I key bombed you.

Do not snap the credit card down on my desk.

You know this one, where you press the

card down with your thumb and use your index finger to bend the front corner of the card up and then release it so it *snaps* authoritatively and loudly on my desk? You just made me hate you!

Do not try to describe someone without ethnicity when ethnicity could be key.

"I gave my claim check to a bellman, and he never came back." "What's he look like, so I can go find him?" "Well . . . he was kind of tall. Not too tall. He . . . I don't know, I don't think he had facial hair. Maybe mid-thirties. I mean, he was dressed like a bellman, but I guess that doesn't help. Um, well, he was . . . about as tall as you?" "Ma'am, was he white, black, Asian?" "Oh, well, Asian." "Okay, that was Jeremy. I'll go find out what happened."

Do not make me use your cell phone.

Sometimes it's necessary. Sometimes the person on your phone has the CC info I need or the confirmation number. I just don't want to use your cell phone. But I guess I have to, so, here, give it to me.

Do not bring up the beautiful weather to people stuck inside at work all day.

That's just one tough side effect of working in a business that accommodates people on vacation. Vacationers, God bless them, sometimes forget that the whole world isn't on vacation too. "Oh. My. *GOD!!* It is so *gorgeous* in Central Park right now!! Look at it out there!! Just look at it!!" Are you fucking with me? Look at it? Just look at it? You must be aware that *all I can do is look at it,* just stare out the lobby doors, and wish to high hell I wasn't working. Next time I have a vacation I'm going to come to your office and rub it all over your face.

Do not ask your husband to ask me something when I can hear you asking him to ask me because I am standing right here.

This one kills me. "Oh, honey, ask him for extra towels." Usually, the husband will just turn to me and raise an eyebrow. If I'm feeling slightly confrontational (or froggy, as they sometimes say in New York), I will just stare back at him. I'll make him do it. Come on, honey, ask me.

Do not hold out your hand for the change you're waiting on.

You know, when I am still counting it out but your hand is there, in front of me, floating in the air, waiting while I count, empty, implying impatience, and uselessly reasserting the fact that the money I am counting belongs to you. Relax, buddy. It's coming. You look like a five-year-old with your hand out like that.

THINGS EVERY GUEST
MUST KNOW

You don't have to pay for the in-room movies either!

Even those of you who shook your heads and blushed when I offered up the minibar might find yourselves morally creative enough to steal a movie. Simply because, whereas the minibar items must be replaced, causing a loss in revenue, for the in-room movie service the hotel usually pays a flat subscription fee, meaning there is no loss of product, no item that needs replacing. Watching a movie and claiming you never watched a movie has no negative effect on the hotel's revenue stream. It just doesn't have a positive one. So stop blushing, and we'll take it in three steps:

1. Watch and enjoy any movie (*any* movie).
2. Call down and say you accidentally clicked on it. Or it cut off in the middle. Or

froze near the end. Or never even started. Would you like them to restart the movie for you? No thanks. You need to go to bed/leave now. Just remove the charge, please.

3. Order another movie, and this time hit up the minibar as if it were an unmanned concession stand!

How to Avoid a Same-Day Cancellation Penalty.

First of all, this little move will not work with anything prepaid online, only "natural" reservations, booked through any channel as long as it's not *prepaid.*

Let us assume, for whatever reason, it's 10:00 p.m. and you have a reservation for this evening. However, you will not be making it in. At all. Should you resign yourself to the fact that you will be charged a no-show fee? Should you erase all memory of the reservation and blissfully hope that no-show fees are *not real* and your credit card will not be charged a full night's room and tax?

The fee is very real. And it charges automatically.

So do this: Call the property directly and ask for the front desk.

"Good evening, thank you for calling the

front desk, my name is Doesn't Matter, how can I assist you?"

"Excuse me, are you the manager?"

If the person says yes, hang up and call back. What we want here is certainly *not* the manager.

"No, I am not. Would you like to speak to the manager?"

"No, actually, I just have a quick request. I think you can help me. Well, I was supposed to fly in late tonight, but my twelve-year-old daughter is sick —"

Let me stop you right there, dear guest. Sure, you need a reason, but what you don't need is a forty-five-minute story. Remember, it's *me* on the other end of that line: I've got about ten minutes left in my double shift, and I've been standing up for thirteen hours straight. Try again.

"No, actually, I just have a quick request. I think you can help me. I've had a personal emergency and won't be able to check in tonight; HOWEVER, I have already re-scheduled my meeting for next week. Do you think you could just shift tonight's reservation to next Friday without a penalty?"

"Sure. Next Friday, the twenty-fourth, all set. Same confirmation number. See you then."

"Thank you."

Done. Now you have a reservation all set for next Friday! Why is that good? Well, tomorrow, whenever you get around to it, call the hotel back (this time no need to inquire about a manager), and just tell the front desk you want to cancel your reservation for next Friday, as you are well within your rights to do. No problem. Fee avoided.

Just in case: When you're pushing the reservation forward, if the front desk agent gets a little uptight on you, a little "unfortunately, the policy is" on you, then it's time for plan C. The *C* stands for "cash." But don't worry, I am not suggesting you spend money to save money. As Steven Seagal said in *Hard to Kill:* "Anticipation of death is worse than death itself." Well, in this case it goes: "Anticipation of getting tipped is worth as much as the tip itself." So get strong inside and say something like, "Listen, I know you have to follow policy and I know you're not interested in my story [*it's nice to hear a guest try to understand our position, it softens us up*], but if you could just move this reservation until next Friday, I promise I'll take care of you when I check in." In this situation, worst-case scenario, the agent says sorry, but no. But most of us will take even the *promise* of a tip. As Wayne

406

Gretzky said (he's an excellent tipper by the way): "You miss 100 percent of the shots you don't take." Or, for a desk agent: "You don't make 100 percent of the tips you don't line up." Me? I'd go for it, maybe hope to have a little cash from you next Friday, go buy some socks with it or something. And when Friday rolls around and I check your reservation and find it dot dot dot. Canceled. Oh, man. I just got Steven Seagaled. You're so slick you must have a ponytail. Which is gross.

If you are going to complain, if you must complain, then, please, eat a mint.
That's it. Self-explanatory. You catch more bees with honey than with garbage. Well, bees love garbage. Damn. Whatever . . . just eat a mint.

I don't want to hear your tragic airline-delay story.
I don't.
At all.

In my opinion, though people are forced to wear name tags, you should never feel comfortable enough to actually call them by their names.
Gluing a name tag to anyone's chest

makes him or her subordinate. Using it without permission implies that you are aware of this fact and, shit, don't mind rudely pointing it out. To pick the name off a tag and use it, whatever your intention, makes employees acutely feel they have lost their personal worth, that they themselves are included in the price. Their mothers use that name on a birthday to ask, "Personal Name, did you get everything you wanted, baby?" What right do you have to use it? Just because you walked into the lobby? My advice is to ask for permission. "Jake . . . may I call you Jake?" Yes, you may. And thank you.

Three ways to turn down a bellman that make you look like a prick

1. *"I'm balanced."* This one is *mythic.* Bell-men bring up this phrase with wrath, disgust all over their faces, yet for years I never actually heard it uttered. But bell-men swear it's said. A guest comes in with bags draped over left and right shoulder, maybe a backpack strapped on tight, a shopping bag hanging from left hand, right hand gripping a roller bag with a carry-on stacked on top. Quite a bit going on. For a few dollars he can lay down his burden and let a nice, hardworking man roll it

comfortably to the room. But upon hearing the offer, the guest turns and says: "No, I'm balanced." For some reason this concept drives bellmen bananas! And then, one winter morning in 2009, I finally heard a guest say it: "I'm balanced." You're balanced? I'm pretty sure you are actually overloaded. And, maybe, a prick.

2. *"I don't want to bother them."* This one was also covered in the book proper (p. 184). Again, these people are trying to make a living. If a stripper writhes over and starts to dance in front of you and you stand up and walk away with your stack of ones, saying, "I don't want to bother her," you sound ignorant of the world and, coincidentally, sort of like a prick.

3. *"I know how to get there."* That is not the main function of a bellman, sweet guest. We are not offering you a GPS. Even ten-year-olds "know how to get there." We are offering you a service. This is about luxury. You sound, again, ignorant of the world. You sound, without a doubt, like a prick.

FYA — FINDING YOUR AGENT

Not all front desk agents are created equally. I've spoken of the power, the power of the crinkly handshake. But I myself have dropped a bill or two on an agent and walked away with nothing from him or her except a nervous smile. And that's fine for me: I'm a desk agent and happy to tip my people just for being my people. But some of you animals expect your money to work for you. Here are a few tips to ensure that it will.

If you haven't already called the property directly and found someone competent to work with, then size up the options upon arrival. No one says you have to fly into the lobby and select the first agent who smiles at you. Hang back. Suss it out. Pretend you need to check your cell phone or something. What are we looking for in our agent? Someone who is efficient and not at all nervous, almost bored. If the agent is overly zealous or nervous, he or she might have just begun working at the property and hence is less capable. Not only does the agent have to be comfortable playing the game; the agent must know the property and system well enough to play it properly. If I see an agent running through check-ins efficiently, I will queue up in that line even if I have to wait. If another, weaker agent says, "I can help you over here, sir," I'll just say: "No thank you. He's helped me before, and I don't mind waiting." Wait for the agent you selected. Don't let social pressure turn you into a coward. Don't let your cowardice put you into a bad room.

Tip UP FRONT. Let the agents know you are serious immediately. I once had a guest talk game the whole check-in: "I'll take care of you. Don't worry. I appreciate your help." In my head I was thinking: "You can't hustle a hustler" (50 Cent). Assuming he was actually going to stiff me, I did exactly nothing. ("I peeped it and slid." — 50 Cent again.) Then, once the keys hit his palm, his wallet came out, and as he walked off, he dropped a baby brick on my terminal. Then, experiencing a moral low point in my life, I said, "Wait! Sir! Hold on, please. Um . . . let me just get those keys back . . . Right. Yeah, you know, I didn't think this other room was available, but it just came up. It's even better." Then I actually *did* upgrade him, slyly hiding the fact I thought he was full of shit and thus had done nothing to help him. So: tip UP FRONT.

At this point here is how I do it: I walk up, smile without showing teeth, give the agent my CC, drop a twenty on the desk, and say, "This is for you. Whatever you can do for me, I'd appreciate it." Boom. If I am after something specific, I will include that as well: "This is for you. Whatever you can do for me, I'd appreciate it: late checkout, wine, whatever."

Finally, if you happen to have a successful experience, then make a point to memorize the agent's name. Jot it down. Damn shame if you ever come back or even if the next day something happens and you need a late checkout, yet you can't recall the name or even describe the person who now, in a way, works for you and would love to help.

STANDARD LIES THAT SPEW FROM THE MOUTH OF A FRONT DESK AGENT

1. All the rooms are basically the same size.
2. Of course I remember you! Welcome back!
3. There is nothing I can do.
4. I appreciate your feedback.
5. I'm sorry the bellman made you uncomfortable. I will certainly alert management.
6. I didn't *mean* to sound insulting.
7. I will mail this immediately.
8. My pleasure.
9. I would like to offer my deepest apologies.
10. We hope to see you again!

BRIEF GUEST SURVEY

1. How would you describe your front desk agent?
   A. Uninterested.
   B. Curt.
   C. Profane.
   D. Rude to your wife.

2. How would you describe your bellman?
   A. Slightly terrifying.
   B. Like being trapped in an elevator with an animal that feeds on money.
   C. Uninterested, curt, profane, *and* rude to your wife.
   D. Bellman? I'm way too cheap to take help. I told him to *fuck off.*

3. How would you describe the cleanliness of your room?
   A. Brought to you by Pledge.
   B. Blood-free at least.

C. Flophousey.

D. *Visually* clean but not *actually* clean.

4. How do you feel the property is managed as a whole?

A. Like a prison.

B. Like a whorehouse.

C. Somewhere between a prison and a whorehouse.

D. Like a prisoner's whorehouse, which sounds really bad.

5. Given the opportunity, would you stay here again?

A. No, thank you.

B. Yeah, *no.*

C. Never.

D. Okay, sure. Whatever. Fuck it. See you next week.

ACKNOWLEDGMENTS

Thanks to Farley Chase at Chase Literary for embracing the project, brilliantly altering its shape, and, finally, aiming the artillery shell at the correct fortress.

My undying thanks to Doubleday's Hannah Wood, who handled the business of me with grace, humor, bottomless intelligence, and once, early on, with inflammatory libelous accusations.

It's impossible to express my gratitude to Gerry Howard at Doubleday for allowing me to work with him. And a direct thank-you to his gimlet eye for ensuring my book wasn't festooned with feckless bullshit.

I would like to thank California for birthing me, North Carolina for raising me, New Orleans for educating me, Paris and Copenhagen for maturing me, and, without question, New York City for making me hard as fuck.

Additionally, I would like to thank:

The New York Hotel and Motel Trades Council.

Short Story Thursdays and all of our members (www.shortstorythursdays.com).

All my friends in Partysburg, Brooklyn, for dealing with *me* while I dealt with *this*.

Every single guest who ever handed me money.

And, most importantly, *every single hotel employee who ever clocked in.*

Finally, my immediate family: David, Nan, and Sarah Tomsky.

ABOUT THE AUTHOR

Jacob Tomsky is a dedicated veteran of the hospitality business. Well-spoken, uncannily quick on his feet, and no more honest than he needs to be, he has mastered every facet of the business, worked in many departments, and received multiple promotions for his service. Born in Oakland, California, to a military family, Tomsky now lives in Brooklyn, New York.

The employees of Thorndike Press hope you have enjoyed this Large Print book. All our Thorndike, Wheeler, and Kennebec Large Print titles are designed for easy reading, and all our books are made to last. Other Thorndike Press Large Print books are available at your library, through selected bookstores, or directly from us.

For information about titles, please call:
  (800) 223-1244

or visit our Web site at:
  http://gale.cengage.com/thorndike

To share your comments, please write:
  Publisher
  Thorndike Press
  10 Water St., Suite 310
  Waterville, ME 04901